The Best
AMERICAN
FOOD AND
TRAVEL
WRITING
2024

The Best AMERICAN FOOD AND TRAVEL WRITING™ 2024

Edited and with an Introduction
by PADMA LAKSHMI

JAYA SAXENA, Series Editor

MARINER BOOKS
New York   Boston

FIRST EDITION

ISBN 978-0-06-337064-7

ISSN 2578-7667

24 25 26 27 28 LBC 5 4 3 2 1

Contents

Foreword

I HAVE A difficult time explaining my job sometimes. When I say I'm a food writer, most people, even my own family and friends, assume that means I'm a restaurant critic. Do I get to travel to all the cool new restaurants? Do chefs give me free food? Can I get them a reservation? (Sometimes; I try to discourage it but am grateful and tip extra well when it happens; and no.) I get it, though. "Food writer" naturally makes people think you write only about eating. It could be a parent's cooking, a dinner at a lauded restaurant, or a sandwich at some counter halfway around the world, but the sensory experience is the point. Because of that, food writing can seem more glamorous than it is, an exercise in pure indulgence and pleasure, its only goal to make you salivate.

Travel writing is met with similar assumptions. It is easy to see the job as a life of free vacations and "experiences," endless room service, the romantic digital nomad traipsing the planet to recommend hotels in which you'll never afford to stay. *How lucky*, peers think, as if work is luck. And, of course, there are the more contemptuous suspicions. The food writer and the travel writer, and often they are one and the same, are frequently imagined to be paid shills, exchanging positive coverage for prime reservations and first-class cabins, laundering press releases through their bylines.

As a reader and sometimes contributor, I have long considered both the *Best American Food Writing* and *Best American Travel Writing* anthologies bulwarks against the worst assumptions of my industry. Because the reality for most of us is neither so privileged nor so corrupt. Every writer I know is deeply committed to honestly portraying the world around them, whether that's the quality of a new restaurant or the emotions that come up in a difficult journey. Through "food writing" I have written about immigration, history, pop culture, labor, and capitalism. The best way I've found to describe what I do is to remind people there is no such thing as food writing. There is just writing with its lens turned toward a particular subject, trying to refract from it a clearer image of the world.

But you're here already, presumably because you love and cherish good food writing and good travel writing, or you want to see what writing is out there to be cherished. When I was asked to serve as the series editor of a new anthology combining the two subjects, I knew I wanted to keep it a place that celebrated, first and foremost, writing. Because no matter how interesting the medieval village in France, or curious the texture of a rare mushroom, if the prose sucks, no one will care. I wanted to showcase just what these broad topics can inspire, and that good writing can mean a poetic personal essay, a thoroughly researched report, and a hilarious blog post. And crucially, I wanted to show that good food and travel writing, while they certainly exist in the pages of well-known magazines and newspapers, can also come from zines, newsletters, worker-owned collectives, and more. In fact, the frequent shrinking of staff at those illustrious publications means the good stuff is increasingly elsewhere.

Honestly, the job is pretty ideal. I just read. I read . . . so much. A lot of this is reading I would have done anyway in my day job, but dedicating more time to it has been a wonderful reminder of just how many people are doing good work (also, it's a fantastic way to keep myself off social media). It has been a joy to comb through the hundreds of submissions this final selection came from, immersing myself in stories of the aesthetics of eggs and hiking through the jungle and gay Thanksgivings. My biggest problem has been seeing things I wish that I wrote. There's a profound jealousy I felt through much of the process, thinking, *Dammit, I wanted to say that*, and, *Dammit, there's no way I could do it that well.* Karen Resta proved that the most well-worn unit of food writing, a personal essay about the food of your childhood, can still be impossibly moving. Talia Lavin's ode to the grilled cheese sandwich possibly pulled me out of a depression, renewing my commitment to finding beauty in the smallest daily activities. And of course, I spend my career in envy of Ligaya Mishan.

There was glory in having my worldview confirmed. But there was also glory in having it challenged. There are pieces in here that made me rethink my shopping habits, butted against what I assumed about spirituality, and showed me culinary worlds I never thought to consider. And Mosab Abu Toha's account of being forced to flee Gaza, and being taken into IDF custody, was an important reminder that showing passports and crossing borders is not synonymous with leisure.

I may have lied before. Yes, food and travel writing are "just writing" on their respective subjects, but in my opinion, their materiality is what makes the subjects so powerful. At the risk of sounding obvious, everyone has to eat, and everyone has to move. These actions are the things that connect us to our world, and whether they're done out of joy or out of necessity, they are visceral and intimately understandable no matter who you are.

Because of that, these are the subjects best suited to allowing us to shift our perspectives and open ourselves up. There will always be experiences you will never have firsthand, people you will never be, or perhaps places where it's not safe for you to go. But that needn't make them irrelevant or inaccessible. You know what it is like to hunger, and what it is like to taste something that brings you back to yourself. You know what it is like to go somewhere and feel new, and to come to a place and feel at ease. Good writing lets you see that knowledge alive in someone else, and then feel it in your own stomach.

This is writing that is going to make you want to eat and to move. I am so proud of the collection we've put together with Padma Lakshmi, whose taste is second to none. This is my first year as series editor, and I assume that with each passing one, I will learn more about what good writing means. But I will remind you that I think it can come from anywhere and anyone, and encourage you to send submissions for the next collection by December 31, 2024, to bestamericanfoodtravel@gmail.com. I can't wait to read them.

JAYA SAXENA

Introduction

THREE YEARS AGO, when I had the pleasure of guest editing the 2021 edition of *The Best American Travel Writing*, I had no idea it would be its last. So, when I heard that the anthology would be revived, albeit in combination with *The Best American Food Writing*, I was thrilled. Food and travel are natural companions, after all. Being asked to return to edit this inaugural edition felt like kismet: my professional life has pivoted around the intersection of the two. And yet, when I sat down to write, I was stymied.

On a drab January day warmer than it should have been, my mother phoned to tell me my father had died—a year earlier. For months, my mother had been feeling uneasy. She kept dreaming about a man she hadn't seen in over fifty years. *Him*: my father. Unable to shake his specter loose, she called in some reliable auntie to sleuth back in India and learned of his passing. No one had thought to tell me.

Several times over the previous year, my mother had asked me if I'd spoken to my father or my half sister. I said I had not. The last time had been two or three years before, when my half sister had called to tell me *her* mother had died and that my father wanted me to be in touch. "He'd really like to hear from you," she said. *I would have really liked to hear from* him *too, all my life*, I thought. I never reached out.

Now, it was too late. I hung up and wept.

Now, I sat before a stack of manuscripts and a laptop, the bright blankness of its screen irritatingly cheerful, anticipatory.

I closed the laptop. I cried again. Rinse, wash, repeat.
What I was crying for . . . I couldn't even tell you.

Twenty-five years ago, I met my biological father for the first and
only time.

Technically, he had met me before—but the last time we'd seen
each other I had been two years old. My parents were meeting
to sign the paperwork finalizing their divorce. Streaks of melted
vanilla ice cream shellacked my chin and stained my blouse, ice
cream my mother had plied me with in the hopes this meeting
would seem to me a happy (or at least not *unhappy*) occasion. The
mess enraged my father, and he chastised my mother for failing
"to control the child." I have no memory of this meeting, and I
have no memories of my father.

On the train from Madras (now Chennai), where I had been
visiting my grandparents, to Bangalore (now Bengaluru), where
I was set to meet my father in the lobby of the Taj Hotel, I wondered if I would somehow recognize him. In the years before that
morning in the lobby, I had seen just one picture of him, a lone
surviving image of my parents' marriage photo. All other photo-
graphic evidence of him had been wiped from existence, torn up
by my mother's family.

As I entered the lobby and scanned it for men of a certain age,
I saw a tall, slim man in a brown suit that hung loosely on his
frame come toward me. My father. Standing across from me was
the man I had searched for in the faces of unknown men I saw on
every trip to India, in restaurants and coffee shops, in stores and at
the beach. My father's face was thin and longish, like mine would
become in the decades after this meeting. I had his nose and his
eyes, more almond and less round than the eyes of my mother's
family.

My father suggested we leave the Taj and head for lunch. He
said he'd like to take me to the private club where he was a member—he seemed proud of this fact. Private social clubs were a relic
of the British Raj, a hangover of the colonial era. Originally designed as exclusive social settings for British elites (signs outside
clubs famously proclaimed, "No Dogs, No Indians"), they thrived
now as exclusive social settings in a culture still enamored with
caste and social class. On the way there, he explained that the club

specialized in Western food and that their sandwiches were exceptionally good.

Eating in India was always a roller coaster ride of flavor, color, textures, and heat. Before every visit back to see my family, I kept a mental list of the things I couldn't wait to eat. On the four-hour trip inland, I had soothed my nerves imagining a bowl of bisi bele bath, a comforting spicy porridge of lentils and rice with vegetables that was a regional specialty. At the very least, I had been hoping for a Mysore dosa, my favorite type of masala dosa—a crispy rice crêpe, smeared on the inside with red chile paste for heat and bite, folded over soft-cooked potatoes tossed with turmeric and ginger. Bangalore was the capital of Karnataka, and these were the specialties of Karnataka cuisine. In a country rich with spices and countless regional curries, I found it odd that he would bring me somewhere to eat a cold sandwich.

The club was a drab place, mostly empty, and nondescript as an office cubicle or a dentist's waiting room. Shades of brown, beige, and tan dominated. The tables in the dining room were made of a cheap, dark Formica, peeling at the corners. The pleather seat pads stuck uncomfortably to the exposed skin on my legs and back. My father rattled off the menu items to me as if I had never learned to read. I settled on a cheese-and-egg sandwich. My father sipped on a glass of beer, so tepid it lacked any trace of condensation. His hand, resting on the table, looked just like mine.

In the auto-rickshaw from the Taj to the club, I had mustered the fortitude to ask my father the question I had been waiting to ask him my whole life. *Why didn't you want me?* I was still in my twenties, and I believed—or at least I hoped—the answer would extinguish my existential fear that I had not been good enough to be claimed. Petrol fumes rose from the sputtering exhaust pipe as we zoomed and zagged through traffic. I could feel the heat of the floor through my thin sandals and the vibration of every pebble and bump along the way. I knew my parents' marriage had been rocky from the beginning, and that my father had not wanted to bring a child into it, but that was all I knew. My father would go on to remarry and have two more kids—ones he actually raised. The wind whipped the strands of my father's comb-over upward, and he used his left hand to smooth down his pate, turning his face away from me as he spoke. "I felt it was best not to disturb your life.

I wanted your mother and you to have a fresh start," he attempted to explain. It was only after watching his "own daughter grow, over the years" that he wondered about me, he continued. I understand now years later that nothing he said could have satisfied.

When the sandwich arrived to the table, it sat limp, lackluster, and lonely on a cheap white melamine plate. The bread was a bad imitation of American Wonder Bread, thin and stale, smeared with a translucent veneer of ketchup. Piled haphazardly between the slices were jagged squares of brittle processed cheese, also white, and a few disks of boiled egg, the yolk powdery and gray tinged at its edges. The conversation en route to the club had left me, unsurprisingly, with no appetite. I did not want to eat, but nonetheless, I took a bite. The sandwich tasted of nothing. I tried to chew, but it felt impossible. I did not take another bite. Flavorless and odorless, the sandwich sat on the table between us, untouched.

In the wake of learning of my father's death, I could not soothe the nebulous pain that came and went, the locus of which I couldn't even pinpoint. Can you miss someone you never knew? Mourn what never was? And now could never be? Grieving without memory is like bleeding without a wound. I couldn't write about him—there was little to say. Certainly, I couldn't write about what so much food and travel writing often circles around: identity, frequently framed in artful odes to a beloved—and a culturally celebrated—dish or place. My father and I had no shared food tying us together, we had never shared a life. He didn't cook for me, didn't train me in the art of family recipes; there was no tradition, no lore, between us. I didn't know any of his favorite foods. Sitting before my pile of pieces to be read, I dreaded confronting what I imagined were other writers' surety about who they were and where they came from, even as I grappled with the mystery of what my father meant to me.

So, when I first picked up Karen Resta's unexpected, unnerving, and painfully great "My Catalina," you can forgive me for assuming it would be, at first glance, some kind of sailing narrative, an environmental call to arms about the island off the coast of Los Angeles. I did not expect an unsparing hymn to a bottle of Kraft salad dressing. The piece is at once a heartbreaking meditation on our desire to be mothered, to be *claimed*, as well as on class, food, and who gets to be the arbiters of taste—and thus what we deem worthy of our attention.

I was surprised in the best way possible by her devoted attention to the iceberg lettuce salad, studded with anemic tomatoes, militaristic slivers of bell pepper, and "insolent" seedy cucumbers, anointed with viscous Catalina dressing, always prepared in the same Corelle bowl, which was, for Resta, her mother's signature dish. Resta's insistence on elevating through careful attention a "condiment [that] would never enter the realm of the well-to-do, or at least not without a hell of a lot of reeducation" reads like an act of defiance. This is a salad no one but Resta would want to reproduce, a salad willfully not Instagram-able, and TikTok resistant, because it is stubbornly anti-aspirational.

I'm not here to knock either platform, exactly—I participate in both, and last I checked, I have no front lawn from which to shake my fist at kids today—but I can't help but think about how these mediums, mediated by influencers, shape our attention. An influencer is always selling something in the end, and the audience's goal is not to discover but to replicate. For so many, what we eat and where we go has become about reproducing an image, about rebroadcasting to our friends, family, and yes, followers, that we too have access to a certain kind of life.

In "How Things Disappear," Jason Wilson, longtime series editor of *The Best American Travel Writing*, considers how the real threat to travel writing, in a world of vanishing outlets for publication, is not the death of the genre, but the death of perspectives from anyone but those who are sponsored by corporate trips and canned PR tours (hello, influencers) or who already have the resources to travel—in other words, the wealthy.

As a college backpacker, Wilson becomes infatuated with the idea of Estepa: a small Andalusian town he reads about in an early, self-published edition of Rick Steves's *Europe Through the Back Door*. With each new edition of the guidebook, Wilson—who has become a professional travel writer—flips to the pages dedicated to Estepa, "revisiting" the sun-drenched, whitewashed village crowning a hill in southern Spain he has still only explored through Steves's writing. On learning an assignment will be bringing him to Andalusia, he grabs the most recent edition of *Europe Through the Back Door*. But Estepa is gone. Disappeared.

Of course, Estepa is still there. In precise, unadorned prose that echoes the unpretentious beauty of the town itself, Wilson leads us from its quiet churches to its orange tree–shaded squares in his incisive essay. It's Estepa's vanishment from the pages of what is arguably the most popular guidebook about Europe for an American audience that is the real subject of Wilson's inquiry. Estepa, it turns out, meets its fate due to "tough editorial calls," but any savvy reader can recognize the publishing doublespeak for what it is: not sexy enough to hold reader attention. And Wilson rightly marks the cut as yet another casualty of the larger forces shuttering one travel-writing outlet after another.

Like Wilson, I worry about who gets to tell their story in this diminished space. But I also worry about what stories we want to hear. Food and travel *content* is as popular as ever, even as enthusiasm for food and travel *writing* may wane. It's content that is inherently attractive, crave-worthy, envy inducing. Aspirational. In good taste. Everything a bowl of iceberg lettuce topped in Day-Glo goop is not, but in which there is so much pathos and beauty.

The more I read, the more I was drawn to pieces like Resta's, pieces that surprised me, that refused to go where I expected. In "Eating Badly," C Pam Zhang writes about the death of her grandmother, a woman who raised her in infancy and toddlerhood, but about whom she remembers little and knows less—including her age or the city of her birth. Grappling with a loss that feels at once both hollow and profound, Zhang never shirks from the razor edge of her own self-awareness, resolutely unsentimental. Naturally, the piece resonated intensely with me. But it also performed a sleight of hand I didn't see coming. As Zhang first orders one disappointing Northern Chinese food delivery after another, before embarking on an obsessive personal odyssey to recreate the foods of her childhood, the reader imagines that *yes!* there will come the payoff. A moment when Zhang, finally tasting the perfect cumin rib, is made a time traveler, delivered into her grandmother's embrace once more. But the payoff never comes. Our readerly sense of what *should* happen just . . . doesn't. And it's a gut punch. It's when Zhang recognizes her mistake that she is able to discern the truth of her grandmother's care. It's a piece of writing so suffused with nuance, and clear-eyed tenderness, that I felt cared for reading it.

But I still couldn't write. And I still couldn't control the erratic crying jags that would come out of nowhere in the weeks following the news of my father's death. I was sick of my daughter seeing her mother weep. I was sick of turning it all over again in my head—my father's rejection, his absence. I was angry that it was taking up so much headspace after a lifetime of working to put it out of mind. I needed to get away from myself. So I invited myself to my friend Punkie's Mardi Gras family get-together.

Punkie Johnson and I met at a card game. I offered her my last taco. Punkie, a stand-up comedian and a writer and cast member on *Saturday Night Live*, is funny as fuck. So, when she let me know she had watched *a lot* of *Top Chef*, I stifled my usual urge to run away. Punkie enthralled me with her quick wit and charisma. Not long after, our friendship was cemented backstage at *SNL*, where I was coincidentally making a cameo. Punkie offered to feed me—to cook for me. I was confused as she led me to her dressing room. There in a space not much bigger than a broom closet, Punkie made entire meals with just an air fryer and a microwave. From a minifridge she pulled a few hot-sausage patties—flown in from New Orleans, her hometown—and proceeded to make me a po'boy with *all* the fixings. Her sandwich was astonishingly good. We became fast friends. As Black and Brown women on TV, both of us felt the need to hustle constantly—our schedules were tight, but we managed to spend a good amount of time together on both coasts.

The fact that I had never been to Mardi Gras might have been the only point of contention between us. But I've always hated parades. Being in big crowds makes me anxious. People massing on Fifth Avenue, no matter the reason, turns me into an insta-Scrooge. I'd always pictured Mardi Gras to be a drunken frat melee.

And also, I loved New Orleans. Hear me out. *Top Chef* had filmed twice in the city, and it remains my all-time favorite filming location. Usually when we filmed it was such an all-consuming experience that I had no steam left for extracurricular adventures. It didn't matter where we were. But NOLA was the only city where I felt an urge to go out after a full day of shooting. I'd wander down to Frenchman Street on my own and hit up this little live-music place that had an El Salvadoran pupusa stand in the back, blissing out on the hot masa and tender, melting cheese, with the band noodling onstage. No matter how stressed or fatigued I might be, xxiiIntroduction

I always felt happy there. Being in New Orleans at any time of the year always felt like a party. Why would you need to turn up that already perfect party with Mardi Gras?

Punkie had little patience for my outsider's take on Mardi Gras. She said what people from the outside don't understand about Mardi Gras is that it's not about the madness and the drinking, though there is a lot of that. It's about spending time with family. Getting together with loved ones. A time to stop and take a break. She went down every year for her mom's birthday on Valentine's Day, which almost always coincided with Mardi Gras. She said repeatedly that sooner or later, I'd have to come with her, come down and experience *her* Mardi Gras, taste *her* New Orleans.

A city I loved, with a spirited and sharp-witted friend like Punkie, was easy to run to.

We had just thirty hours, both of us with deadlines and work obligations over our heads. When I land at Louis Armstrong International Airport, Punkie is there curbside, leaning against her father's pickup truck, arms spread wide. "*You ready to party?*" she bellows. She's wearing a purple, green, and gold striped beanie—the colors of Mardi Gras, slightly askew over her locs. Miraculously, the beanie, which she wears the entire trip, never falls off. I'm baffled by her insistence on picking me up at the airport, something I don't do anymore even for my own mother.

As we climb into the truck, a pearlescent platinum Ford F-150 with an extended cab, Punkie starts running through her list of food spots. Emphatically, Punkie states, "They *ain't* no Antoine's or *none* that tourist or fancy shit." Mid City Seafood, Manchu, Daiquiris & Company (which I quickly learn to just call "D Shop"). I hadn't heard of any of them. It wasn't a hipster's list, it was a personal list, places she and her friends had hung out, places her family had frequented. Each spot was a marker on her own individual timeline, her own New Orleans. A non-white New Orleans, it felt to me. I hadn't been to New Orleans in over ten years, but my food experiences there had been largely conscribed by *Top Chef* and its guest judges, an undoubtedly whiter and chef-forward experience. At this point in my life, I no longer have much interest or patience for haute cuisine. Likewise, my taste has waned for breathless reporting from tables set by chefs who think manipulating a tomato until it's unrecognizable is God's gift to the universe. I don't care about making the perfect Sazerac or going to Commander's Palace. I'm drawn to places where the faces in the dining room, not just the kitchen, are brown and black. The food is often bolder: the flavor is turned up, there is more intensity on the plate.

But before we start ticking off Punkie's list, I have just one request for her: a stop at Dong Phuong bakery and restaurant, where we're supposed to meet up with Nini Nguyen, one of my favorite *Top Chef* alumni. "Aw *yeah*, you not fucking around, P." Punkie seems impressed with my bona fides, though I have no idea where we are going. I ask Punkie if she needs the address, but she scoffs at me. We barrel down a multilane highway, until, about half an hour from the airport, we hit New Orleans East. This is where the earliest Vietnamese refugees settled in the mid-seventies, after the fall of Saigon. Dong Phuong has been a beloved hub of this community since the early eighties. It's also become a Mardi Gras tradition: from early January right up until Fat Tuesday before Lent, at 7:00 a.m. sharp, a line forms out the bakery's door and snakes around the block, filled with people waiting for that most New Orleanian of treats, king cake. The family-owned restaurant sells about 60,000 king cakes every season, each one of them handmade.

The line is gone when we pull into the parking lot around noon, as the king cakes have sold out hours before. But I'm not here for the king cake. I'm here for a taste of Nini's childhood. She grew up eating at Dong Phuong with her grandma. Both of us were raised by our grandmas, both of us were Asian girls growing up in an often alienating American world. Nini, with all her talent, resilience, and grit, certainly doesn't need my protection, but I feel protective toward her.

Nini greets us with a wide grin, her long, shiny black hair swinging in the wind. Inside, we sit down, and she immediately hands us each a red envelope for Tet, or Vietnamese New Year. Nini orders for all three of us and in minutes, every inch of the table is covered. But even among the steaming bowl of bún bò huế (noodles, beef, pork, ham, ham hock, and bricks of fried tofu swimming in a dark broth garnished with thinly sliced onions) and the platter of bánh hỏi (small bundles of rice noodles meant to be topped with grilled shrimp, thinly sliced short ribs, and fried sausages, folded in lettuce leaves along with fresh basil, cilantro, and pickled vegetable), the pâté chaud stands out.

Golden, flaky hockey puck–size pastries, pâtés chauds are at once a classic Vietnamese dish and a direct reflection of French colonialism in Vietnam. The buttery puff pastry reflects the influence of French baking techniques on Vietnamese cooking, much like the baguette in a banh mi. I rip a pâté chaud in two. Inside is a glistening surprise of oozing braised pork with onions. My mouth starts to water. The pastry is soft and fluffy, somehow not soggy from the stew inside. Biting into it tastes so good, my shoulders drop. The pâté chaud is light, buttery, and airy until my teeth sink into the center. The warm pork stew, silken with cooked-down vegetables and fat, is savory, unctuous, and comforting. It is perfection. A soft, textural meditation that is at once quiet and thrilling. Nini and Punkie chat effortlessly—making friends comes easily to them both. They compare notes on where they went to high school and the best places to eat in New Orleans East, laughing easily.

Hugging Nini goodbye feels like leaving family. Her body is full and soft against mine. Back in the truck with Punkie, I watch the city unfold outside my window. I can't believe it's been five years since Nini's season of *Top Chef*. I still remember the étouffée she made in Kentucky, delicate and complex, a marriage of New Orleans and Vietnam in every bite. That étouffée stole my heart. In one glorious, elegant bite it captured what it means to be of two worlds, two cultures.

The Johnson family home sits on a quiet street in the middle-class Gentilly neighborhood, in the 8th Ward. The sidewalks are spotless. Lawns are trim and neat. Punkie's mom, Mary, answers the door. Her voice is a sweet, long drawl that rises at the end of each phrase. I greet her and hand her a brown bag with a king cake Nini somehow nabbed for us—"It's from Dong Phuong," I tell her. "*Aww, baae-baee, na ain't you so sweet*," she says, smiling warmly. The house is aggressively air-conditioned, fastidiously clean, and homey. Punkie's dad, Kevin, enters the kitchen moments later, readying the supplies for the parade. A retired New Orleans police officer, he has a salt-and-pepper Afro that adds a four-inch halo to his already considerable height. I feel easy around Punkie's parents. Punkie's house reminds me of the homes of my high school friends, where I spent so much time as a teenager back in La Puente, California.

At the Krewe of Bacchus parade route, we meet up with Punkie's nephew Miguel, her cousin Duke, and his wife Megan. The family has secured a spot remarkably close to the barriers—having a retired cop for a dad helps. I settle into a proffered lawn chair and accept a healthy pour of reposado tequila from Duke. Punkie and I split a foot-long hot dog. Very quickly the sun begins to set and the parade is in full swing. There are marching bands interspersed with brightly lit floats. Beads fly in every direction. I am almost impaled by a flying plastic sword the size of a small ruler. I work my way up to the barrier easily and am in spitting distance of where each majorette, flag twirler, and drumline make the turn from Napoleon to St. Charles. It's all so . . . *wholesome.* The blare of the high school marching bands is electrifying. As each band comes through, we whoop and holler, cheering them on. The Roots of Music Marching Crusaders, a band comprised of what look like mostly middle schoolers, is my favorite. Punkie points out all her alma maters. She has moved schools *a lot.* I know I am tipsy because I film at least nine identical videos, eight of which I will never use for social media or watch again.

A couple of hours and several tequilas in, a cold wind kicks up, and we have had enough. We pile into Punkie's dad's pickup. The radio is tuned to an old-school hip-hop station, and I feel dislocated in time. It's easy to believe for a moment that I'm sixteen again and back in the San Gabriel Valley. Kevin drops us off at the D Shop. Punkie worked here for a year when she was younger, and I imagine her dad dropping her off then too. Punkie orders what seems like half the menu: po'boys with roast beef, po'boys with hot sausage, po'boys with fried shrimp. *This* is the birthplace of our dressing room meal, I realize. The site where Punkie learned the sacred mysteries of proper po'boy assembly. The sandwiches come out fully dressed—lettuce, tomatoes, pickles, and mayo—and shredded iceberg snows on the table as we take our first bites. The bread is crusty, airy and chewy, giving way just so to pressure as you bite into it. Punkie and I eat like we've never eaten before. I barely taste the tomato or pickles. The shrimp in the po'boy feels like popcorn shrimp. It's piping hot, crunchy, snapping under my teeth and burning my gums.

Punkie dips her sandwich in ketchup. She must be drunk if she's doing that, I think. I search for hot sauce and the only thing available is Crystal, a staple in New Orleans where it originates. Crystal hot sauce is not really hot sauce, though—more like orange-tinted water with a tang, training wheels for children who are still teething, perhaps. It will just barely keep your sandwich from tasting like nothing. I wonder where they're hiding the Tabasco.

Outside D Shop, Kevin reappears faster than I can call an Uber. I never had a dad I could call to come pick me and my friends up. I am so, so glad Punkie does. For a minute, Punkie's New Orleans feels like my New Orleans, a place I could belong, where I am welcome, where I can relax into being someone's kid. Where someone knows where I am, what I'm doing, and they'll come rescue me from my own dumb decisions.

Back in Gentilly, we gather in the Johnson family bar room, a one-room structure detached from the main house. There's a billiards table and a working Pac-Man arcade game circa 1985. Jackpot! Family portraits, Sears Portrait Studio style, from what appear to be the eighties and nineties, line the walls. I peer at the photos of Mary and Kevin, seeing their clothes and hair evolve over the years, searching for something in the photos that will reveal how they've remained so steadfast, so *together*, across the decades. Next to a fridge packed with soda, beer, and goodies, there is a long bar. The Johnson Family Bar Room is a choice hangout spot. Punkie is always playful, very sweet and loving, but watching her now, she seems softer, more *relaxed*. Like there's nothing to prove. The toughness with which she usually armors herself just isn't there. I recognize the shift: it's how I feel with my family, in India. I'm grateful to her that she let me come here.

I am terrible at pool, and Punkie tries to be patient with me. She is a good friend. We mean to go out and hit some live music spots on Frenchman Street, but we never make it out of her mom's bar room. I pull the rip cord around one a.m.

The next morning, Duke and Megan, who have now fully cosigned our tour of gluttony, wait with Punkie outside my hotel in their minivan. The hours that follow are a blur of potato salad and chicken. A Styrofoam box of wings from Manchu rivals yesterday's pâté chaud—biting into a wing, the crust shatters into a million savory bits in my mouth. No grease, perfect salinity, only what I pull with my teeth comes off. I cannot deny the perfection. We drive through the 7th Ward past brightly painted Creole cottages and shotgun houses to get to our last stop of the day: Mid City Seafood, Punkie's favorite spot to get crawfish. We pull up in front of a long, low, faded-orange storefront, which to my untrained eyes looks more "liquor store" than seafood emporium. A redheaded Vietnamese woman manning a long counter lights up when we come in. She and Punkie flirt, while I peer through the glass divider running the length of the counter. Behind it sits an array of chafing dishes laden with ham hocks, crabs, shrimp, king crab legs, corn, potatoes, boiled eggs, sausages, and, of course, crawfish. She promises us that if we "wait for ten minutes, you get the good ones." I'm still so full I'm uncertain I'll be able to do much damage. My alarm increases when Punkie orders *eight pounds* of crawfish. Registering my disbelief, Punkie chastises me. "We can't be out here eating in the streets, so we gon' take 'em to my mom's. I can't be arriving with no two pounds for seven people."

Mary is unperturbed by the ridiculous amount of takeout we thrust at her when we arrive back in Gentilly. She spills an avalanche of crawfish onto a giant tray she sets in the middle of the dining table. We get to work. Punkie is like a machine. She efficiently plucks and sucks all the flesh and delicious juices from each critter. I'm usually squeamish about the head, but here now, I gleefully suck as much as I can from each head I rip off. The juice is briny, pungent. Every so often there's a note that feels too deep of the innards of the thing, but I carry on. The shell gives way, a thin, crisp breaking, exposing soft, spongy meat that is sweet and seasoned just right, bright and earthy, redolent of lemons and smoked paprika.

This is my last meal in NOLA. Juice runs down my arms, drips from my chin. I've tucked a paper towel into the collar of my top, but it's not up to the job. Before I have to contemplate the ruin of my blouse, Mary appears behind me. I can sense her body close to mine as she drapes a dish towel over my chest, securing it just below the nape of my neck. "Ya need somethin' thicker to absorb it all, *baae-baee*," she gently chides me. I glimpse an alternate universe where I know my daddy, my parents are married, and I can come home anytime and drink, play pool, letting loose with my kin, knowing exactly who I am and where I come from.

Before I head for the airport, we gather on the front lawn for photos. There's a just-before-prom vibe to it all, as we wrap our arms around each other's shoulders and reconfigure, facing this way and that to keep the sun out of our eyes. I'm headed for security and an anonymous airport lounge, not a ballroom, but I feel a surprising lightness in me I can't quite parse. I had gone to New Orleans to blow off some steam with good company. But Punkie had given me not just herself, but her family. Their easy acceptance of me had soothed the gnawing hunger of rejection. The trip hadn't answered any questions, there were no epiphanies on the table. But it had allowed me to just be, and to receive an embrace I hadn't known I needed. Even if only temporarily, it rendered answering the questions less necessary.

Maybe that's why, less than ten days later, I'm on a plane to India for a seventy-two-hour trip. It seems crazy, but my stupor has lifted enough in the week since I've been back from NOLA that when I'm invited to speak at the Ideas for India conference, I think, *Why not?* The conference is in Mumbai, on the opposite coast from Chennai, just too far for a such short trip—I won't be able to see my family.

Then I'm onstage. And the host asks, "How do you persevere in spite of all the difficulties, to become the person you are today?" Suddenly, I'm struck with a rough case of *mention-itis.* I can't help but talk about my father. I think I'm talking about my mother, about the sacrifices she made for me, but what's coming out is: "I never knew my father." Within minutes of exiting the conference center, I'm rearranging my return flights. I'll have just a day and a half in Chennai, but I need to go home.

Like Punkie, my aunt Neela meets me at the airport, but instead of a pickup truck our ride is a golf cart. She's come to fetch me, just as she did every summer of my childhood, when my mother sent me back for the three-month stay that would ensure I'd remain Indian. A breeze off the Coromandel Coast twines between us, the air supple and mild. At our grandparents' flat, which Neela has taken over and remodeled, I drink tea, my cup refilled wordlessly at regular intervals. For the first time in too long, I am truly at rest. My aunt Papu and my uncle Ravi are there, and we share a simple meal of yogurt rice.

Fortified, I drag Neela to Nalli, a famous sari and fabric shop. There are almost forty Nalli shops across India today, in cities like

Delhi, Mumbai, Bengaluru, Kochi, Ahmedabad, Kolkata, and Hyderabad, but Chennai is the original birthplace of this temple of textiles. I've been obsessed with it since I was a kid, obsessed with the bolts of silk—cobalt and magenta, ivory and rust, tangerine and marigold—that reach all the way to the ceiling. It was where everyone, and I mean *everyone*, bought their wedding saris and regular daytime saris, as well as men's suiting. I'm on the hunt for a dress for my friend Sohla's baby girl. I want to surprise her with a special outfit for her daughter's *annaprasanam*, or first food ceremony. Such gladness in having a baby to shop for. The silks, tightly woven, slip coolly between my fingers as I consider them, then settle on the perfect little dress in a plaid of bright orange, purple, blue, and red. A traditional Madras fabric, from old Madras.

At my cousin Akshara's new home I can see the Indian Ocean through the living room window, lapping at the sand of Elliot's Beach where I had played as a child.

At my great-aunt Chinnu's, a TV broadcasts a cricket match. The younger sister of my grandmother, she is her spitting image (as well as her only living sibling). I haven't seen Chinnu chithi since 2017, but she looks just the same. When I hug her, I can feel she is smaller than she used to be. She smells of Pond's and coconut oil. Her voice is still just as scratchy, her smile just as wide. God, it's good to see her. When I hand her the box of sweets we picked up along the way—Mysore pak, fudgy squares of sugar, besan flour, and ghee—she opens it right away. "Do you know," she asks me, "that I still play cards with Mrs. Balagopalan every week? Shall we call her?" Mrs. Balagopolan was my third-grade teacher. She rode a scooter to school every day with her sari fluttering behind her. I loved her. To my surprise, she had been keeping tabs on me all these years. When we speak, I promise her I'll come for tea next time I am home.

That night, the family gathers. My aunt Banu and my uncle Vichu are the first to arrive. Like Akshara and Chinnu, they live in the neighborhood. Everyone lives in the neighborhood. After my grandmother died, Neela moved into this apartment, where we all grew up. I think about how, in the old days, this was all our home. How when Vichu and Banu had kids—my cousins Rajni and Rohit—they continued to live here. They all slept in the big bedroom; my grandparents had the other bedroom, with Neela and me sleeping on the floor, rolling up our bedding each morning. Eight people living in a home that was no more than 1,200 square feet. Sometimes ten, if others came to stay for a while, which they did. I hug Banu. She, too, has grown thin. There is more gray in her long, braided hair.

My uncles in their cricket jerseys sit together on the settee. My aunts mill about in the small kitchen. Neela has bought a new stove, to replace the two-burner one we grew up with. No wonder the women were always cooking. I lie on some pillows on the green marble tile, which has remained unchanged my whole life. There is no need for AC. The tile is cool, cool enough that soon my feet grow cold. Banu tells us she has a surprise for us. She holds up a jump drive and explains that she found some old cassette tapes and had them digitized. Singing begins to fill the room. It's my grandfather. Then my grandparents, singing together. Papu says she never heard my granny sing. Neela says that after they moved down from New Delhi she stopped. The speakers emit the strains of a cheeky ten-year-old Neela and another cousin, Vidya, dueting, hamming it up.

Neela sets a small Eversilver (stainless steel) bowl of rice and lentils, kneaded into a porridge with her fingers, on the floor beside me. I eat quietly, tears escaping the corners of my eyes as I listen to the voices of my grandparents, both gone now. The sounds of my childhood echo through the apartment in which we all grew up, as I lie on the very floor where my grandmother once fed us by hand.

And then comes a very small child's voice. It's me. I am three years old. I am singing a song about an old man who wants a bride. I sing in perfect Malayalam, a language I no longer speak.

I don't need to know why I'm grieving, just that I am. I can just be with it. What is absent has so much to tell me about what remains present.

Once I stop pushing for an answer, writing returns. As I read through the manuscripts splayed across my desk, I can see that so much of the writing I'm drawn to deals with absence and loss, missing pieces: what we don't have words for, what we don't eat, where we can't go, the choices we don't have, what escapes our attention.

There are few, if any, tidy conclusions. What is left is expansiveness. Answers, tidiness, so often describe limits. These essays leave us, instead, in their refusal of neat completion, with possibility. This is not the kind of possibility that our relentlessly positive culture insists on. The cheerful adage inscribed on HomeGoods word art and inspirational Instagram squares, a "possibility" that is aggressively productive, that points toward the consumer's joy of more, more, more. A future happy ending.

Instead, these pieces offer the possibility of seeing anew, of examining how we make and assign meaning, whether or not our premises are sound, as in Marian Bull's sly and uncompromising takedown of our pastoral fantasies "Orange Is the New Yolk," in which she interrogates the current incarnation of the ideal egg; or in "The *Titan* Submersible Was 'An Accident Waiting to Happen'" by Ben Taub, not so much a lesson in hubris as it is a quiet but savage indictment of our American love affair with "disruptor" culture.

They offer us, the reader, the possibility of sitting with unknowing, with its discomfort, and attending to the grief that arises.

Mosab Abu Toha writes, "'Hope' is a difficult word for Palestinians. It is not something that others give us but something that we must cultivate and care for on our own. We have to help hope grow." This observation comes toward the end of his essay "Unsafe Passage." He traces his multiple brutal and heartbreaking dislocations in the wake of Hamas's October 7 attack and Israel's war in Gaza. We move with him, first from his family home in Beit Lahia, then from the refugee camp in Jabalia to which they've fled, then from the Rafah border crossing after he's taken into custody by the IDF, and finally, from Palestine entirely, as he and his wife and young children find safe harbor in Cairo.

I write this as we are eight months into the war, and over 40,000 killed with no real or tangible end in sight.

It is only after leading the reader on a journey he was forced to undertake, every step of which is suffused with sorrow and fear, that Toha speaks of hope. He and his family have arrived, finally, to the Egyptian Travelers Hall on the other side of the Rafah border crossing. They receive an emergency passport from the US embassy (Toha's son, Mostafa, was born in the United States). A minibus takes them to Cairo. It is only then that Toha muses on the poem "A State of Siege," by the Palestinian poet Mahmoud Darwish, who himself lived in exile for much of his life. *We do what jobless people do /We raise hope,* wrote Darwish. This is, of course, a translation from Arabic. Toha draws the reader's attention to the idea of "raising" hope. "The verb *nurabi,* meaning to raise or to rear, is what a parent does for a child, or what a farmer does for crops," writes Toha. This is not a passive hope of American platitudes, but a laborious act of self-determination, of enduring love.

This, for Toha, is not a happy ending. Parents, siblings, lifelong friends remain in Gaza. He does not know and cannot know if they will be safe, if he will see them again. He doesn't know what comes next. But he can hope, and does, leaving us in the realm of possibility: "one morning I sit at my friend's beautiful wooden desk, in a room full of light, and write a poem. It is addressed to my mother. I hope that the next time we speak I can read it to her."

There are twenty-one pieces in this collection, each one arresting in its own right, each an act of possibility, each capturing a moment in time that can never be replicated. They range the globe from Dakar in Senegal, Michoacán in south-central Mexico, to the Camino de Santiago in Galicia, Spain. There is pleasure in spending time in the company of their intelligence, grace to be found in their bravery, beauty in their surprise, their possibility. I for one never expected an essay about grilled cheese to make me cry. But Talia Lavin's "Notable Sandwiches #75: Grilled Cheese," written with the religious fervor of an initiate, impossibly sincere even as it winks at you, is both a blessing—of the "small and perfect thing"—and a kind of benediction, as is each piece here. Her wish for the reader is my wish for you as you read these pages: "Every joy erodes; survival necessitates that no state be fixed. But we can hope for its return, as light returns. I hope you find your small perfect thing, and in doing so welcome joy's arrival."

PADMA LAKSHMI

The Best
AMERICAN
FOOD AND
TRAVEL
WRITING
2024

NAVNEET ALANG

"New American," "Fusion," and the Endless, Liberating Challenge of Describing American Food Right Now

FROM *Bon Appétit*

TAKE A LOOK at the sorts of restaurants that were celebrated on best-of lists this past year by the *New York Times, Eater,* and here at *Bon Appétit,* and you will see a mishmash of cuisines. Rooster & Owl in DC features cornbread, banh mi, panzanella, *and* tabouleh. At Elvie's in Jackson, Mississippi, the menu careens from "New Orleans–style baked oysters to pork tonkatsu, vegetable lumpia to redfish amandine, shrimp remoulade to cacio e pepe," as the *Times* puts it. Bonnie's in Brooklyn flirts with a new vision of Cantonese American food, its menu including salted duck egg-custard French toast, and cha siu done two ways: as a hash for brunch, or as a "McRib" at dinner.

The current moment in American food is pushing the boundaries of what "American" means—resolutely taking what was historically not considered American and making it so.

Yet amidst this burst of creativity and invention, a question has emerged: What do we call the kind of food that defines how Americans eat now? Instead of being neatly confined by geography or a single culture, the food of cutting-edge chefs pulls from varied cultural backgrounds, as well as the cities where they learned to cook. Such cooking, like the things that defined this year's best-of lists, blends cuisines and cultures in a way that we don't quite yet have a name for.

Or, rather, we do have names for it, but none of them quite work. In the past, chefs, food media, and diners called this food "fusion." But the cooking that first garnered that label eventually fell out of fashion, because instead of innovation, it too often resulted in the sort of thing worth putting on mocking listicles (think: burritos filled with spaghetti). Fusion is now "a hydra of a slur" according to *L.A. Times* critic Bill Addison, a way of flattening difference, nuance, and history.

In restaurant reviews and think pieces, we instead started calling similar, more judicious forms of mixed cuisines "New American." Writing in the *L.A. Times* in 1991, Ruth Reichl pointed to California as an epicenter of "the new" in American cooking, one that saw an emphasis on eclectic takes on regional or international ingredients. From the early eighties and on, New American grew to encompass nearly any kind of food that draws from global cuisines to adapt American staples—think a mac and cheese topped with lines of Kewpie mayo, or slices of rib eye served with nuoc cham on the side.

But in the last few years, "New American" has fallen out of favor too, with numerous publications lodging complaints that aren't too far off from the criticisms of fusion: that so-called "foreign" food is used as cheap marketing, something international thrown in to make the familiar seem exotic. Now, like fusion, New American is a label used for derision as much as description. Recently, when food writer Ashlie Danielle Stevens asked on Twitter what the term brings to mind, answers ranged from "gentrified soul food classics" and "mid roast chicken and carrots with the tops on" to, more pointedly, "unseasoned bullshit."

But if fusion's become something of a dirty word, and New American is falling out of vogue, where does that leave us? Writers and chefs alike have been scrambling to come up with new ways to describe this distinctly modern, American form of cooking. Food writers have lately suggested New New American or, more interestingly, chaos cooking—a sort of devil-may-care approach that, as Avish Naran of Los Angeles restaurant Pijja Palace tells *Eater*, means chefs are "cooking our experiences, not our ethnicities."

It's an exercise that feels necessary. As silly as a label may feel, finding a name that encapsulates a restaurant's menu can be helpful too. Giving something a name makes it recognizable to us as diners or writers, but also influential forces including Google and Yelp. Words have currency, in more than one sense of the term.

Whatever label we give it, though, it will describe a regular part of life in America today. So much of what's deemed "fusion" or "New American" is just what happens when hungry third-culture kids get home from school and blend together things which, to them, aren't novel or separate to begin with.

After all, when chef Suresh Sundas puts burrata in the middle of a plate of black daal at DC's Daru, is that not both American and new—in the sense that it is a product of the time and place and country in which such a mixture occurs so fruitfully?

People are yearning for something, well, new: a label that food critics, chefs—and anyone who loves to eat—can give to what is, in equal measure, both new and distinctly American.

"New American" got its start in Berkeley, California, in the seventies at Chez Panisse. At the time, the cuisine it described didn't have much to do with pulling flavors from around the world. Chef Alice Waters and her peers drew from the same tenets that were informing French culinary movements around that period: simplicity, freshness, and an attention to sourcing local ingredients. Eventually, the *New Yorker* suggested that Waters had invented at least part of "New American" cuisine, one where the farmers market dictated the meal.

The term came at an ideal time. American food was expanding and evolving, and writers and diners alike were looking to mark a change from the meat-and-potatoes midcentury food that you might have seen in *Leave It to Beaver* or *Mad Men*. In 1984, Jeremiah Tower, who had worked as the chef of Chez Panisse, picked up what Waters was doing and ran with it. His cooking pulled from the canon of classic American cooking, then added *something*—like, say, a Cajun remoulade or a ginger cream. At Stars, Tower's restaurant in San Francisco, he served dishes like local grilled lamb with ancho chile sauce, avocado salsa, and cotija cheese. The restaurant was a smash hit and became a who's who of A-list celebrities and fawning food critics. In 1986, Tower published his first cookbook, *New American Classics*.

In the early 1980s, other chef personalities such as Wolfgang Puck and Jonathan Waxman began using influences from various Asian cuisines in their cooking, and along with "fusion," the term "New American" started popping up to describe it, according to the *Chicago Tribune*. The Austria-born Puck didn't, say, put bulgogi inside a samosa, but he took something roughly familiar to white

Americans like a chopped salad and added a few "Chinese" twists like soy sauce and sesame oil to make a "Chinois salad."

In all of these early examples, New American meant the addition of an "exotic," foreign, non-white *flair*. It's a mentality in which food seen as "not from here" was looked at by entrepreneurial, mostly white restaurateurs as a kind of raw material to be mined and refined and, eventually, sold at some celebrity chef's newest outing in Vegas.

It's not a coincidence that most of the genre-defining New American cooking came from white restaurateurs, with the exception of notable chefs such as Roy Yamaguchi, a pioneer of Asian fusion fare. There's the longstanding question of who has historically been allowed to call their food "American" and to whom it appeals when a certain kind of novelty emerges. Puck himself says that he knew his second restaurant, Chinois, had really become something when Elizabeth Taylor, Madonna, and Warren Beatty started eating there; if Hollywood stars are a barometer of anything, it's the cultural appetite for what's considered new.

But while white chefs were finding success cooking with "exotic" ingredients, chefs of color were (and sometimes still are) confined and typecast. Many non-white chefs today bristle at the ways in which their cooking has been constrained, such as the old trope that an Asian chef is expected to only cook Asian food. Couple that with the ongoing frustration around cultural appropriation and the trend of white influencers profiting off exoticized "foreign" practices, and it's easy to see why labels become such contested ground. I am reminded of Kentucky-based chef Edward Lee insisting in a 2014 episode of the television show *Mind of a Chef* that his cooking, even when it includes his Korean influences, is American. Like the other side of the coin, that assimilationist approach has its appeal for the reason specific labels do: they're demands for an expanded definition of what it means to be American.

And it certainly has expanded. In the last half-decade, the landscape has developed. The makeup of award-winning restaurateurs has diversified, and at least in the last few years, it's not just white chefs who have been celebrated for food that skips around the globe. And while plenty of chefs have found original ways to describe their cooking, Google, Yelp, and the other crowdsourced platforms often still clump these restaurants together under the New American umbrella.

At Kasama in Chicago, you can get a sandwich of "shaved pork adobo, longanisa sausage, and giardiniera" or a corned beef breakfast with garlic rice and fried egg. Yelp calls it Filipino and also "American (New)," a little parenthetical to let you know this isn't just diner food. Chef Andrew Black's Oklahoma City restaurant Grey Sweater defiantly says it has "no allegiance" in its menu, which might feature Norwegian scallops in a pool of Jamaican coconut milk sauce. Yelp also calls that restaurant "American (New)." New American cuisine can cross borders too. In Toronto, swanky Vela also gets called New American despite only technically being one of those two things. But it, too, shares the tropes of the genre: scallops with Thai nam jim, octopus with tamari and togarashi. New American might be vague, but it is also recognizable.

In the absence of other language, New American is, perhaps, the simplest (and sometimes, most reductive) description of what these chefs are doing: pulling from an array of contemporary resources to reflect something about dining in America.

But just because "New American" is the best we've got doesn't mean it's good enough, or that it isn't obscuring something by being so generic. We can—and should—do a better job of acknowledging the individuality that actually makes food culture in America so striking right now. Using a label at all suggests the existence of a cohesive American cuisine, when what really defines American food right now is how far-reaching and all-encompassing it can be. This is not the French-inspired cooking of the eighties and nineties. New bids into the canon like "New New American" or "chaos cooking" are encouraging attempts to describe what's happening in American food culture right now, but much like the term they intend to replace, don't quite describe all that American cooking has to offer at this moment. How quickly will we find those labels to be outdated too?

When food media went through a racial reckoning in 2020, part of the fallout was precisely a call for more specificity. The complaint about Alison Roman and "the stew"—a chickpea dish heavy on turmeric that was close enough to many South Asian dishes to raise more than a few eyebrows—the objection was less about who owns what, or who has a right to use which ingredient, than simply a desire to call something by its right name.

It's why "New American" as a term simply doesn't work anymore—if it did at all. It once claimed to look forward, but now in fact looks back: to a time when it was simply assumed that the default in America was whiteness, and what was new about New American was new to most in the country—when Wolfgang Puck adding Asian ingredients to his menus still seemed "daring." But that isn't the case anymore. Kimchi, sumac, curry spices, lemongrass, fish sauce—these are ingredients now so ordinary you'll find them on mass-market cooking programs such as *America's Test Kitchen* and *Cook's Country* on PBS.

Today, part of what is driving novelty in American cooking, and landing restaurants on best-of lists, is a more purposeful, specific mindset. Chefs are finding their own ways to describe their cooking—and perhaps providing useful keys for how to read this culinary landscape.

When Eric Brooks and Jacob Armando put their own twist on red sauce Italian at Gigi's in Atlanta, the results—beef carpaccio with rice crackers, polenta with caviar, fettuccine alfredo with fermented chili breadcrumbs—might well be called "New Italian American" (they call themselves, quite simply, an Italian kitchen). At LA's Anajak Thai, Justin Pichetrungsi took over his parents' decades-old establishment and the results are almost a too-on-the-nose expression of what second-gen, third-culture American cooking looks like: Thai Taco Tuesdays, Southern Thai-style fried chicken, Kampachi sashimi with a Hainanese ponzu. It describes itself as Thai—but with the very American addendum that "Anajak is one big f*cking party." And at Nami Kaze in Honolulu, chef-owner Jason Peel takes the already multicultural cuisine of Hawaii and adds in not just Japanese touches, but also Levantine labneh and za'atar, Southeast Asian satay sauce with summer rolls, and beets with gochujang.

Eater described Peel's approach as "grounded in the Islands and exposed to the world." It's not a bad way to think of American food right now: rooted somewhere, but also reflecting the fact that the Americans cooking and eating it come from places where the food cultures are far different from what's historically been considered American.

Yet on Nami Kaze's website, rather than New American or Japanese American, what it says in large sans serif is "Japanese + American." The hyphen is gone, replaced by a plus sign. If you were to squint a bit and read it symbolically, you have the "yes and" of labels. It's a good way to capture what is actually going on: there isn't a single thing emerging in American food culture at this moment, but a constant process of addition that is taking the American and making something, well, new.

Sure, that interpretation is probably a little optimistic; nothing in the mess of national and ethnic identity is actually that easy. So much of how we define ourselves comes down to the subjective practice of what feels right. Chefs like Edward Lee may prefer the simple, declarative "American." Others seek a combination, like Taiwanese American, Korean American, Neo-Italian American—and yes, hyphenation can be imprecise and clunky in its own way. But each attempts to avoid the ambiguity in obscuring an intentionally made cuisine. And more precision does perhaps get us closer to clarity. In general, when it comes to thinking about the miasma of appropriation, history, race, and the hundred other things currently troubling the food world, even a little more specificity seems like a good thing.

American food is constantly evolving and, in turn, evading labels. We can follow some general ethos: Say where its various influences are from. Take descriptors from places like Google and Yelp with a grain of salt (good advice for any topic). But also: Use a hyphen or a plus sign or whatever else to suggest that where something is from doesn't wholly determine where it's going.

The nearly impossible challenge here is describing the way the present is constantly giving way to the future. Then again, that's part of the challenge, charm, and beauty of eating in the United States in the first place. It's constantly pushing forward, blending and creating and inventing until something radically new—even cuisine defining—emerges. It's not just new and American, it's "American, and." Filling in that blank is exactly where the promise lies.

BETSY ANDREWS

The Science of Savoring

FROM *Saveur*

THIS PAST JULY, I turned sixty, and I started thinking more about my health. To me, the idea of healthy eating has always been a drag. I'm from Philadelphia. I want my cheesesteak. The aroma of caramelized meat and onions, the luscious goo of the Whiz, the burn of the long hots, the pillowy heft of the roll. Popping statins to quell my cholesterol, I've long eschewed diet culture in favor of truly enjoying my meals.

But recently, something changed. The cheese and long hots are gastrically challenging, the bread is bloating, and the meat is a climate-damaging guilt trip. How, in that context, can I continue to love my cheesesteak? I am a food writer. Culture is ostensibly my subject and privilege. Yet I wonder how often I actually enjoy my meal, being prone to scarfing down lunch at my desk by day, then posting photos of fancy restaurant food by night. When I worked at *Saveur* in its onsite days, all the recipe testing, product samples, press meals, and long hours fueled by expense-account pizza meant weight gain. We called it the "*Saveur* 30." We were privileged eaters, but I'm not so sure we were pausing to actually savor our meals.

In recent years, nutritionists and dietitians have started centering the idea of savoring—the pleasure of tuning in—as a way of improving our relationship to food. Many of them work with people who've cycled on and off diets all their lives. Is there something for non-dieters like me to learn? Can I have my cheesesteak and eat it too?

The *Oxford English Dictionary* defines savoring as, "In modern use, to taste with relish, to dwell on the taste of, also figuratively, to give oneself to the enjoyment or appreciation of." With eating, the enjoyment is both figurative and literal because it is not a simple act. "People don't eat nutrition; they eat food," says registered dietitian and wellness and nutrition expert Tamara Melton. "They're looking for flavors, textures, temperatures, sounds. Pleasure hormones in our brains get turned on once we start eating."

Beyond that hit of dopamine, lots more happens. In *Gastrophysics: The New Science of Food*, psychologist Charles Spence, head of the Crossmodal Research Laboratory at the University of Oxford, invites us to imagine eating a peach. "Your brain has to bind together the aromatic smell, the taste, the texture, the color, the sound as your teeth bite through the juicy flesh, not to mention the furry feeling of the peach fuzz in your hand and mouth."

Your thalamus processes that information and filters it to your cerebral cortex, where it's connected to a slew of associations and memories. If you pay attention as you eat, slowly savoring each bite, those random thoughts organize themselves into a deeper enjoyment of your experience. As Spence told me when we spoke, "It's like the pleasure of standing in front of a work of art and the transformative moment when you understand it and cry, 'Aha!'"

That's precisely the type of pleasure that chef and psychologist Caroline Baerten promotes. Founder of Brussels' Centre for Mindful Eating and Nutrition, Baerten is a disciple of Buddhist teacher Thich Nhat Hanh, who popularized mindfulness—being present in the moment—through books like 2014's *How to Eat*. During retreats, Hanh guides attendees in eating a single raisin. "Thanks to 100 percent attention to what I was doing, I was blown away. I had never tasted a raisin in such a profound way," says Baerten. Stopping to savor a single raisin is likely a laughable proposition to the 39 percent of North American workers who basically never break for lunch (despite 94 percent saying they're happier when they do). Mindful eating, then, is triage. You do what you can, taking a moment or two during eating to focus on your sense of smell, taste, or touch, checking in with how you and your body are feeling.

After work, mindfulness can mean turning off the television and setting the table to essentially feel like an invited guest in your own home. "It creates this almost sacred moment where we can find this pleasure while we are eating, through the senses," says Baerten.

A growing body of research points to the long-term psychological benefits of mindfulness. It's an antidote to "an epidemic of stress," says Dr. Lilian Cheung, director of mindfulness research and practice at the Harvard T.H. Chan School of Public Health and author, along with Hanh, of *Savor: Mindful Eating, Mindful Life*. The research backs her up. She also cites studies showing mindful eating's association with decreased binge eating and a higher-quality diet.

That doesn't mean, nor do studies show, that mindfulness works for weight loss. "Viewing mindfulness and savoring through the lens of diet culture is problematic," says clinical psychologist Alexis Conason, author of *The Diet-Free Revolution*. "I'm about tuning people in to what feels good and doesn't. Allowing ourselves to have food is a radical act when we're told most of our lives that our pleasure is gluttonous."

Proponents of intuitive eating, another anti-diet approach, are even more explicit about the need for pleasure. As Evelyn Tribole and Elyse Resch, the method's cofounders, write in *Intuitive Eating*, "When you eat what you really want, in an environment that is inviting, the pleasure you derive will be a powerful force in helping you feel satisfied and content." You can use satisfaction to achieve balance, whatever the size of your body, so that your enjoyment of food is the driver behind experiencing a comfortable level of both hunger and fullness.

Savoring your food, ultimately, helps you savor the rest of your life. Indeed, intuitive eating's connection to "numerous adaptive psychological constructs" has been asserted in studies. "People have better moods, self-compassion, and they're less connected with eating disorders and pathology," Tribole notes. "They're able to engage in life."

Yet, savoring doesn't have to be an all-in process. Intuitive eating dietitian Christy Harrison, host of the *Rethinking Wellness* and *Food Psych* podcasts, notes, "For people who are restricting or binging, savoring can be overwhelming. Distraction—looking at their phone, being out with friends—can be helpful." Savoring doesn't have to be, and for some people shouldn't be, a solitary act. Meals with friends and family, if uncomplicated, can help you really connect with yourself, with others, and with the food you're eating.

The social context is how Melton, cofounder of Diversify Dietetics, a nonprofit promoting diversity in the field, approaches savoring. "Think of a group of friends sitting around eating. They all dig in and go 'Mmm.' Social pleasure comes from that collective experience," she says.

For Melton, whose father is Trinidadian, an essential part of helping people savor their food is honoring the culture it came from. "Often food is the one thing people can experience from home multiple times a day," she says. "Let's take away the stigma that what you are feeding to your family is not healthy just because mainstream culture says it's not. What do you like to eat? What memories is it bringing back? Celebrations, family, customs—is there a reason why you are craving this kind of food?"

Where does all this leave my cheesesteak and me? Well, I'm biologically programmed to crave it, for starters. "From an evolutionary perspective, there must be a reason we have dopamine," Baerten said. "Pleasure pulls us toward something. The question is, what gives you not just superficial pleasure but profound, soul-based pleasure? That has to do with connecting with deeper layers within yourself and others." She wasn't talking about cheesesteaks, of course. She was thinking of the way you savor broccoli from a grower you come to know at the farmers market. But I certainly feel connected to my family and my community when I'm back in Philly and eat my hometown sandwich.

The next time I order a cheesesteak, I will tune in to what feels good and what doesn't, as Conason says, and not eat it with so many gut-challenging long hots. I've also been thinking about something Cheung suggested: "We're in the habit of saying, 'I don't have enough time for lunch, so I'll eat while meeting the deadline,'" she said. "One way of savoring your food is spending 10 minutes doing nothing but eating. If you're in a hurry, save the rest for a snack. You'll get hungry later, and you can have the food again and appreciate it." Then she mentioned how on Okinawa, one of the planet's so-called blue zones, where people live to be in excess of 100, they make sure to eat to only 80 percent fullness.

I'll eat my cheesesteak, not like I normally do, while driving. Instead I'll slide into a booth at the local joint, unwrap the sandwich carefully, ponder the sensations of the meaty, melty filling and its sturdy roll as I eat it, until I feel I am just this side of "Oy, I am stuffed." I'll rewrap what's left contemplatively, and look forward to savoring it the next day, when I feel hungry again.

JOHN BIRDSALL

The Gay Roots of (Ugh)
Friendsgiving

FROM *Shifting the Food Narrative*

"THERE WAS AN uproar in the IRS offices here over canceling an upcoming Thanksgiving office party potluck," the artist Edward Gallagher told a reporter, "when the straights said they wouldn't share food prepared by gay employees."

This was in 1984, mid-November. Gallagher had built a piece of street art in the plaza outside the Federal Building in San Francisco: four open coffins, each stuffed with a mannequin—a businessman, a housewife, a little kid, a cliché gay—all linked by transfusion tubes connected to blood bags in hospital IV hangers: a protest of Reagan's policy of silence and neglect and slashing health agency budgets, that AIDS was righteous retribution from a vengeful God, not a public health crisis.

Gallagher stood by to study the reactions of passersby, and this is how he heard about the canceled potluck. Many who walked around Gallagher's installation were unmoved. "Most say it's a gay disease and a gay problem and the gays should solve it themselves," Gallagher said.

Thanksgiving would be subject to a similar calculus. There would be 4,251 known deaths from AIDS in the US that year (surely a gross undercount that hints at the neglect—in eight years in the White House, President Reagan would preside over more than 89,000 reported deaths). Nancy Reagan inadvertently took a sip of water from her homosexual hairstylist's glass and summoned the White House physician to ask with alarm if maybe now she had *it*.

Thanksgiving 1984 saw the first dedicated dinner free of charge for people with AIDS and HIV and their friends and partners in San Francisco. A year later, the event drew 500 people to a performance space in the Mission. The SF AIDS Foundation supplied some of the food, the rest was potluck style from attendees who were able to cook. Volunteers offered rides, helped some of the fragile guests to the party.

Mainstream opinion held that gays were spreading the disease everywhere that November: let the promiscuous animals spread their gay sweat and saliva over their gay turkey and gay yams; spread the deadly droplets and miasma of doom around their own kind.

And so (cue the magic wand glissando harp), Queer Thanksgiving was born. In the early 2000s it would morph into *Friendsgiving*, a word I do not like (a glib, cloying word). And this rebirth, if you will, would erase the history of political urgency around Queer Thanksgiving. Long after the eighties came to an end, this indie holiday, this alt-Thanksgiving, would be rehabbed like some Chip 'n' Joanna family fixer into bland and sunny open-concept lifestyle content: as Friendsgiving.

Thanksgiving has always had a tradition of the unattached from home—so-called holiday orphans, people unable to make it back to blood family because of distance: students, soldiers, workers; but Friendsgiving became this different thing, a conscious staying away.

I like Eric Kim's story in the *New York Times* describing LGBTQ expressions of Friendsgiving, especially a quote from Queer chef Tony Ortiz: "So many of us aren't able to build strong connections with our families because of our Queerness. It makes me think about the strength of my bonds with my chosen family, how much deeper that connection is because of our shared identity. It can feel deeper than blood."

Elane, who is one of my oldest friends, has scarred memories of holidays at home, which she left when she was sixteen.

"The first Friendsgiving I can think of under that (sort of) name," she tells me in an email, "would have been one with my then-fiancée Jules, in San Francisco, in a Victorian/Edwardian/ etc. house that belonged to neither of us. I'm sure I would get the guest list wrong (because I am terrible about that stuff, having been taught to forget, not to remember) but I do know that Jules (wine rep and poet) was there . . . more lesbians were there, and [the chef] Traci Des Jardins was there. Both Jules and I were cooks—

loved cooking, loved all the sensual and giving aspects of it—and
we had agreed/volunteered to manage it.

"Please know: I don't remember us as having done the whole
thing, but it's hard to remember when attraction and food and
hosting are involved."

Remembering is key, though.

The roots of Queer Thanksgiving stretch deep, deeper than 1984,
when the IRS employee potluck was scrapped. By at least 1971, two
years after Stonewall, the gay civil rights org Society for Individual
Rights was putting on annual Thanksgiving dinners in San Francisco,
free and, at a time when Queer bars were segregated, open to everybody. These dinners offered clear messages of Queer freedom—in
place, or maybe next to, flickers of nostalgia about Thanksgivings
at grandma's house in the bad old days of the deep closet, the conviction that we are Queer family. That instead of celebrating some
mythic patriarchal past, Thanksgiving could mark collective hope for
a future of liberation.

Since 1978, when Dan White assassinated Queer Supervisor
Harvey Milk and Mayor George Moscone at City Hall just days
after the holiday, Thanksgiving was a time of Queer rebellion in
San Francisco. Each year on November 27, hundreds marched
down Market Street to protest police violence and the lack of
legal protections for Queers. In 1983 protestors highlighted
another injustice: the lack of federal AIDS policy in Washington.
In late October 1985, a pair of AIDS protestors chained themselves to the front doors of a federal office building. They called
it the Vigil—a spontaneous action demanding a level of basic
humanity from the White House, Congress, and the judiciary,
i.e., ending their toxic hatred of Queers (granting access to
experimental AIDS drugs, committing money for research, prosecuting discrimination against people with AIDS . . .). It was
doomed to fail, of course. Still, other protestors joined them,
and on Thanksgiving, supporters delivered a potluck to activists
bundled in coats and blankets. They ate stuffing, green bean cas-
serole, yams, and pie from paper plates balanced on their laps.

Gay bars also put out spreads for Queer Thanksgiving—
the Gangway, SF Eagle, and all the silly, dumb, and charming
bartender wink lines: *You fixin' to get stuffed and basted tonight,
darlin?* . . . the wet Jockey shorts contests and go-go boys and

drag . . . pecan pie and poppers and things with lush promise and maybe even the power to black out the growing-up traumas in Davenport or Dinuba and a killing accumulation of day-to-days lived in the closet . . . the Dykesgiving potlucks, or—to rinse the bitterness of colonialism and patriarchy and animal exploitation clean out of the holiday—Harvest gatherings, where acorn squash baked with mounds of chestnut stuffing were totems of the womb; of the cosmic cycle of fertility and Womyn power.

James Oseland, one-time editor-in-chief of *Saveur* magazine, former judge on *Top Chef Masters*, and author of the World Food series, was a Queer presence in the early SF punk scene. James was a student at the SF Art Institute in the early eighties, and a friend there got a grant to make a documentary about the performance art scene in the East Village. They spent three weeks shooting in New York in November–December of '82, as James recalls, a lot of it centered on the Pyramid Club, which was like some cultural incubator for punk and drag and art, the place where RuPaul, Lypsinka, and Lady Bunny got famous downtown; where Nirvana played its first NY shows; where Keith Haring hung out. Anyway, they were shooting there, and in artists' studios, basically a bunch of shitty squats. "Lo and behold," James says, "our being in New York was coinciding with Thanksgiving, and I've never been a great Thanksgiving fan—the foods of that holiday hold zero sentimental value for me—but I do appreciate the idea of a meal that we have once a year either as a literal blood family or with people we *understand* to be our families.

"Anyway, I heard about this gathering, in someone's big old storefront loft on Avenue C, maybe, this big, big space, and it was a potluck. There were maybe 35 to 55 people there, basically all vying for the Nina Hagen costume award. But what was so touching to me—even to this day—was the sincerity of the endeavor, and the natural-born instinct of these people to gather together and carry on this tradition that's inside people everywhere to connect over a meal. I was really struck by how delightfully uncynical it was. Like Norman Rockwell in the East Village of the 1980s."

My own hazy memories of alt-Thanksgiving (let's call it '85), drifting down to Marc's flat on Haight Street after our own dinner, walking up to this sprawling potluck in the later stages of dissipation, dozens of people kicked back, splayed, me ransacking scattered bottles of wine to piece together a glass as the needle drops *again* on "This Charming Man" . . . shaggy, brown-stained joints still circulating, powders being snorted from a table somewhere on the periphery, and *Oh my god you have to taste Margo's pumpkin mousse cake would you ever in a million years guess it was tofu,* and it's warm and sweating on the table in the absolutely wrecked kitchen, sliced up, fingered, picked at, and of course it's fucking delicious and of course I'd guess it was tofu . . . *Why pamper life's complexity / when the leather runs smooth on the passenger seat?* . . . and then piling into somebody's car to zig through empty streets to the Stud, packed and *quivering* with the DJ's take on Madonna's "Holiday"—sonically embroidered, appliquéd, and quilted—and it feels like the home we always hoped to find, or try to make if we had to.

A home in that zone of exclusion, exile, and belonging—of need and the end of need—where alt-Thanksgiving lives, forever and everywhere. It's where every alt-holiday lives.

Orange Is the New Yolk

FROM *Eater*

AN EGG YOLK is precious; a hundred are terrifying. In an Instagram reel from last year, a pair of disembodied hands tips a large metal bowl full of neon-orange yolks into a well of flour, an act whose ostensible purpose is to make fresh pasta but whose effect is to freak me out. The wet yolks cluster densely as if just emancipated from a sac, the sort of potential life form that portends doom in a sci-fi movie: *When all of these hatch, we're fucked.* Without this shock of near-unnatural color—which ranges from clementine to cadmium—the video would lose its effect; the yolks are so dark and so plentiful you worry they might fight back. But with the whisk of a fork, their borders disappear, and they become a thick, placid pool of goo. The video ends before they get the chance to become dough. In recent years, these shockingly orange yolks have infiltrated America's supermarket shelves, boasting virtue and vitamins. At your local upscale grocer you might find a robin's-egg blue carton of "heritage free range" eggs from the Happy Egg Co., six of them blue and six of them brown. The label is a dusty cobalt, interrupted by a bright orange circle: a yolk, naked and flashing you from its cracked-open shell, no white in sight.

Last spring, my boyfriend brought a dozen of these eggs into my kitchen. They seemed harmless at first, but when he scrambled them, I found myself eating a plate of eggs closer in color to Bugs Bunny's carrot than a simple French omelette. Later, I fried one next to my last CSA (community-supported agriculture) egg, laid in the Catskills by a pasture-raised hen. Once transferred to a bowl of rice, they looked like a clone experiment gone wrong. The CSA yolk was a deep goldenrod, fat and happy looking. The Happy Egg yolk was such an aggressive reddish orange it looked like a pustule.

The specter of those radioactive yolks haunted me. Clearly, they were meant to make me feel good about myself, but their effect was uncanny. We have become so desperate for the all-natural, I realized, that we will pay a premium for its simulacra. And in an effort to appease us by proving the natural, healthy habitats of their hens, egg companies will supplement their feed with things like marigolds, turmeric, and beets to greenwash a perfectly suitable yellow yolk. According to a spokesperson for Happy Egg, their proprietary corn-and-soybean chicken feed includes "micro ingredients like marigold that provide additional nutrients to ensure the health of our hens."

As we have boomeranged back from the egg-white omelet's late-twentieth-century tyranny, the egg has become the poster child for all-natural, accessible, "whole" foods ready to prove their virtue once you crack them open. And as the last decade's farm-to-table and locavore movements (and, importantly, their aesthetics) have gone mainstream, the "farm egg" has become ubiquitous, its yolk an object of our undivided attention. We want it jammy, that sludgy midway between soft- and medium-boiled. We want it over easy, its yolk sploojing across the plate. And we want its color to convince us that it was not hatched in some animal-welfare hellscape.

Egg carton marketing, which is at best opaque and at worst a pernicious lie, would have us believe that the hens who imparted these eggs to the bourgeois grocery-shopping class are twirling through pastoral fields like Maria in *The Sound of Music*. The yolk is the purest representation of this dream, a bright-orange ball of flavor and "good" fat that dazzles the eye, fills the belly, and soothes the conscience. Earlier this year the high-end egg purveyor Vital Farms launched an ad campaign in which couples propose to each other not with diamonds, but Vital Farms eggs. Inside these shells, if you follow this swell of marketing logic, lies not just the secret to happiness and virtue, but life itself. The state of the yolk today tells us more about ourselves and our desires than it does about the egg that laid it.

While egg-white omelets seem outré in our current era of virtuous fats, America's relationship with yolks has a deep and complex history. The yolk phobia of the late twentieth century arguably began in the 1950s, when the biologist and physiologist Ancel Keys popularized the idea that high levels of cholesterol increase the risk of heart disease, an idea further reinforced by the landmark Framingham Heart Study. By the 1960s, the relationship between cholesterol and cardiovascular disease had been established; in the ensuing decades, scientists and farmers alike created low-cholesterol eggs. Egg whites sold in a carton boomed. But by 1959, the American Heart Association was insisting that villainizing cholesterol in eggs "is unjustified from existing scientific evidence and is depriving persons of a 'very good product.'"

It took almost fifty years for this idea to catch on. The origins of our recent yolk worship can be traced to the late nineties, when a few influential chefs were buying ingredients from local farms and educating their diners about it. As the farm-to-table movement and the locavore movement and the Slow Food movement swelled throughout the aughts, the egg was freed not just from nutritional jail but also the dogmatic strictures of breakfast: "Put an egg on it" became a popular way to level up a dish. In 2008, it even spawned a zine with the same (though purposely misspelled) name.

Four years before that, Momofuku Noodle Bar opened and began serving bowls of ramen topped with poached eggs. Thanks to the restaurant's runaway popularity, "the soft egg became a ubiquitous hipster entity," explains the food writer Charlotte Druckman. By the late aughts, the egg had been given a bespoke agrarian rebranding: In 2008, Frank Bruni lamented the redundancy of a "hen egg" on the menu at Momofuku Ko; the following year, Eleven Madison Park was serving a poached "farm egg with Parmesan foam," topped also with brown butter hollandaise and asparagus. The egg's luxury came as much from its implied provenance as it did from garnishes like caviar and hollandaise: the diner might assume that the chef had sourced the egg from a farm where the chickens' asses were being wiped with non-GMO Charmin.

The rise of the farm egg on fine-dining menus also coincided with the Great Recession, an era when "a lot of fine-dining chefs started looking into ingredients that had been considered trashy or ugly," says Druckman. "They would make the ingredients 'refined,' and charge more but pay less." As chefs like Momofuku's David Chang moved toward a more casual aesthetic, eggs began to colonize menus along with offal, bacon, and doughnuts. A sous vide egg, popularized in the States by the late-aughts ramen boom, "is something that's snobby in its technique, but it's a staple food for everyone," Druckman points out.

With those sous vide eggs, the popularity of ramen also laid the groundwork for the future of the now-ubiquitous jammy egg, which, with its molten, sludgy, ideally deep-orange yolk, has since become its own object of desire. It's difficult to locate the first use of the phrase "jammy egg," but *Bon Appétit* certainly vaulted it into the lexicon of the masses. A 2017 spread in the magazine called "Put an Egg On It," written by Chris Morocco and Amiel Stanek, put forth a primer on fried, poached, and boiled eggs to suit the modern "egg-topped age." Last in the package was "the jammy soft boil," which instructed a strict six-and-a-half-minute boil and an ice bath plunge for "exactly the egg we want luxuriating in our ramen or getting cozy with soft grits."

"There was this collective feeling that eggs were just everywhere," Morocco remembers of the package. The egg "becomes this visual language that is a gateway to so many things," he says. The jammy egg in particular is "a preparation that crosses all kinds of culinary boundaries and is so readily adaptable to virtually any type of dish." The fact that it takes under ten minutes to cook helped smooth the jammy egg's transition from restaurant fetish object to home cook favorite.

The spread of the farm-to-table movement also endowed the jammy egg with more virtuous undertones. "The orangey, burnished, reddish yolk also became its own kind of signifier for this 'better egg,'" Morocco says. "That color became synonymous with free-range, free-running hens that have access to the outdoors and are able to actually eat the foods that they're most naturally geared towards."

That color played to our subconscious appetites: in the world of food marketing psychology, yellow and orange make people hungry; red makes them feel passion. Add some messaging that claims color as a signal of farm-to-table virtue, and you have a product so appealing you could sell it to hens. The ease with which companies can obfuscate the origins of these eggs—and convince us of their virtue—further deepens the divide between animal and cook. As consumers grow ever more alienated from the animals, crops, and laborers involved in producing the ingredients we buy, more and more producers have made an effort to remind us that they come from farms, creating a strange feedback loop of ignorance. We have been taught to equate color with better treatment and better nutrition, whether it's true or not.

Consider the fifteen different egg options at Mr. Mango, a Brooklyn grocer near my yoga studio. One comes in Styrofoam, but still claims its eggs are "sourced from family-owned farms" and encourages shoppers to "meet the family farmer whose hens laid your eggs." Next to it are Happy Egg Heritage eggs, and eight more free-range or pasture-raised brands, almost all with labels that show a few (not too many!) hens, pecking their way through rolling hills or pastures.

The labels on the egg cartons contain more disclaimers and promises than a Notes app apology: tended by hand; small family farms; happy hens; ethical eggs; no hormones; no antibiotics; no animal fat; all-natural; certified organic; 300mg omega-3s; lutein + ZEA [zeaxanthin]; non-GMO; certified humane raised + handled; fresh air and sunshine; freedom to forage outdoors year-round. Vital Farms even publishes a faux newspaper (one page) about their "outdoorsy girls" that's tucked into their $12 cartons.

All of this copywriting is telling the same story, which can be summed up as "We're not like them!" *Them* being the industrial farms whose eggs turn up at lower price points—I recently saw a dozen sold for $2.19—in Styrofoam containers at your local grocery store. These are the farms that often stack chickens on top of each other and stuff them with GMO feed, breed disease, wash their eggs with bleach to sanitize them, and squeeze out as many eggs as possible from bedraggled hens who must lay in view of their comrades' corpses. These farms turn the chicken, as authors Page Smith and Charles Daniel explain in *The Chicken Book*, into "an industrial process whose product [is] the egg."

If you walk the aisles of Mr. Mango or just about any feel-good grocery store, a binary narrative might appear in your brain. There are the bad farms—Styrofoam carton, diseased hens shitting on each other—and then there are the good ones, whose hens are happy and free to roam, and lay eggs abundant with nutrients and vibrant color.

In reality, that binary is a spectrum, and a muddy one. Yes, factory farms wreak environmental and ethical havoc. And it *is* possible to buy eggs from hens who have lived a much more humane and carefree life than you have. (The easiest way to do this is to buy directly from a small farm whose practices you've researched or asked them about.) But the middle ground between those places is far wider, and more common, than egg labels would like us to think. And where the question of flavor is concerned, the equation becomes even jammier.

The flavor of an egg—watery and wan or rich and lively—owes itself to the choices of a farmer. So too does the color of its yolk. Those choices begin with the breed of hen purchased and the living conditions provided for those hens; they end with variables like washing, refrigeration, and distribution.

At Ramble Bramble farm in Huntington, Vermont, Jamie Skye Bianco raises chickens for both slaughter and laying, as well as dairy goats, sheep, and lamb. All of the farm's products are certified organic, and its laying hens are heritage breeds including the black copper Marans, which can lay copper-colored eggs with such a striking and sought-after hue that they have their own color charts. Their yolks, too, are a deep golden orange.

The black copper Marans are some of the most expensive hens to raise per laid egg: While hybrid breeds used by industrial farms lay six to seven eggs a week, Marans lay anywhere from zero to four times a week, a rate that gradually decreases to zero before the end of the hen's average eight-year lifespan. Marans take up to forty weeks to mature; industrial hens can take as little as fourteen.

"Raising that type of bird, you can't sell enough eggs unless you're selling to a really niche market," Bianco says. "From the position of a market farmer, you might be able to get twice as much selling Marans eggs, but you're really only getting about a quarter of the eggs in a given season." The Marans, though, is prized not just for its egg color, but the rich flavor hiding inside.

Throughout the year at Ramble Bramble, the hens graze on the refuse from the farm's other operations. In the fall, they peck at fallen apples that have been turned to a sweet mulch by the tractors that drive over them, which creates a marginally higher sugar level in the eggs that lightens the yolk. Some farms with heavy composting operations or lots of pigs will raise chickens atop compost and manure piles, "and that has its own flavor" that it imparts on the eggs, Bianco says. "It obviously doesn't taste like *shit*, but it does have a particular flavor because it's predigested pasture, so to speak, and they're picking out both the bugs in the compost and the predigested stuff. But your ordinary person is not going to pick up differences like this."

What happens *after* the egg exits the chicken also has an effect on flavor. At Ramble Bramble, Bianco waits as long as possible to wash their eggs, in an effort to stave off degradation. In the US, farmers must wash eggs before selling them to remove the "bloom," a protective coating added in the cloaca just before laying that keeps the egg safe from bacteria. Immediately after the wash, an egg begins to dehydrate, and the inner membrane lining—the thin white clingy stuff that can make peeling a freshly boiled egg such a pain—begins to degrade. This process leads to a breakdown of the protein and fat bonds inside the egg that keep a yolk delicious, vibrant, and jammy. Refrigeration also affects the chemical composition of an egg, decreasing its viscosity and increasing its wateriness. Crack a freshly laid, healthy egg onto a plate or pan, and you'll see the yolk sit proudly above the white, like a napping Gudetama; the white, too, will have a clear demarcation between the firmer inner white and the looser outer white. An old, long-washed, long-refrigerated egg will spread out in the pan.

And what about color? What about the molten-red yolk that once terrified me but so many people chase in a Marans? According to their website, the Happy Egg company's contracted "family farmers" raise copper Marans for the orange-yolked heritage eggs and speckled Legbars for the blue-shelled eggs, and give them "a specialized and more premium feed." The Happy Egg website points out how "spoiled" their "egg-laying queens" are, roaming and eating "tasty bugs" near play kits and swings. If you're unsure of the results this environment creates, you can visit a page titled "9 Pictures of Heritage Egg Yolks That Are Undeniably Sexy."

I asked Bianco about the likelihood of a mass-market egg producer using supplements to turn their yolks orange. "If you are a larger seller," they said, "or a market seller using hybrid birds that make watery eggs with no interesting color, the only way you're going to get the results you're looking for is some kind of coloration through diet."

Of course, there's no health risk to consumers if farmers are sprinkling marigolds into their chickens' feeds. But this tinkering still leads consumers to conflate yolk color with health benefits and increased flavor that they're not likely enjoying—some anonymous taste tests have shown little difference between the flavor of "farm eggs" and factory-farmed eggs. Yolk color preference varies between countries; egg farmers can use Yolk Fan, which looks like a deck of paint colors, to calibrate their feed to consumer preferences. Shoppers pay for the idea of the benefit, not the benefit itself, a discrepancy that the color of the yolk further obscures. Scientists have found that visual cues can affect the flavors we taste even more persuasively than what we smell or taste. A darker yolk might taste more delicious if only because of its rich color, not the protein and omega-3s it hides.

The mass-marketing of amber yolks serves only to further distance the consumer from the farm. Such greenwashing gives the well-intentioned shopper the illusion that they are making choices in line with their own beliefs—and saves them the trouble of going to a farmers market and asking an actual human farmer how they raise their eggs—but obfuscates the specific choices carried out by producers and farmers.

For Happy Egg, those choices have resulted in a class-action lawsuit claiming that its eggs should be labeled as "free-range" instead of "pasture-raised." In the UK, PETA has allegedly filmed inside a number of farms owned by the identically named but entirely unaffiliated Happy Egg Co. and found overcrowding, large swaths of muddy dirt instead of peckable grass, and dead birds left to rot among those who survive them. While the animal welfare nonprofit can skew militant and sensationalist, its alleged footage underscores the often stark differences between what people expect from their feel-good supermarket eggs and the way those eggs are actually produced. Keeping farm animals always entails a bit of control: even at the microfarming level, animals are there primarily to produce food. But the great scam of industrial greenwashing is convincing consumers that the animal welfare and sustainability that smaller farms often prioritize is easily scalable, without sacrifice.

In recent years, this conflation of health and flavor with yolk color (and even shell color) has granted eggs, and particularly their yolks, a sheen of wellness that was unheard of two decades ago, when the country was still under the spell of the egg-white omelet. The egg yolk is now sexy in the way that selectively placed body fat and overhydrated skin are sexy—it promises an abundance of life. The egg has long represented fertility, but now it has a proprietary money shot: Breaking into the seven-minute egg sitting regally atop a composed salad offers a safe-for-work form of ejaculation that feels decidedly wholesome.

On social media, the egg yolk has become a matinee idol. At the now-shuttered Konbi in Los Angeles, the menu's star was an egg salad sandwich which, when split open, offered a centerfold of jammy yolk. At Manhattan's 4 Charles Prime Rib, if you add the $3.99 "farm egg" to your $36.99 double wagyu cheeseburger, you receive tableside service wherein a white-gloved server pierces the egg's yolk and pours it over the burger, raising it up for a long and dramatic stream as if it's Basque cider. The VIP List girlies claim this bit of theater *changed their lives*. It has, predictably, become a TikTok sensation.

For home cooks, eggs remain the ultimate Instagram bait: They're cheap to buy (inflation notwithstanding) and easy to make, and even a luddite with an iPhone 4 can get a nice shot of a fried egg. Eggs are easily recognizable and easily broken: see an intact yolk on a TikTok and you already know what's coming, like the twelfth kill shot in a John Wick movie. Despite all that repetition, it's still fun to watch someone's knife cut into a fried or soft-boiled egg and watch the yolk conquer the rest of the plate.

Dan Pelosi, who shares recipes and cooking videos on Instagram under the name @grossypelosi, has posted countless egg photos, which means he has years of data on the ways in which a yolk can drive us crazy. Aside from pasta, "eggs are the thing people talk to me about the most," he says. "The orange yolk is huge—they think that you have to go to some special place that's on a different plane to get an orange-yolked egg." In reality, he gets his Vital Farm eggs from the bodega. "I'm a sucker for it," he says of the orange yolk. "It doesn't taste better, but it's pretty, and I care about aesthetics."

Many people, Pelosi says, are still nervous about cooking an egg—they think they'll mess it up, or get salmonella from undercooking it, or gross themselves out by overcooking it. Eggs are accessible and familiar, but require finesse, a perfect foil for our neuroses.

Seeing them on a screen, however, turns eggs into an idea, a consumer product to coo at. When I ask Pelosi about why the piercing of a yolk is so appealing—even after we've been seeing it for a decade—he offers a little giggle, but his explanation is more chaste than the one I'm imagining: "I mean, have you ever popped a pimple?"

Orange yolks have become a useful tool in professional food photography too. Susan Spungen, a cookbook author and food stylist, has used Happy Eggs for photo shoots. "I do think that getting that shot where the yolk is running has always been a food styling moment," she says. "Those dark amber eggs really do look good on camera—there it looks natural. If the yolk is really pale yellow, it just doesn't have the same impact. But I made pâte sucrée with [Happy Eggs], and I couldn't even use it; it looked dyed." She thinks that the farmers may feed their hens turmeric for that extra glow.

Spungen was the founding food editor at *Martha Stewart Living* when it launched in the early nineties, and believes that it was none other than the magazine—and its eponymous founder—who planted the seeds of our current egg enthusiasm. "She was an early adopter of keeping [heritage breed] chickens," Spungen says of Stewart. "Martha would bring her eggs from her farm in Westport to the test kitchen." The magazine even ran a multipage showcase of heritage breeds, with a dissertation on the joys of keeping them.

Backyard chickens became a foundational part of Stewart's DIY-luxe ethos, in which she turned homesteading into class performance for the upper crust. To wit: In 1995, she launched a collection of paint colors inspired by the shells of her Araucana hens' eggs. Although they were discontinued in 2012, they continue to loom large in the cultural memory. When I mentioned to my boyfriend's mother that I was writing about egg yolks and Martha's influence in the world of egg worship, she let out a gasp of recognition and exclaimed, "*Araucanas!*" Stewart's strategy—to expose those interested in homemaking and cooking to the luxury and aesthetic of good eggs—both echoes and inverts their promise: While the egg is cheap luxury, she turns it into luxury-luxury. Almost thirty years ago, her paint sold for over $100 a gallon. (More recently, she wrote about the trays of wheatgrass she grows in her greenhouse especially for her "happy, healthy chickens.")

Like a yellow yolk, a blue shell doesn't say much about the life of the chicken who laid it, or how flavorful its interior goo might be. But from a consumer perspective, it appears as precious as a gem that begs to be shown off. And consumers are all too willing to comply: At Gohar World, a recently launched tableware company from chef and artist Laila Gohar and her artist sister, Nadia, you can buy a $328 wrought iron "egg chandelier" to display your brown and ecru and blue eggs, regardless of whether you plan to cook them. (Does one remove the eggs one by one for cooking, until the chandelier is finally bare?) The piece's impressive frivolity underscores the egg's new role as status symbol: Martha may have placed hers in a handwoven basket, but Gohar World insists on elevating them—literally—as design objects. To finish the look, you can purchase a set of six lace "egg dresses," complete with black ribbon. "Why just eat your eggs," the product description reads, "when you can dress them up, too?"

I have had spotty luck perfecting the jammy egg. *Bon Appétit*'s six and a half minutes leave me with a loose, snotty white near the yolk; seven minutes and about twenty seconds usually gets me closer to the ideal, but the edges of the yolk begin to set and turn pale, an aesthetic sin that evokes the specter of the hard-boiled yolk, whose chalky texture has yet to find its resurgence.

But some people hope that moment is nigh, including Moonlynn Tsai, the cofounder of Heart of Dinner and a former partner at the Malaysian restaurant Kopitiam in Manhattan. When Kopitiam opened in 2015, she remembers, someone on Instagram shared a photo of the restaurant's nasi lemak, a dish topped with a halved hard-boiled egg. "Everybody was like, 'How dare they cook it to that point? That's disrespectful to the egg—do they not even know how to cook a proper egg?'" Tsai says of the comments. "And I just remember sitting there like, *This is a literal direct attack on our culture and upbringing.* Just because you're seeing a different style of egg [than what's] popular nowadays, it doesn't mean that this is a bad egg."

Tsai, who is Taiwanese, grew up eating her mother's tea eggs, would crumble the seasoned yolk, using it "almost as a topping on my rice." Unlike a runny yolk, which can evade you once it's exposed, a hard-cooked yolk is willing to be put into service. It can be seasoned, turned into a condiment for rice or even steak tartare. "It's like a sponge," Tsai explains, eager to soak up whatever flavor we want to assign it.

Tsai recently ate a hard-boiled egg that may be a bellwether of things to come. Lingo, a new Japanese American restaurant in Greenpoint, Brooklyn, serves a smoked tamago sando, which arrives as delicate rectangles of egg salad sandwich topped with bold lines of salmon roe. Chef Emily Yuen hard-boils the eggs for ten minutes before marinating them in mirin and soy and then smoking them; finally, she mashes them with Kewpie mayonnaise, seaweed, and Sichuan pepper. A hard boil is essential, Yuen says, for a sturdy and flavorful egg salad; a runny yolk would get lost in the mess of dressing.

Perhaps if recession-style cooking brings us back the deviled egg and egg salad, it might also revive that single-use kitchen tool, the egg slicer. Can't you picture Great Jones, foremost purveyor of *What if it was the fifties again?* aesthetics, making one in "broccoli" or "taffy"?

If you are one of the millions of civilians who still fear the egg, do this: boil it until each cell of its yolk can be held between the fingers without running away. Find yourself an egg slicer, and watch as the firm white bends to its wires, succumbing to the soothing regularity of pattern. A soft, calming yellow will appear between the cracks. You'll realize it was never so complicated after all.

SHARANYA DEEPAK

India's Beef with Beef

FROM *The Baffler*

WHEN JUNAID KHAN was a young boy, his mother, Saira Begum, would return home close to nightfall. She would squat next to an open fire to cook rotis for her hungry son, who would smear them with butter. "Junaid would eat rotis in whole gulps. I had to stop him before he ate too much," Saira told me one summer evening in 2019. She lives with her relatives in a small brick house in Khandawali, a village in Haryana near New Delhi. When we spoke, she lay on her divan. In a corner stood a desk on which Junaid would study. Like many women in her village, Saira is a farm laborer whose income—four thousand rupees per month in 2019, or fifty-seven dollars—does not ensure food for her family at all times. She owns one buffalo, however, that she milks and uses to plow the land that she works. Food is scarce in her home, but the white butter she made with buffalo milk was delicious and filling for her children.

Junaid was sixteen years old when he, his older brother Hashim, and two friends were attacked on a train in Haryana in June 2017. The boys were commuting home from an Eid shopping trip and a visit to the mosque when they were asked to vacate their seats by a group of men. When I visited Saira's home, Hashim explained that the men noticed they were Indian Muslims and threatened to beat them if they didn't move. "They were older, larger, and Hindu," he recounted, as he fiddled with a photograph of Junaid. "They kept calling us *beef eaters*," he continued, along with other faith-based slurs. "Whenever they said the word *beef eater*, they became more violent and coordinated in their attack. It was like the chant brought them together." During their argument, the men stabbed Junaid with a knife. They threw the boys out at Asaoti station, where Junaid succumbed to his injuries from the assault and died.

Junaid Khan's lynching is one of several incidents of its kind that have frequently occurred in India over the last decade. They are commonly referred to as "cow-related violence," a subsection of crime in which those under suspicion of eating, selling, or transporting beef are searched, humiliated, mauled, and even killed for supposedly violating a cow, an animal which Hindus consider sacred. A 2019 report titled "Violent Cow Protection in India" notes that, between May 2015 and December 2018, at least forty-four people were killed in such attacks. According to the report, this violence occurred across the country; the victims were largely Muslim, indigenous Adivasis, or Dalits, members of India's lowest caste. In most cases, attackers in these incidents were *gau rakshaks,* or self-styled cow vigilantes, operating either individually or in organized groups. Frequently Hindu, they were often members or affiliates of the ruling Bharatiya Janata Party (BJP) government.

In 2015, a fifty-two-year-old Muslim man named Mohammad Akhlaq was dragged out of his house with his son and beaten to death by a mob on the suspicion of storing beef in his fridge. When Akhlaq was killed, the Hindi-language magazine *Panchjanya* published a piece in defense of his killers. According to the article's author, Tufail Chaturvedi, seminal Hindu scriptures "order killing of the sinner who kills a cow. It is a matter of life and death for many [Hindus]." All nineteen accused in Akhlaq's murder—one of them a son of a local BJP leader—were released on bail. Sixteen were later congratulated in person by a local politician, as if to reward their actions.

History and Hypocrisy
While India's present government and media claim that the consumption and slaughter of beef is practiced only by foreigners, invaders, and miscreants, the history of beef consumption in India tells another, more complex tale. As anti-caste jurist and social reformer Bhimrao Ambedkar wrote in his 1948 book *The Untouchables: Who Were They and Why They Became Untouchables,* vegetarianism was first institutionalized in India in the fourth century as a move to reinforce rule by the Brahmin caste. (An architect of the Indian constitution adopted in 1950, Ambedkar fought against the caste system, arguing that its abolition was necessary for democracy in the fledgling Indian nation-state.) Before vegetarianism was claimed as central to Hindu culture and life, as writer Mukandi Lal explains in his 1967 essay "Cow

Cult in India," the slaughter of cows on ceremonial occasions was considered auspicious in ancient India. Lal notes this was especially commonplace among dominant-caste Hindus; *gomedha*, or the slaughter of the cow, is even mentioned in the classic Hindu epic the *Mahabharata*.

However, a change occurred under the king Ashoka, who converted to Buddhism in third century BCE and declared Buddhism the state religion of India. Lal explains that while eating beef was initially a visible practice during Ashoka's reign, animal slaughter was eventually discouraged by Buddhists in order to promote ideas of *ahimsa*, or nonviolence. To defeat their rivals in the politics of purity, Brahmins followed suit. They began to oppose cow sacrifices, deifying the animal instead. In *The Untouchables*, Ambedkar writes that, "without becoming vegetarian the Brahmins could not have recovered the ground they had lost to their rival namely Buddhism . . . This happened because the Brahmins made the cow a sacred animal. This made beef-eating a sacrilege."

The taboo on eating beef would later be heightened by the emergence of the "Krishna cult," as Lal puts it. Lal details how fifteenth-century Hindu saint and philosopher Sri Vallabhacharya, who founded a Krishna-centered sect of Hinduism, translated the *Bhagavata Purana* from Sanskrit to Hindi, the language of the masses. Vallabhacharya's translation and commentary on the text characterized Krishna as the most human incarnation of God. "Therefore, as the Krishna legend appealed to the common man in India, Krishna's cow became the cow mother (*Gomata*) of every Hindu," Lal explains. This is the beginning of *gau raksha*, or cow protection, in which protecting the animal became a way for Hindus to demonstrate their devotion and loyalty to the Hindu community and those that made its rules. The sanctification of cows and condemnation of cow slaughter were also useful tools for Hindus to combat Muslim influence. Lal asserts that dominant-caste Hindus became "even greater protectors of the cow" in response to Muslim conquests in the subcontinent, declaring beef eating as a "foreign" practice despite the growing popularity of Islam over the centuries among Indians, especially those of oppressed castes.

Purity Politics
Today, even as large communities across the subcontinent eat beef, most Brahmins remain vegetarian—a lifestyle they've

tried to normalize as an unquestionable part of Indian national identity.

For the last eight years, under its present leadership of the Narendra Modi–led BJP, India has drastically shifted to the Hindu right. Recent years have seen pogroms against working-class Muslims in the country, as well as the passage of laws that undermine the citizenship of Indian Muslims and prevent interfaith marriages. The BJP government is aided, funded, and backed by the ninety-year-old Rashtriya Swayamsevak Sangh, a Hindu extremist organization which supported Modi's rise to power. Together, Modi, the BJP, and the RSS make no qualms about the mission to build a Hindu Rashtra, or "India for Hindus," at the cost of its religious minorities. The BJP and RSS is resolute in their mission: everyone who obeys their terms is Indian, and anyone who doesn't is not.

In this environment, the BJP has pushed vegetarianism as fundamentally Indian, despite the continued predominance of meat consumption throughout the country. Recently, the *Economic and Political Weekly*, an Indian academic journal, found that more than 60 percent of India eats meat. Vegetarianism thrives only in the Hindu-dominated central part of the country's northern region. In India's northeastern states, less than 2 percent are vegetarian; West Bengal and Kerala, known for their meat dishes, are home to less than 5 percent. But under the BJP, the Hindu vegetarian's claim that meat eating is a foreign, miscreant practice is validated. In Khandawali and surrounding areas, both legal and vigilante punishment for selling and eating meat—especially beef—is severe, resulting in death in many cases.

The BJP and its supporters are not the only ones reinforcing these myths around the ubiquity of vegetarianism. These biases are also incredibly prevalent in the cultural sector. Take, for example, how the National Museum in India banned meat-based dishes from a 2020 historical exhibition on the food of the civilization of Harappa after officials from the Ministry of Culture expressed concern upon seeing meat on the menu; or how meats like beef and pork are seldom visible on *MasterChef India*, the show even going fully vegetarian for one season in 2015. The myth of Indian vegetarianism is also upheld by the dominant-caste Hindu diaspora in the West, where India's vegetarian dishes are viewed as the most "authentic" cuisine of the country. Zahir Janmohamed, an Indian American writer and host of *Racist Sandwich*, a podcast about food and politics, told me that it's the universality attributed to Indian vegetarianism in the diaspora that makes it a harmful tool for stereotyping South Asian cultures. The fact that vegetarianism is often seen as connoting purity and altruism by Western cultures is a boon for dominant-caste Hinduism and grants a degree of acceptance to the far-right Hindu agenda against beef. "It's like Indian Muslims don't have agency to claim a linguistic, regional, and culinary identity," Janmohamed explained. "In the diaspora, Hinduism, vegetarianism, and 'Indianism' go hand in hand."

For the Love of Beef

While beef remains undocumented in the Indian culinary canon, the meat has been essential to many around the country, especially those who work the land and rear cattle. The public declaration of the right to eat beef has taken many forms in the last decade, one of which is the formation of "beef festivals." These festivals have been organized across India by students' associations, particularly those headed and formed by students from the Dalit caste. In 2012, for example, Dalit students at Osmania University in Hyderabad, Telangana, organized the university's first beef festival, challenging the Brahmanical lens through which food is usually viewed. The event was stormed by the Akhil Bharatiya Vidyarthi Parishad, the youth wing of the RSS, who attacked the students and ransacked the venue. Other such festivals organized on university campuses were also threatened and attacked by the ABVP.

In 2017, the BJP government instituted "beef bans" across the country, closing slaughterhouses and further encouraging the terrorizing of beef eaters. In response, the BJP's actions were criticized as acting against India's federalism and flattening the country's varied eating cultures. Additional festivals and protests reemerged across India in a movement to resist the bans, especially in states like Kerala and West Bengal where beef is regularly consumed. Eating beef biryanis, kebabs, and curries in public became acts of rebellion against the BJP's actions. Public beef consumption, then, is a method of critical protest, one that resists the Hindu state's imposition on food cultures and directly confronts the vegetarianism dominant castes herald as supreme.

The bias against meat eating by those in power also hampers initiatives to fight hunger. The bans on beef and the vigilantism that

imposes vegetarianism deny adequate nutrition to those who need
it the most. Food rights activist, public health doctor, and researcher
Sylvia Karpagam spoke to me about how the Bangalore-based nonprofit Akshaya Patra Foundation was criticized for disallowing onions, garlic, meat, and eggs in their midday meals for malnourished
children. "Eat your green leafy vegetables, they will say. Even though
it has been proven that liver and other animal proteins are the most
effective and nutrient-dense sources of nourishment. Why is bias
enforced on the stomachs of those that it historically excludes?"
Karpagam asked. Food is not just about consumption but a matter
of taste, she argued. "The mouth salivates, the brain receives signals,
the food settles. To eat is to be moved, fulfilled, comforted. Would
you feed your own children bland food they resented? Would you
give them tablets instead of a warm meal?" Karpagam described the
Hindu vegetarian's idea of a "balanced meal"—including only lentils, rice, vegetables, and dairy—as a construct of privilege, catering
to those who have constant access to food.

When I spoke to Gogu Shyamala, a Telegu-language Dalit writer
and women's rights activist, she echoed Karpagam's frustrations.
Shyamala's work often focuses on the dominant-caste suppression
of oppressed-caste eating cultures. Her writing expresses criticism
and amusement at Hinduism's institutional preoccupation with
the cow while speaking directly to the Brahmanical authority that
denies food, land, and dignity to people like herself. "To this day /
have you reared a pair of bullocks? / A pair of sheep? / A buffalo
or two?" she writes in her poem "Beef, our life." "Do you know of
cattle fuzz? / What, in the end, do you know my friend / but to
say, 'don't eat beef?'" "To me," Shyamala explained on the phone,
"beef eating is a personal choice. It is related to land, cultivation,
and culture, and for many Dalit citizens of India, it is part of their
livelihood and lifestyle."

Down-and-Out in Lucknow
Despite beef being eaten with relish by communities around India, it is still hidden. The suppression of beef as food or culture
from public life has also been detrimental economically. The beef
bans, surveillance, and incidents of violence committed by the government, cow vigilantes, and other right-wing Hindu groups have
directly impacted the livelihoods of butchers and small-scale meat
sellers across India.

It was a scorching day in June 2019 when I traveled to Billoch-pura, part of the old city in Lucknow, Uttar Pradesh, and home to the Qureshis, a caste of Muslims who make up the community of butchers in the city. There I tried to speak to butchers about how their lives were affected by the bans on beef and meat selling. Lucknow has a large appetite for all meat, and especially beef. Its most beloved foods include *nihari,* a slow-cooked stew swiped up with fat, flaky breads called *kulchas,* and the *tunday kebab,* which is a dish of buffalo meat blitzed with spices that is famed through-out India's north. I spoke eventually with a butcher named Shahabuddin Qureshi. As we talked, he cut mangoes for the chil-dren gathered around him. They held the fruit upside down and watched the pulp leak onto the floor. Somberly, he recounted an incident that occurred three weeks prior, where a group of men in saffron scarves roughed up three others on the street outside his shop's window for holding a plastic bag, which the attackers suspected held pieces of beef. Qureshi's quiet shop is only one of the twenty still open in what once was a bustling market for meat in Billochpura. I met with several other butchers before Qureshi; all of them expressed a fear of retaliation from vigilante groups and refused to talk.

The butchers of Billochpura used to source their meat from a slaughterhouse at Kursi, a forty-minute drive from the neigh-borhood. Following the 2017 beef slaughterhouse ban insti-tuted by Uttar Pradesh's militantly Hindutva chief minister, Yogi Adityanath, the Kursi location was shut down, and the butchers were forced to buy meat from small-scale operations farther away from their shops. "When the ban came, they told us that it was temporary," Qureshi said. "They wanted to build slaughterhouses with amenities, hygiene, cleanliness. Slaughterhouses that didn't leak into the rivers and pollute them," he added. "But they never built these or gave us the resources to build our own—they simply closed the slaughterhouses down." Several butchers have lost their livelihoods in Billochpura. Work is hard for those who continue, and both butchers and customers remain fearful. For many male members of the Qureshi community, trained to be butchers from a young age, gaining employment in other communities is close to impossible, Shahabuddin said. "It's hard work, carving meat. It needs precision, and training. It is an art—like tailoring, or car-pentry. Everyone is concerned about what they eat. Tourists will come to Lucknow to eat kebabs, but where will they come from? Does anyone know?" he asked.

What Was Once a Golden Bird

In India today, cow vigilantes continue to attack and torture people. Indian Muslims are especially targeted, often accused of selling beef or stealing cattle. In 2021, a Muslim biryani vendor in Delhi was forced by Hindu right-wingers into closing his stall after selling meat during the Hindu festival Diwali. In March 2022, a twenty-six-year-old Muslim man in Tripura was lynched by a mob for the alleged theft of cattle. The following August, the relative of a man accused in a cow-slaughter case in Muzaffarnagar, Uttar Pradesh, was tortured by the police. Two months later, another Muslim biryani vendor's food cart was vandalized and forced to close in Sardhana, Uttar Pradesh, after he was accused of selling beef at a Hindu festival—this despite the "meat" being soya, a vegetarian meat substitute.

As Indian vegetarianism gains mass appeal by way of the Western diaspora, its presence in India continues to be used to deny people adequate nutrition and to enact violence on the citizens that Modi's government is attempting to exclude. While in the past decade there have been stories of resistance to the state and the ruling elite's imposition of vegetarianism, tales of grief and mourning crowd the conversations surrounding Indian food. In Ghasera, not far from Junaid's village, a group of Meo Muslim singers has begun to write songs about victims of recent cow-related violence. In one such song, they sing of how a young Junaid's life was snatched from him in mere minutes. "What was once a golden bird / The India of yore—now a living hell." As she boiled water for chai for her sons and me in her home, Saira watched videos of these singers on Hashim's phone. When she added tea to the water, she realized she had no milk and sent Hashim away to bring some from the store.

After he left, Saira reminisced about a young Junaid taking a motorcycle back and forth from their house to the same store to which she had just sent Hashim. Junaid would stuff his pockets with biscuits for him and his siblings, the sweet and salty snacks fueling him as he studied on the same bed on which his mother now sat remembering. "The people that killed him reduced him to one thing and one thing only," she said. "Why are these the only stories I have to share?"

The Hungry Jungle

FROM *Outside Magazine*

I LIE HALF naked and miserable in a puddle of my own sweat. I open the tent flap to breathe, but there's no relief, even at midnight. *Who comes to the Guatemalan jungle in July?*

Yesterday's hike was rough, but the 15 miles today were raw pain. The mosquitoes were so vicious that by mile two even our local guides had asked to borrow our 100 percent DEET. Bugs here suck down lesser repellent like an aperitif. Nothing provides complete protection.

Our destination is La Danta, one of the largest pyramids on earth. It's located in the ruins of El Mirador, a centerpiece of Maya civilization from 800 BCE to 100 CE that was abandoned nearly 2,000 years ago. There are no restrooms, no gift shops. In fact, the site is still being excavated.

This is where Angela and Suley want to get married. So, accompanied by a pair of guides, a half-dozen pack donkeys, and their ten toughest (or least informed) friends, the brides are determined to march us sixty miles over five days through Parque Nacional El Mirador in northern Guatemala to La Danta to say "I do." It's our second night on the trail.

I close my eyes and wait for Tara, aka Tent Dawg, to start snoring. I met her forty-eight hours ago. Broad shouldered and sharp jawed, she looks like she could win a car-tossing competition or spit and hit Mars. A major in the US Army, she's been training soldiers on how to survive in the field since before *Survivor* was a tiki torch in Mark Burnett's eye. Back in the small town of Flores, the night before we all set off, she'd said something about a kidney condition with a shrug. Nothing fazes Tent Dawg.

I slip out of our nylon cocoon to pee, swimming through the

liquid night. Humidity 83 percent. Cicadas buzz from thick-vined shadows—the jungle's twenty-four-hour booty call.

The misshapen moon shimmers like a mirage. I drop my underwear and flash a rounder moon at the donkeys. A languid tail whips a fly. Because my body temperature nearly matches the outer world, it's hard to feel the boundary line. So I watch to be sure the piss is pissing. At least it runs clear; I've been pounding water to replenish the gallon I sweat off every hour.

No sound emerges from our five tents, just green-black humming in all directions, 1.6 million acres of primeval rainforest teeming with the richest biodiversity in Central America. I shake my hips, pull up my skivvies, and float back to my tent.

I flop down and remind myself, *This is the opportunity of a lifetime*, when a mosquito the size of a Winnebago chomps my left butt cheek. The pain is electric but passes quickly. After frantic swatting and cursing, I drift off, anesthetized by this single dart.

It was not a mosquito.

Four months before this trip, in April of 2017, I sat in a collapsible chair at a campsite in Joshua Tree, California, avoiding eye contact with the breakfast of sardines I had to force down.

"Yes!" I said, before Angela finished her question.

I'd met her years ago when she was a subject in a documentary film I'd directed, and we became friends. An Arab American medic in the Army, Angela met Suley, a Mexican American enlistee, and couldn't resist her thousand-watt smile. Despite the recent repeal of Don't Ask, Don't Tell, the policy had left its scars. The military still didn't feel like a safe place for their love. Although Angela had once dreamed of being a lifer, she quit and Suley followed suit. They launched new careers and big plans for life as wife and wife.

As Joshua Tree's cold March winds blew dust around our campfire, I swaddled Angela and Suley's drowsy Chihuahua inside my parka, keeping us both warm. They told me they planned to marry in Guatemala—something about the Maya ruins, a handpicked crew, almost all women, did I want to come along?

I didn't want details, I just wanted in.

I was a single thirty-nine-year-old living and working in Los Angeles, freelance writing and making films, and my life felt rife with uncertainty. This trip offered a chance to grab on to the one thing I knew about myself. I'd ascended the peaks of the High Sierra, explored the bowels of the Grand Canyon, and snow camped across north-central Colorado's Gore Range. My future was a cloudy mess, but I knew this: *I am an adventurer.*

To be clear, I am not a fearless adventurer—I'm paranoid about viruses and parasites, and have a phobia of ticks. Growing up in Syracuse, New York, a hotbed for Lyme disease, didn't help. Anything insidious or invisible is my enemy. Give me something I can see and fight, not a freeloader sucking out my life force. (Yes, I have low-grade OCD and watched *Alien* at an impressionable age.)

But at this moment I wanted to say yes and feel grand for saying it. I'd fallen out of trekking shape; I needed to prove that I still had the stuff. There would be plenty of time for fear. *I am the kind of person who says yes.*

Had I been listening, I would've heard that almost everyone on the trip was professionally fit and ten years younger than me: a soldier, a martial artist, two physical therapists, and several fitness instructors. My regimen of strolls on Venice Beach and Sunday morning flop yoga wouldn't cut it with this crowd.

Had I been listening, I would've heard Angela describe her dream wedding: "A super-trek to a remote destination that we all barely survive but bonds us forever—like how Suley and I met in the Army!"

Had I been listening, perhaps I would've said no. Instead, the conversation turned to breakfast. Angela gestured to my sardines. "They're not so bad if you hide them in the eggs," she said. The Chihuahua squirmed against my belly.

I peeled back the tin and threw another oily stinker onto the campfire skillet. As it popped and sizzled, I heaved a spoonful of orange whitefish roe into my mouth. *Just get it done.*

I was choking down sardines and roe at the behest of my acupuncturist. He said that this diet would help prepare my body for the harvest of my own eggs a few weeks later, and I'd learned not to question his methods. (At least it wasn't the encapsulated deer placenta this time.)

I wanted a sexy adventure buddy and a safe, reliable co-parent to have children with, but he hadn't appeared yet. Refusing to settle for the wrong guy had felt plucky at twenty-three, but at thirty-nine seemed more like a game of chicken with the universe. Freezing my eggs stretched out the road a bit longer, but it might be for nothing.

A fertility clinic is the one place in Los Angeles where you can't hide from the realities of aging. I'd never felt less in control as I dropped ten thousand hard-earned freelancer bucks to take my best shot at having a baby. I'd have eaten the sardine can itself if the doctor suggested it.

When I returned to Los Angeles from Joshua Tree, I shot up my abdomen with expensive medicine for several weeks leading up to the egg-retrieval procedure. I didn't have a partner to help me prep the injection site or hold my hand as I stabbed the dripping needles into my subcutaneous fat. My only companion was the paid model in the injection tutorial video produced by the medicine's manufacturer. Night after night, I'd mimic her manicured hands—long after I'd memorized the steps.

A month before Guatemala, with my eggs successfully retrieved and on ice, I sat across from a travel-medicine doctor in Santa Monica. She'd already vaccinated me for dengue fever, hepatitis A, and tetanus, and given me a bottle of Malarone to ward off malaria. I filled out a form detailing my history with giardia, a parasite in contaminated drinking water that causes diarrhea, exhaustion, and, in my case, so much weight loss that my college basketball coach worried I'd become anorexic. I'd caught it five times on wilderness treks, even when no one else did. "I don't know what to tell you," she said. "I guess bugs just like you."

"What about ticks?" I said. "Do ticks in Guatemala carry Lyme disease?"

"Honey, they got *something*," she said. She handed me a prescription for a single doxycycline pill the size of a baguette. "Anything bites you, take this. No hospitals in the jungle. And get the best tweezers you can find."

I stopped at a drugstore on the way home.

I open my eyes in the misty jungle dawn, grateful to have dozed a handful of hours. Tent Dawg continues her Darth Vader breathing, perhaps dreaming of rappelling from a helicopter or choking out a python. I sit up and listen, hearing only the guttural wail of a howler monkey declaring his territory. The other tents are still.

I start to lie back down, but a tight sensation between my legs grabs my attention.

*

I face away from Tent Dawg, cross-legged, and peel off my underwear to inspect. Nothing. *But what is that ache?* I pull my right labia aside and my field of vision snaps into a tunnel.

Behold my nightmare: a tick has bitten my vagina.

The predator is massive—the size of a pencil eraser—with a revolting blood-brown shell and mandibles that rival *Jaws*.

A dizzying heat rushes to my face. I feel the urge to tip headfirst into an imaginary hole. A voice from some deep place rises. *We've trained for this, Johnson.*

I grit my teeth and pull out a brand-new pair of Mr. Tweezermans—excuse me, Dr. Tweezermans—from my pack. I flip on my phone's flashlight and assume the butterfly position.

The good part about being bit by a jungle-grade arachnid on the lady taco is that the folds of the labia make it hard for the little jerk to get traction. I spread my labia with my left hand, slit my eyes, and dive into surgery.

The creature squirms and plunges for deeper velvet, legs in blind fury, cruel mouth desperate for flesh. But my wrath will not be evaded. *Not today.* I grasp its beady head with a firm hand and yank up once, exorcizing the demon from my holy garden.

"Fuck you," I hiss. I dump it into a plastic sandwich bag and smash out its guts with a rock. I swallow the enormous antibiotic pill in one gulp.

Tent Dawg wakes up, fresh as springtime.

"I've had a negative life experience," I say.

She rolls over and I relay the ordeal with the gravitas of Obi-Wan Kenobi describing the destruction of planet Alderaan.

She bursts out laughing. I decide I hate Tent Dawg.

At breakfast I am, perhaps, a little unhinged.

"I just want everyone to know that I was bitten by a tick on the vagina," I announce.

The group looks up with full cheeks and wide eyes. Ashley, a bubbly blond yogini who weighs as much as my left leg, offers me tea tree oil from her stash. I splash on so much that it feels like my undercarriage has been power-washed with Listerine. I thank her for this kindness.

Angela pulls me aside. "Hey look," she says, "If you don't want to go on with us, I totally get it. That sucks. One of the guides can take you back."

Just say yes and this will be over. But her tone is so compassionate, so ready to let me off the hook from this hellish trip, that it soothes me out of my tantrum.

The tick is dead. I took the pill. I'll be fine.

I slap gaiters over my hiking boots and we single-file out of camp for eight more miles through the bush.

Another breathless dawn sags over our heads on the third day, but I feel light in a way I haven't since I boarded the plane at LAX. No matter what else happens, we've made it to El Mirador. Now we just need to climb the La Danta pyramid and pull off a secret wedding.

A moment before we leave camp, Suley decides she needs a pre-wedding beauty treatment. She plops on a stump, douses her hair with a water bottle, and shakes off the excess. Ashley uses the tiny pair of scissors from the med kit as Angela brushes bits of hair from her beloved's shoulders. "Look how prepared I am," Suley says, showing off her underwear waistband, which says: TUESDAY. Today is Tuesday. Angela smiles. It's time to go.

I think we're climbing over natural ridges and hummocks to get to the La Danta pyramid, crown jewel of El Mirador, but our guides, Alejandro and Luis, explain that we're actually climbing over the half-digested bones of a capital city that would take lifetimes to unearth. With an estimated population of 200,000 at its height during the third century BCE, El Mirador was the nerve center of a densely settled network of towns and villages. But the city declined and was largely abandoned in the first century CE.

This collapse didn't mean the end of the Maya. But it did mark a low point for civilization in the region. Why did so many of its inhabitants abandon this place, never to return? Warfare? Shifting trade routes? Alien invasion? Richard Hansen, an archaeologist who has conducted research in northern Guatemala for over four decades, points to drought and deforestation as the culprits. Over millennia, the jungle swallowed this once-mighty metropolis—no small lesson for a group of Americans about the fate of a society whose power outstrips its wisdom.

Despite aching feet, sopping armpits, and a blossoming case of jungle butt (think adult diaper rash), adrenaline inflates my lungs as we approach the massive pyramid, which is easy to mistake for a sleeping volcano in the canopy.

Angela asks Alejandro and Luis if we can spend a few minutes

alone atop La Danta for a period of "quiet meditation," and they
hang back. Although the Maya were no strangers to homosexual-
ity and may have incorporated it in some shamanic rituals, things
changed when the Catholic Spaniards arrived in the 1500s. Gay
marriage is not recognized in Guatemala today. A gay man and
two trans women were killed in a single week during Pride Month
in 2021, and at least 19 LGBTQ+ people were murdered in 2020.
Alejandro and Luis seem cool, but Angela can't risk complete
honesty. (Also, I've changed the guides' names lest they suffer
consequences for being party to our expedition.)

So why choose this spot for their wedding—somewhere that neither woman has personal ties to, in a country hostile to their love?

"I know there were gay people in these communities," Angela
says. "I can't quite explain it, but I feel connected to them. I don't
want to be disrespectful; I hope the Maya spirits understand."

Besides, neutral ground doesn't exist for Angela and Suley.
When they announced their engagement back in the States, members of their families cried—and not in the happy way. Despite
getting their marriage license in California, the couple didn't feel
safe having a public wedding during the first year of the Trump
administration. Choosing peak rainy season has assured them of
precious privacy. We have not seen, nor will we see, another tourist the entire week. This is what a history of trauma yields. When
you've been forbidden to be yourself for so long, a lost city feels
like home.

We approach a rickety wooden staircase scaffolded onto the
side of the pyramid. Two hundred and thirty-six feet to the top.
Lacquered with sweat, I grab at the skeletal railing to hoist myself
up platform after platform. My ego refuses to be left behind by
my younger, fitter comrades. *So what if my lungs explode?* The sun
beats down upon my pale body as I squint and adjust my hat and
sunglasses against its full equatorial force.

We spill out on top of the pyramid and dump our daypacks into
the shade of a single tree. The rough slab is the size of a modest
backyard deck, with nubs of ancient steps on one side and a simple
wooden railing to prevent falls on the other.

We're standing on sacred ground. No one speaks. Our guides
had told us that in the midst of the Maya's environmental crisis,
they had sacrificed everyone from babies to nobility up here—a
futile attempt to appease gods for human errors. I'll later learn

that there's no evidence of human sacrifice in Maya rituals until centuries later. But right now, the story of spilled blood feels true.

Looking out, it's hard to imagine a bustling city or the degraded landscape that followed. All I can see, all anyone can pay attention to, is the great green ocean roiling to the horizon.

The brides slip identical crisp white shirts over grizzled hiking pants and straighten their sweat-soaked bandanas. Joby, a mountain-biking med student, steps upon a rock-cum-pulpit and pulls her hair into a bun to officiate. Tent Dawg, the ring bearer, assumes her post with military posture.

Suley stumbles over her opening lines. Angela takes her hands. These two souls, so full of passion and conviction, choose their own holy words and cast a spell over their future. I have never felt anything close to the bond these women share. Merging with another person requires a kind of faith I've distrusted and resisted. But this altar was made for transformation.

The midday sun kindles the white of their shirts into incandescence. I am the weightless reflection of this glow. My body, dearest friend and burden on this journey, appears to have gone missing. In its place the jungle buzzes—a cacophony of life in every direction, vibrating with its inescapable, insatiable, many-mouthed maw, the sound of life's deep yearning for more. I am that yearning. For to witness love like this and bless it amid the primordial is to be absorbed. To become part of it.

When I feel my body again, I realize I can't stop smiling. Life to life, creature to creature, the buzz bounces and refracts and compounds everything in its wake with an intoxicating hunger that hits like joy.

After the ceremony, hugs, and a thousand photos taken from every angle, we notice dark clouds rolling in from the west. Rather than climb down, we stand our ground in the stultifying haze. Not even a leaf moves. As the tallest person on the highest promontory, I should be worried about the approaching veins of lightning—but the ceremony has left me invincible. I raise my aluminum hiking pole in defiance. Lightning could no more strike me down than it could shatter the whole of La Danta.

Moments later, when the heavens wash our stinking, ecstatic bodies clean, we shout like children who've known no greater pleasure. Then, having dumped its violent bounty upon us, the sky moves on.

In a final touch of magic, when we make it back to camp, we find that our guides have decorated a long table with a plastic, fruit-patterned tablecloth. It feels like the Ritz-Carlton. Alejandro and Luis present us with a pineapple upside-down cake and a magnum of Ron Botran.

My eyes widen and find Angela's with the same question. *Do they know about the wedding?* But no. Today is Tent Dawg's birthday, and they wanted to surprise us. The air dissolves into toasts and merriment while the red sun sinks below the horizon. I gorge my body with sugar and caramel-vanilla rum, offering a small blood sacrifice to the mosquitoes who float like spirits above the feast.

On the last morning, I wake up cocky and hungover, and vote to take the shortcut back. Everyone agrees. *Let's abandon the trail and beeline to Carmelita for an early lunch!* The jungle isn't so terrifying after all. We've tamed it.

We haven't tamed shit. Two hours later, our progress slows to a crawl. I follow Alejandro, who slashes his machete against the interminable, intestinal green at every step. Rainy season has yielded super-growth that he didn't anticipate. The leaves are so enormous, I imagine curling into one to serve myself up as a spring roll for whatever hungry giant patrols this ramble.

No wonder people get lost and die in this park. Angela tells me that Alejandro saved Luis's life out here years ago. That's how they met. My stomach flutters.

We pick our way through swamps that stink of death and sulfur. A gang of monkeys hurl branches at us from a tree. I spy a scorpion two feet from my toe and lunge past it. A fer-de-lance, notorious rainforest serpent, pokes its venomous yellow chin out of the muck and I stop breathing. *Or is it a vine? No matter, press on.*

Thick mud paints my purple gaiters gray; I look like I'm walking on concrete stilts. I use my hiking poles to peel pancakes off the bottom of my boots every fifteen minutes.

Trying to enliven the mood, ever-sunny Suley interviews Diana with her GoPro. "So," she chirps, "what did *you* learn in the jungle?"

"It doesn't matter what percent DEET you use, the mosquitoes still bite you." Diana has a bite on her eyeball.

Suley turns to Joby. "What did you learn in the jungle?"

"Don't go in the jungle," Joby deadpans.

Luis assures us there's only a mile or two left. "Twenty more minutes!"

Twenty minutes pass. A dour silence falls.

Estela's knee gives out. Tent Dawg, suffering a nasty bout of trench foot, shuffles like a zombie, but she insists that Estela ride the donkey. None of us yet know that Tent Dawg is also suffering from gout and renal failure precipitated by our salty diet and dehydration.

"Twenty more minutes!" Luis says.

By hour five, everyone stops talking. The only sound is our sludgy trudge and the rhythmic whack of the machete. By hour six, I stop thinking. My quads and calves scream and fire on autopilot. Bugs can't get traction on my skin, glazed in a slime of sweat, sunscreen, and DEET. No mind. Only motion.

One foot in front of the other. Keep going. Another sardine on the skillet. Another date. Another injection. Mimic the manicured hands. Don't stop. Left foot, right foot, left foot.

Hours (or minutes?) later, our troop lands on a rare dry patch of dirt. Bodies bend over knees. Hands clasp the backs of heads. Lungs suck and exhale.

Alejandro slices a bamboo cane and guzzles water from its hollow core, then offers it to me. Even he looks cooked. Tent Dawg is dead last. Her soaked shirt slings from the angles of her frame. Her face glows with a ghostly yellow tint.

Luis, shirt off, smile forced, can't resist. "Only twenty more minutes!"

Rage boils up my throat, but before it can release, Ashley, our gummy bear of light and positivity, beats me to it. She wheels on the group with bulging eyes and clenched fists and screams, "You can't do this to people!" followed by a shriek that would appall a howler monkey.

Who is she yelling at? Luis? Angela and Suley for bringing her? Perhaps she's yelling at the jungle itself. But the jungle can do whatever it wants to people. As far as the ticks and the scorpions and the fer-de-lance are concerned, we're just another soft-skinned mammal.

Another body to swallow in the mud. Another city to devour.

I dart my eyes away from Angela's and choke back a giggle. Someone snorts and tries to cover it with a cough. I stare at the ground, but it's too much. The group erupts into laughter. Resistance is futile. Resistance is suffering. The jungle will eat you. So be eaten.

My future is a cloudy mess, but I know this: *I am an adventurer.* And an adventurer is someone who surrenders to the unknown even when it's uncomfortable, even when it's horrible, because once you've been absorbed, nothing else will do.

When we set forth this time, I feel a new sense of calm. It *is* only twenty minutes before we happen upon a small bright clearing and turn right to see beautiful Carmelita with its rusty corrugated roofs, dirt roads, and a single horse in a pasture. We have been released.

The group's mood soars into blue skies—hugging, singing. Blood rushes to my head and washes the backs of my knees, down my stiff calves, and between my toes.

After cervezas and enchiladas prepared at Alejandro's home by his wife and daughters, we pile our smelly bodies into a passenger van and head off for Flores. I sit shotgun and hold the muscles of my thighs. *Thank you, thank you.* The jungle whips past my window at impossible speed.

Suley taps my shoulder from the seat behind and points her GoPro at me. My hair is wild, and my face is dirty. I'm proud of looking this bad. I tell the camera, "I just feel alive."

I'm a thousand feet high and flying in this magical old van. I am La Danta, and the roiling green ocean, and the scorpion lurking in the muck. I am a tick on the cosmic vagina. I do not fear not finding love or missing out on motherhood. There's nothing I cannot do in this life.

It will be a few days before the giardia sets in.

TALIA LAVIN

Notable Sandwiches #75: Grilled Cheese

FROM *The Sword and the Sandwich*

IN WRITING ABOUT the grilled cheese sandwich, I find myself with little to offer but praise. It is difficult to encounter such a thing and not overrun the page with the fervency of my gladness.

This is not a column where I will carp and complain—about air-fryer grilled cheeses, or fancy gourmet grilled cheeses, or Kraft-single grilled cheeses, or the proper application of butter, or the appropriate pan, or the degree and nature of the condiments. To me, each grilled cheese is enough, and more than enough. In this world so full of slaughter and fire, where doubt and monstrosity abound, this much is clear to me: the grilled cheese is a small and perfect thing. And how many of those are there?

So my position on the grilled cheese is unabashedly booster-ish, and moreover, it is agnostic toward ingredients and prove-nance. To your grilled cheese you may add caramelized onions or avocado; bacon, turkey, or ham; chutney or cornichons. Make it with Wonder Bread or a freshly baked eighteen-grain country loaf sourced from fields you cultivated yourself in a cantilevered sky-farm with the finest hydroponics. Add goat cheese or smoked gouda or aged cheddar or unidentified plasticine processed cheese product; heat it in a pan or over a flame, under a broiler, in a dutch oven, or with an acetylene torch. I do not care. You have composed something perfect with your own hands. You have made something that will warm and satisfy you. You have, for a small moment, partaken of the act of creation that grants the human animal its sliver of divinity. You have done so by means of the grilled cheese sandwich.

From two perfect things—bread and cheese—arises a more perfect union. In contemplating it and its lessons I think of this fragment from Fernando Pessoa's "Odes":

To be great, be whole . . .
The whole moon, because it rides so high,
Is reflected in each pool.

Each grilled cheese sandwich is entirely itself, like the moon is its whole self in a barrel of water. What else could it be? It is enough. To encounter it is to encounter something made for pleasure which gives pleasure in the beholding and in the consuming.

The simplicity of the sandwich engenders its own kind of awe: an internal pause at the perception of this unalloyed good. Describing that complex emotion makes me think of another poem, by Eugenio Montale, about the perfection of lemon trees in bloom, the "hushed miracle" of it:

. . . Even the poor
know that richness,

the fragrance of the lemon trees.

You can be too poor or too ill or too overwhelmed to obtain a grilled cheese sandwich, but the thought of one is attainable to anyone; the ideal is there, pleasant to the mind parched of gladness.

I imagine a wheel on which I am turning dizzily and perpetually on the verge of falling off, and then I think of the small and simple and perfect thing, and the wheel judders to a halt and I am blessed with stillness. Joy changes you, it smashes the dark wheel: considering the grilled cheese sandwich I am, as Nicole Callihan writes, *all moonshine on the snowbank, clockwise back to a better self.* This thing is humble, not hallowed; it provides not ecstasy, but satisfaction, which is easier to obtain and less giddy to receive. You can hold it in the palm of your hand and be content.

Consider this: each grilled cheese sandwich is a reflection of all other grilled cheese sandwiches that have come before it. All are part of a great whole that rings the world in fat and starchy warmth. Each grilled cheese sandwich bears commonality with each other grilled cheese, in all their guises; it is easy to get wrapped up in the particularities, the innumerable recipes, easy to cavil and quibble and doubt, but perhaps better, and certainly more gentle, to regard the grilled cheese sandwich as an ideal, a thing-in-itself. Faced with this perfect thing, the idea of the small good whole, I am pleased and undone at once.

I am hungry for joy lately. Perhaps you are too. The grilled cheese sandwich for me is an object of consistent joy, which is different in kind than the transcendent ray-through-the-clouds joy that graces any life too rarely. Perhaps that makes it more valuable; reliable pleasure, ordinary pleasure, is as common as light and as necessary. It is only in the consideration of it that I come to appreciate how this mundane thing can be an object of desire and delight. With effort and after much contemplation I think myself toward joy, and welcome its arrival. Life must be leavened by joy to rise; stand and let it in; it approaches with soft footfalls and is easy to miss, or to begrudge in petulance or fervor.

Denise Levertov, too, writes about the pleasure that arrives through effort:

Gull feathers of glass, hidden

in white pulp: the bones of squid
which I pull out and lay

blade by blade on the draining board—

Still, life can't all be squid bone and glass feathers; some pleasures must be simple. As I ponder joy I long for it and for ease; for senses immured in pleasure, for a mind upturned by wonder, for the small good moment prolonged forever.

It is, on the whole, a good thing that our senses are dulled and subsumed by care. Should we stop and observe each perfect thing—the vast, for example, fireworks of dying the trees are now engaged in, as they are each autumn; the coarse grass stems on the brown ground; the silky peel of an apple; the way cold water feels on the tongue—if we were to feel them completely, we would have no time for any of the rest of it. We would bathe in wonder and cease there, in the pathless woods of pleasure. Nothing would get done and no one would get born; we would be lost in admiration.

I can think of worse ends but admit the inefficiency of astonishment. Still, I think there could be more room for it. More joy.

Every joy erodes; survival necessitates that no state be fixed. But we can hope for its return, as light returns. I hope you find your small perfect thing, and in doing so welcome joy's arrival. I recommend going to your kitchen and finding a loaf of bread, and adding to it cheese, and adding to that heat, and from this meeting of good things, attaining a moment of satisfaction to which you may return at any time. Toward that benediction I end this column with a return, to the poem of Montale and his lemon trees, and its magnificent ending, in which the sun pours forth in gladness; may you too be gladdened; there are still small perfect things in this bad world, grilled cheese, and lemon trees.

> The illusion wanes, and in time we return
> to our noisy cities where the blue
> appears only in fragments
> high up among the towering shapes.
> Then rain leaching the earth.
> Tedious, winter burdens the roofs,
> and light is a miser, the soul bitter.
> Yet, one day through an open gate,
> among the green luxuriance of a yard,
> the yellow lemons fire
> and the heart melts,
> and golden songs pour
> into the breast
>
> from the raised cornets of the sun.

My Favorite Restaurant Served Gas

FROM *Bitter Southerner*

IT STARTED ON date night and in Jr. Food Mart, my obsession with Mississippi restaurants that served gas.

This was date night in 1984.

Ofa D, my grandmama's boyfriend, would come over Friday nights in the summer. Ofa D wore head-to-toe camouflage decades before it was in style, then out of style, then back in style to wear head-to-toe camouflage. He smelled like tobacco and, most importantly to everyone in Forest, Mississippi, Ofa D had an actual Coke machine in the front yard of his trailer. Not the goofy plastic kind, either. The kind where you had to pull out the ice-cold bottle. As quiet as it was kept, Ofa D was the sexiest man in Forest off of that fact alone. Ofa D would pick Grandmama and me up maybe twenty minutes before *The Dukes of Hazzard* came on Friday evening.

They'd sit in the front cab of a raggedy Ford listening to a Tina Turner tape. I'd sit in the back, next to burnt-orange pine needles, a few broken lawnmowers, and all forms of rust. Friday nights smelled like dead chickens, piney woods, browning water, burning yard, and the insecticide that the mosquito man sprayed over every mile of Forest.

Grandmama didn't wear her Sunday best, or even her Friday best, to Jr. Food Mart on date night with Ofa D. She'd drape herself in this baby blue velour jogging suit sent down from Mama Rose in Milwaukee. Grandmama was the best chef, cook, food conjurer, and gardener in Scott County. Hence, she hated on all food, and all food stories, that she did not make.

But Grandmama never, ever hated on the cuisine at Jr. Food Mart, our favorite restaurant that served gas.

I have no idea what I wore any of those Friday nights. I just knew that there was no more regal way to move through space in Forest, Mississippi, at eight years old, no matter how you were dressed, than the back of a pickup truck near dusk.

At this time of evening, even on a Friday, or maybe especially on a Friday, there were more gangs of TGIF dogs roaming the roads than people walking to and from work. But I swear, even the gang of TGIF dogs were jealous of how we looked going where we were going on Friday night.

I loved everything about where we were going. I loved the smell of friedness. I loved the way the red popped in the sign. I loved how the yellow flirted with the red. I loved that the name of the restaurant started with Jr. instead of ending in Jr. Like, Food Mart Jr.

I loved that we could get batteries and gizzards. I loved that we could get biscuits and Super Glue. I loved that we could get dish-washing soap, which was also bubble bath, which was also the soap we used to wash Grandmama's Impala, and the good hot sauce in the same aisle. I was eight years old. I never knew, or cared, that my favorite restaurant served gas. My Grandmama and Ofa D were deep into their fifties. They seemed to never know or care that our favorite restaurant served gas, either.

I suppose there were choices of where you'd eat out in Forest. There was a Pizza Inn. There was a McDonald's. There was Penn's Fishhouse. There was Kentucky Fried Chicken. But there were no choices in what we'd eat on Friday. Ofa D would order a box of dark meat, a Styrofoam container of fried fish, and a brown bag filled with 'tato logs. Grandmama would grab a box of a dozen donuts. Grandmama and Ofa D would let me pick my own cold drank. I picked the six-pack Nehi Peach or RC Cola every single time.

Maybe thirty-five minutes later, I'd eat myself into a lightweight coma while Grandmama and Ofa D lightly petted and pecked each other on the couch with the week's greasiest lips. This was our practice.

This was their romance.

I would have to get kicked out of college in Mississippi, then transfer to a school in Oberlin, Ohio, then go to graduate school in Bloomington, Indiana, then get a job in Poughkeepsie, New

York, at twenty-six before I really understood that my favorite restaurant served gas, and this discovery didn't happen at a gas station or restaurant in any of the places I went to school or worked.

I was driving back to Mississippi with my partner, a Black woman raised in the Northeast, when she commented how there were so many more McDonald's and Subway restaurants connected to gas stations on I-81 South. "Isn't it just so American that we will eat anything right next to literal oil and gas."

The sentence shocked me. I'd never, ever thought about what it meant that so many restaurants on the way down to Mississippi from New York were parts of gas stations. That revelation tasted like crude oil. It didn't taste fried at all. I remember saying, "Gotdamn. That's so foul."

And I'm still sure it is.

But I'd never really thought about the fact that my favorite restaurants, as a child, as a teenager, as an adult returning to Mississippi, nearly all served gas. And I never, ever thought of them as gas stations that served food. That is, until I moved back to Mississippi to teach and write in 2015.

Oxford, Mississippi, was, in many ways, as far from home as one could imagine. That's where I came back to Mississippi to teach. But there were three restaurants that served gas between Batesville and Oxford that honestly gave my memory of Jr. Food Mart a run.

This is where the story gets a bit shameful, because though my favorite restaurants serve gas, and a staple of restaurants that serve gas is fried chicken and fried fish, I haven't eaten meat in thirty years. Granny worked the line at the chicken plant my entire childhood, and I saw enough the few times I visited her at work to feel some kind of way about those little chickens, and the way the humans paid to kill, clean, slice, and wrap the chickens were paid.

Still, the restaurant that serves gas leading to the square has the best chicken-on-a-stick ever, I've been told. They definitely have the best fried potatoes, I know. The restaurant that serves gas on the other side of the square has the best banana pudding I've had anywhere other than Grandmama's kitchen.

And the restaurant right off I-55, at the first Batesville exit, where Highway 6 takes you to Oxford, has the best pecan pie and sweet potato pie on earth. They only sell it by the slice, though, and on my worst days—which were also my best days in Oxford—

I'd drive down to Batesville, pick out two pieces of each, look over at all the fish, chicken, potato salad, macaroni and cheese, greens, and green beans and just feel so happy to be home, in a place where brutality leaves bruises, and a place that truly expects incredible restaurants to serve gas.

I missed that up North.

Yet it is the experience of eating food from restaurants that serve gas that really elucidates our American, or our deeply Southern American, conundrum. Our practices are literally poisonous. Mississippi charges me a tax for driving a hybrid car. It literally charges me for not wanting to fuck up our environment more. And. But. The friendships we make while experimenting and/or surviving the poisonous parts of Mississippi are what make our lives and definitely our childhoods—if we are willing to mine them— heavier, and actually most wonderfully Southern.

I missed that up North.

My grandmother had her 94th birthday last week. It was the first birthday we've had for her where the only people left (alive) were family, except for one woman who was slightly younger than Grandmama. This woman knew me and thought I should have known her. She introduced herself as Ms. Joyce. Ms. Joyce made all the food for my Grandmama's birthday, and apparently she was the person I'd paid to cook for Granny before she had to move in with my Auntie Sue. Ms. Joyce, I learned that day, also was a head cook at Jr. Food Mart all those decades ago.

I found a time to tell Ms. Joyce thank you for the birthday food and for the food she made at Jr. Food Mart. I asked her if she thought of Jr. Food Mart as a restaurant that served gas or a gas station that served food. Ms. Joyce said she thought of Jr. Food Mart as "my damn job."

She said she was the cook, the custodian, the shopper, the manager, the security guard, and the server. All for minimum wage. She said the job was actually the worst job of her life in terms of pay and labor, but she never had a better time at work because she got to love on her people every Friday night. Ms. Joyce compared Friday nights at Jr. Food Mart to Saturday evenings when the bus from Jackson would arrive in Forest and all these parents and grandparents would see kids who'd moved to Jackson.

I told her I understood, and said that my favorite restaurant still serves gas. Ms. Joyce looked at me and said, "Oh, okay," then hugged Grandmama's neck and said, "I miss my job. But I'm shole glad not to be washing them damn dishes and fooling with them gizzards no more."

My favorite restaurant served gas.

My favorite restaurant served gas.

My favorite restaurant paid its most important asset, a human we called Ms. Joyce, as little as one could get paid to work in any restaurant. She was paid as little as one could get paid while smelling, and sometimes pumping, gas for folks unable to pump until her shift ended at 11 p.m. This, now, is part of my favorite restaurant memory too. And while I smell the memory as deeply as I've smelled anything in my life, I'm shole glad Ms. Joyce ain't cooking, cleaning, or washing no more damn dishes in any restaurant on earth that serves gas.

I do miss her 'tato logs, though. I can't even lie about that. I miss our date night.

JORI LEWIS

Our Daily Ceeb

FROM *Orion*

WHEN I FIRST moved to Dakar in 2011, I lived in a small apartment in the compound of a Senegalese family, an in-law unit with its own entrance through the garden. The apartment was basic. A hot plate and a dorm-style fridge became my kitchen. A small room with an air conditioner that never worked served as living room and office. The bedroom faced the front of the house, and I could hear the traffic on the busy road outside, the loud conversations of passersby, and the parties at the Catholic high school across the street. I always slept fitfully there, sensitive to all these sounds of life; it would feel as if I had just dozed off when the muezzins of at least three different mosques would start their morning calls.

There was no reason for me to get out of bed that early, though, and I would squeeze my eyes shut until I heard the metal shutters of the *butik* (corner store) open in front of the house. It was a place of orderly chaos: at the entrance, bottles of propane that everyone uses for cooking; at the counter, hard candies, cookies, and salty snacks for children; to the side, a refrigerator stocked with Fanta, water, and yogurt; in the back behind the counter where clients weren't allowed, shelves of canned peas, beans, meat, containers of shelf-stable milk and juice, pasta, dish soap, bug spray—everything you might need in a hurry in the middle of cooking or cleaning. At the counter itself were big bags of *ceeb* (rice) and a scale to measure it out by the kilogram.

During the day, the shop owners alternated between news programs and music stations playing the latest from American to Nigerian and back to Senegal's beloved mbalax, which mixes jazz, salsa, funk, and hip hop and subordinates all the forms that make it up to the implacable beat of traditional drums. All day long, a playlist of the greats, old and new: Thione Seck and his son Wally, Coumba Gawlo and Viviane Chidid, and, of course, Chidid's former brother-in-law, the king of mbalax, Youssou N'Dour.

My defining mbalax experience happened down the road from that apartment, at N'Dour's club Le Thiossane (a word that means "tradition" in Senegal's dominant language, Wolof). The first time I went, the owner himself took to the stage after midnight and did not leave it for a few hours, swigging water now and again to keep that golden voice going. Occasionally, the drummers would speed up their hands and spin a dizzying beat, and the show dancers would move to those wild drums, hopping so fast their feet barely touched the ground.

One of the minor songs N'Dour is known for is a paean to Senegal's pride and joy, *ceebu jën*: a mix of rice, fish, and vegetables cooked together in one pot. It's not the most sophisticated piece of songwriting—basically a recipe set to music—but what it lacks in cleverness, it makes up in enthusiasm: "Ceebu jën . . . What could be better? It's a blessing from heaven . . ."

In *Un Grain de Vie et d'Espérance*, a meditation on the culinary culture of Senegal, novelist Aminata Sow Fall transforms a traditional ceebu jën of broken rice colored red with tomato concentrate into a "platter of tiny rubies" and covers it with a "kaleidoscope of beautiful gifts offered by the earth to the eye and palate."

The first gift is the fish itself, whether a thick cut from a corpulent grouper or a skinny *Sardinella* filled with bones; both might find their way to the bowl after being stuffed with a mix of parsley, garlic, and pepper. Overshadowed by the glory of the fresh fish is the fermented shellfish, an essential element that imparts a bit of its funk to the whole meal. Then a rainbow of vegetables follows: a green cabbage, an orange carrot or pumpkin, a greenish-yellow bitter eggplant, a red or yellow Scotch bonnet or two, and a white cassava root. And, finally, no ceeb could be called complete without a bit of the crunchy rice from the bottom of the pot for you to eat with your portion, or a dollop of a tangy tamarind sauce that includes the pods for you to suck on, or a bit of *nététou*, a mash made from fermented locust beans. If you are lucky enough to be served a variation called *ceebu jën bu weex*, white ceeb made without tomatoes, you might also get a slippery sauce made from a mix of hibiscus leaves and okra.

I am obviously a ceebu jën lover, maybe even a connoisseur. I have eaten ceebu jën in Dakar restaurants, seated at a table with a fork and knife, and I've eaten it in people's homes, sitting on the floor around a communal bowl as is customary. I've eaten variations that could be barely identified as such, with just the basics, a mound of rice, a bit of fish, and a tired vegetable or two. And I've eaten feats of gastronomy, like the one my Senegalese sister-in-law pulled off at Christmas last year when she made a version with copious vegetables, shrimp, three types of fish, and dozens of bite-size fish meatballs. There is a ceebu jën for every occasion and an adaptation for every pocketbook.

When UNESCO added ceebu jën to its list of "intangible cultural heritage," along with kimchi in Korea, lavash in Armenia, and the cuisine of Michoacán in Mexico, the whole of Senegal preened. Ceebu jën is, Fall writes, a dish that both sings and dances. And it does; ceebu jën is mbalax itself, a mix of the modern and traditional, its rhythm so insistent that you almost forget everything else.

Generosity is a core value in Senegal. If you come across a group of people sitting around a communal bowl for their midday meal, whether in a city or in a village, one of them will call out to you in Wolof, saying "*Kaay lekk*—Come eat." If you're wise enough to accept, everyone will shift slightly on their knees until a sliver of space emerges, and you will be handed a spoon or encouraged to eat with your hand (always the right, never the left).

In the 1780s, French slave trader Dominique Harcourt Lamiral wrote about seeing something of this when he lived in the region: "The Negroes are very hospitable. They will never eat any food without offering some of it to everyone there. It even often happens that visitors arrive, sit down, and eat without being asked." Today, that communal plate would almost always involve rice, but in Lamiral's day it was a couscous made from millet.

When another slave trader, Alvise Ca' da Mosto, sailed his ship down the coast of West Africa in 1455, he visited a country ruled by a leader called the "Budomel," which suggests he was in the central part of Senegal—a region called Kajoor where a "Damel" reigned. There, he noted, the climate and landscape were not suitable for most cereal crops except for millet, a hardy grass that grows in poor soils and resists the droughts so common on the desert's edge.

For hundreds of years, successive mariners, slave traders, military men, missionaries, and gentleman scholars made similar observations, opining on how people used millet to make various types of porridges and couscous. Such travelers loved to talk about the spectacle of women working in pairs around a mortar to break down the hard millet grains into flour, putting their whole bodies into it. The women sang special songs to pass the time: "It was the good Lord who gave me millet / And asked me to grind it for him."

Millet even shows up in Senegal's most famous folk tale, about a motherless girl named Koumba, who is sent by her evil stepmother to wash a spoon in the distant ocean. Along the way she meets an old woman with only one arm, one leg, and one eye, who gives Koumba an ear of millet to grind in a mortar and it turns into a copious amount of couscous before her eyes. (Koumba eventually makes it to the ocean to wash her spoon.)

Aminata Sow Fall begins her book not with ceebu jën, but with a sensuous description of a *cere bassi salté*, a couscous royale. Ideally, the millet couscous would have been rolled by hand and mixed with *laalo*, a powder made from baobab leaves. The cook would sprinkle some white beans and dates or raisins, along with a bit of stock, creating a kind of pilaf. The sauce is its own production, full of chefs' secrets, but has a rich tomato base and is simmered with a hearty dose of lamb, beef, or chicken (maybe all three) and a selection of vegetables—carrots and cassava, sweet potatoes, and a special gourd. Once served, after eaters have made good headway into the tomato sauce with its veggies and meat, the hostess might pour a bit of milk into the bowl to mix with the cere for the perfect last bite.

Historical records tell us that people back then cooked millet-based dishes with meat or fish in much the same way as one does now with ceebu jën. And when something like ceebu jën made an early appearance, public opinion was lukewarm—mixed-race cleric David Boilat, writing in the 1850s about the customs of Senegalese society, noted: "The Wolof do not find rice as fortifying as couscous."

Today, millet still appears at every key moment of a person's life in most of Senegal. When a child is born, the family prepares a thick millet porridge to distribute to well-wishers. When a couple is married and move in together, their first meal should be millet. And when a person dies, millet must be served at the funeral. In times of uncertainty, people make and give away millet. Millet is for chasing away ill stars and calling in blessings.

But some millet dishes have suffered from a kind of prejudice over the years. My Senegalese husband likes to tell a story about the time when he lived in Dakar as young man and went searching for a millet porridge called *fonde*. He grew up in a small town down the coast and was used to eating millet, a habit more common in the country than in Senegal's cosmopolitan capital city. On this occasion, he was hanging out with his urbane Dakarois cousin, who saw him as a hick, so when my husband said he was off to a fonde stand in the neighborhood, his cousin drew him close and, in a low tone, told him to keep his voice down. Eating the porridge, it seemed, was like waving a sign to proclaim how poor you were.

My husband laughed it away, never letting a little snobbery get in the way of his love of fonde for breakfast, for *cere taalaale* (millet couscous with a light onion-tomato sauce) for lunch, for more fonde for dinner, and for millet beignets as snacks.

Given the long history of millet and its cultural importance, why then has it now been consigned to the second rung in Senegal's culinary landscape? Why is ceebu jën more a part of humanity's intangible "cultural heritage" than cere bassi salté?

The emergence of ceebu jën in the late nineteenth or early twentieth century is likely due to a confluence of colonialism and cash-crop agriculture. It was a period in which the French were expanding their administrative footprint, conquering most of the country we now call Senegal and consolidating large swaths of the interior into a thing called the colony of French West Africa. During this time, Senegalese farmers started cultivating more peanuts, sparked by a demand from French soap makers for a suitable oil for their industry. Farmers might have grown peanuts on a small scale before, but now the market was so insistent that they started to put more land into peanut production, land that might otherwise have been dedicated to growing millet. Early on, French administrators and merchants recognized that inciting farmers to abandon their staple crops might create food shortages, but instead of promoting a more balanced approach, they developed an alternative plan. In 1857, the colonial governor wrote, "Let Senegal produce [peanuts] instead of grains, and we will bring them rice"—rice brought on French ships from other colonies in India and Indochina.

Today, Senegalese people eat about 125 kilograms of rice a year, on par with South Korean (124 kilograms) and Chinese (126 kilograms) consumers. If you invite someone for lunch and serve anything else—say, millet—you might hear a variation on this phrase: *Suma lekkul ceeb dafay mel ni lekkuma dara*—If I haven't eaten rice, it's like I haven't eaten anything.

Rice production has expanded, tripling over the last decade as part of long-standing attempts to make Senegal self-sufficient by growing it on the heavily dammed Senegal River. But Senegal's population is growing too, and the amount of rice each person eats per year keeps rising. The idea of becoming self-sufficient in rice production is an ever-shifting target, one that becomes a bit more distant every year. Part of me always wonders if it's worth all the effort—all the irrigation water, the fertilizers, the pesticides, the downstream water pollution, all that the process of growing paddy rice close to the desert requires. Meanwhile, a recent study showed that farmers have stopped planting millet in some parts of Senegal, a move that researchers believe is negatively affecting the diversity of the grain in the wild. Wild cousins retain traits that may be useful in a changing climate and are, the paper says, "a reservoir for future adaptation"—a reservoir now in danger.

Despite the effort to ramp up rice production, most of the country's rice is still imported—more than 70 percent. Such dependence on imports means that Senegalese consumers are deeply vulnerable to the vagaries of world commodity markets. They are one bad Thai or Indian growing season away from a food crisis. All because some French colonial administrators nearly two hundred years ago decided that the peanut trade was too import- ant for them to care whether people here could grow the food they needed to live.

So, where does that leave the country and its culinary traditions? Yes, ceebu jën is a product of colonialism—and yes, it still ignites the ingenuity and creativity of millions of home cooks every day. Yes, colonialism and, later, urbanization, structurally altered the palates of people, priming them to desire rice to the exclusion of other grains. And, yes, no matter how diminished, those grains are still here—at least for the moment.

Millet couscous—the deluxe cere bassi salté itself—does make at least one yearly appearance in most Senegalese households, on Tamxarit, known to the rest of the Muslim world as the Feast of Ashura. On that occasion, there's a run on precooked cere in stores, although traditionalists spend hours, even days, rolling tiny balls of couscous by hand. The sauce itself, with all its secrets, often takes all day, and cooks try their best to impress. In the evening, the family assembles to stuff themselves on couscous and meat, and then couscous and milk. After that, the Taajaboon starts, a festival of transgression, as boys dress up as girls and girls dress up as boys and they go from house to house with their bright selves, their joy, and their drums or makeshift instruments, dancing and singing and asking for gifts of money or even more couscous. This has always been my favorite holiday in Senegal, a sort of mix between Thanksgiving and Halloween. I like to think that the Taajaboon, which does not seem connected to religious commemorations of Ashura, is a survivor of some pre-Islamic harvest festival where the community celebrated the new millet crop with extravagant revelry.

At the end of her book, Aminata Sow Fall writes that there's a story behind everything we put on our plates. "Our cuisine is the pure product of our history," she writes, both its triumphs and its sorrows. On Tamxarit, I'm always convinced that millet could, one day, reclaim its story. And maybe it can, starting with those boisterous children doing their enthusiastic Taajaboon. After all, you need to grow up with millet to fully appreciate its finer qualities, its rich and slightly sour flavor. Rice is a neutral vehicle for sauces; it conducts flavor instead of asserting much of its own. On the night of Tamxarit, some families leave a handful of couscous out for the ancestors, an offering, because millet is more than a food. It's a conductor of a different kind, a mode of communication, an instrument to get closer to the gods.

JORI LEWIS

Tell Me Why the Watermelon Grows

FROM *Switchyard*

THE AIR CONDITIONER was malfunctioning. When I bought the car used in January, the owner said she had just fixed it, but here I was on a steamy August day on the Atlantic coast of Senegal, with the vents pouring hot air into the already hot car. So, it was my imminent dehydration talking when I skidded to a stop in front of a roadside fruit seller's table. I was once told by a grandmother, who lives in my seaside village but grew up in the northern dry regions where the Senegal River winds across a crispy and prickly savanna not far from the great desert, about a watermelon varietal called *beref*, which is cultivated mostly for its seeds but also serves as a kind of water reserve.

"There's water that you can drink from it like a coconut," she said.

In the north, she explained, if you're traversing the flat plains under a white-hot sun, and you see a watermelon in someone's field, you can just pull it up, take it, break it open, and drink. It's your own portable oasis. "Nobody forbids it," she told me. The watermelon is for everyone. It was not yet the season for them, but I was overheating, my lips and throat dry, and the idea of a watermelon, even an out-of-season one, seemed suddenly like the ideal solution to my predicament.

Most of the watermelons that Senegalese farmers grow for the local market have rinds that are light yellow green or occasionally a deep evergreen, but the watermelons at this roadside stand were moss colored and covered with forest green stripes, indicating that they were probably grown for the European market, where buyers might expect the fruit to look a certain way.

A couple of centuries ago, Europeans might have been more open-minded about the watermelon's appearance as plant hunters and naturalists searched for the keys to the plant's past. When David Livingstone, the famed missionary-explorer-colonialist, journeyed across the Kalahari Desert in the 1840s and 1850s, he wrote that he had come across a surprising wild plant that he thought was yet another type of watermelon. "In years when more than the usual quantity of rain falls, vast tracts of the country are literally covered with these melons," he wrote, the fruit's thick rind secreting away the rain's bounty for the future. "Some are sweet, and others so bitter that the whole are named by the Boers the 'bitter watermelon.' The natives select them by striking one melon after another with a hatchet, and applying the tongue to the gashes. They thus readily distinguish between the bitter and sweet."

I like this idea of sweet watermelons coexisting with bitter ones, each type influencing our perceptions. The watermelon is a generous fruit: the flesh of one can feed a dozen people and can parent hundreds of melons with its seeds. Cultures throughout the ages have, and still do, interpreted the watermelon as a symbol of good luck and fertility, a plant whose great fecundity might be shared with you. But in the United States, more than a century of racial denigration has cloaked and clouded this primordial symbol of solidarity, generosity, and abundance, transforming it into something almost unpalatable for many Black people. Of course, the watermelon itself is not to blame, but throughout its botanical, cultural, and social history, it has been a vehicle for our ideas about community, survival, and what we owe the future.

At the fruit stand, I searched the oblong bodies for one with a yellowish oval discoloration, the telltale field spot. Only one of them had it, so I picked it up to listen to it as I often saw my mother do, tapping its bottom like a naughty child. But I didn't know what I was listening for, not really. She could never quite put it into words herself—just something about how this or that one sounded "right." When you cut into it, the "right" watermelon (for me and my mother) has a fuchsia red color, the deeper the better; a delicate smell; flesh that is tender but not mushy, watery but not spongy, just firm enough for the lightest of chomps; and the sweet flavor of endless summer. Once I got the watermelon home, I chose a big knife to stab it in the middle and then worked the knife around its circumference until I could pry its two halves open. Then I slit a chunk from its belly and tasted it right there in front of the sink, the juice trickling over my fingertips. It was perfect.

When I was a child growing up in Springfield, Illinois, my family hardly ever bought watermelons at big supermarkets with faraway supply chains that might have left us with a mushy melon. Instead, we waited until we saw a farmstand or sometimes just a pickup on the side of the road—as long as their sign said: BEARDSTOWN WATERMELONS. We'd swoop in to buy one or two, straight from Beardstown, Illinois, the self-proclaimed Watermelon Capital of the United States.

Today, the road from Springfield to Beardstown is lonely, a two-lane highway that passes almost nothing but fields of corn and soy decorated by seed signs, those flags from corporate nations who offer flashes of yellow and orange and red as the car whizzes by: AGRI GOLD, CROP TECH, NUTECH, ASGROW, DEKALB, FS, BRANDT, BECKS, PIONEER. I was headed not to Beardstown proper, but a few miles away, to Arenzville; metro Beardstown, if you will. It shares the feature that makes the Beardstown watermelon the best, or so they say: the sandy soils on the Illinois River's banks. Roger Hendricker runs the Sandy Springs Farm in Arenzville, which has been in his family ever since his Hendricker ancestor came over from Germany in the nineteenth century and settled in Illinois.

"Right here where we're standing on this river bluff, my great-grandfather raised his family and he raised watermelons," he told me when I visited in late August. "And then my grandfather raised watermelons. My father did. And we've been raising melons," he said, gesturing to his stepson, Mike Powell, who mostly tends the melons now that Hendricker is in his seventies and can't bend and squat like he used to.

And bending and squatting is a must, because their six-acre field of organic watermelons resists much mechanization. From some paces away, the patch looked like nothing to me, looked like weeds, but when I got closer, I saw the trailing vines with watermelons hiding amid the vegetation. A listing scarecrow stood, but barely, a faulty sentinel against incursions by varmints who are, in fact, rarely crows. Here and there I could see where a deer bit into or stepped on a watermelon, where a coyote dragged one to a clearing for a snack, or where a raccoon sat down for a feast. Powell said the raccoon damage is the nastiest; the animal will make a hole in the melon and scrape out the insides with its front paws as well as they can but leave behind a lot of liquid that will soon start to ferment and smell.

"It kind of looks like a slushy," said Powell, but not one you'd want to drink.

This part of Illinois had been in a moderate drought this summer, probably a problem for all those corn and soy growers I saw on the road, but Hendricker noted that the watermelons were doing just fine. "Our vines are healthier than a lot of years. We haven't had this disease problem," he said. By disease he means the assortment of mildews, wilts, and blights that typically affect the watermelon plants as the summer goes along. "And that could be due to the lack of rain," Powell added, "because, of course, the more rain you have, the more fungus can grow."

That made intuitive sense to me since some watermelon cultivars, like the one in northern Senegal, or wild species, like the ones in the Kalahari, seem to thrive in arid regions, storing water away for times of need. But Zhangjun Fei, a researcher at the Boyce Thompson Institute in Ithaca, New York, later told me that the varieties of watermelon we grow today, after millennia of breeding to focus on bigger sizes or sweeter fruits, have lost some of their ability to fight diseases and to withstand the harsh conditions of the deserts of their forebears, which are much more extreme than the Illinois River basin.

"A crop that is taken care of by humans, they are kind of spoiled," he said. "They say, 'Even if I don't have this ability to fight off disease, I still can survive because people are treating me well.'"

Fei said that as the climate changes and diseases evolve, farmers will need more ways to raise healthy watermelon crops—and not just growers in the United States like Hendricker and Powell, but also farmers in China, which produces more watermelons than any other country in the world, more than 60 million tons in 2020 compared to the next highest country, Turkey, with just 3.49 million tons, or to the United States, with its modest production of just 1.7 million tons. Fei said that researchers all over the world are finding solutions for the watermelon's future by investigating its past.

I was a self-conscious teen. I couldn't help it. I had landed on the bright side of the tracking machine, but there were only ever a couple of other Black kids in the honors and AP classes that formed the rhythm of my life. I often felt on display, singular, strange. I remember once having a conversation with my father about something I was self-conscious about as the only Black person around, although I can't remember what. Was it someone who wanted me to play basketball? Or to dance? Or to speak like the sassy Black women they saw on TV? Was it a request to do something or wear something or, even, eat something? I think it must have been about food, because my father told me that he used to avoid eating watermelon in front of white people when he was younger. I knew then without knowing firsthand that watermelon was wielded by racists as a cudgel, but I never imagined that he might have deprived himself of the juicy melon, not the least because it was ever present in our house during the summer.

"For more than a century and a half, the watermelon has been a staple in America's racist diet," writes sociologist David Pilgrim in his 2017 book, *Watermelons, Nooses, and Straight Razors.* "The depiction of black people eating watermelon has been a shorthand way of saying that black people are unclean (the fruit is messy to eat), lazy (it is easy to grow), childish (watermelons are sweet and colorful), overly indulgent (especially with their sexual appetites), and lacking ambition (the watermelon presented as satiating all needs)." Pilgrim is the founder and curator of the Jim Crow Museum at Michigan's Ferris State University, and he says the museum has hundreds of racist images and objects encapsulating this stereotype, including "banks, plates, wall hangings, aprons, towels, ashtrays, toys, firecrackers, cookie jars, match holders, dolls, souvenirs, doorstops, lawn jockeys."

Historian William Black traced the origins of the racist association of Black people with the watermelon to the period after Emancipation. Many formerly enslaved people farmed and sold watermelons, a crop that they had often grown in their kitchen gardens in the beforetimes. The watermelon was, for them, an instrument of self-sufficiency, a way to survive and even thrive. But that soon changed. "White southerners," he writes, "waged a campaign within popular culture to transform the watermelon into a symbol of black people's unfitness for freedom—an utter negation of the meaning black people had given the fruit." Black reports that during Reconstruction, as early as 1866, southern newspapers often reported on supposed watermelon thefts by Black people, a kind of fixation that he says stood in for white anxiety about what they perceived as the violation of their property rights and political authority. In 1870, Tennessee legislators even proposed the so-called "watermelon bill," which would have made trespassing a felony and stripped those convicted of their voting rights. It did not pass but eventually other types of legislation across the south would have the same effect: widespread disenfranchisement of Black voters that endured for nearly a century, and in some ways still endures today. In the meantime, Reconstruction-era white supremacists used popular culture to vilify Black labor and initiative when it came to cropping and selling watermelons, and, of course, the Black consumers eating them.

In addition, traveling minstrel troupes literally spread the "watermelon man" archetype in live form—a blackface actor with big red lips, toting his watermelon, scheming to get more watermelon, giving up everything for a slice. That archetype moved across the United States and beyond it to Europe, Asia, Africa, and South America, one hateful performance at a time. Historian Chinua Thelwell told me that while researching his book *Exporting Jim Crow*, he came across a reference to an American group that performed its racist repertoire in Durban, South Africa, in 1881, including a song called, "Oh That Watermelon." The stereotype did not take root on the African continent as well as it had in the United States—Thelwell found only a handful of references to the watermelon being used in this way—but in the United States, such blackface songs, musicals, and theatricals carried over onto the silver screen. The 1915 Ku Klux Klan classic *Birth of a Nation* included a scene of Black people (many of whom were white actors in blackface) having a watermelon-filled celebration.

My father, who was born in segregated Arkansas in the 1940s, would have grown up inundated by advertisements, postcards, films, and TV shows that depicted Black people as watermelon-eating buffoons of either the happy-go-lucky-and-ignorant or the thieving-and-conniving types. My mother, born in segregated Chicago during the same period, said she remembers being stung by a watermelon joke on a nightly TV variety show, maybe *The Johnny Carson Show* of the 1950s. Martin Luther King Jr. remembered refusing to eat watermelon in mixed company when he was at seminary in Pennsylvania: "I didn't want to be seen eating it because of the association in many people's minds between Negroes and watermelon," he told a journalist from *Redbook* in 1956. "It was silly, I know, but it shows how white prejudices can affect a Negro."

And Dr. King was not alone. It was enough to make whole generations of Black people self-conscious about eating watermelon. Psyche Williams-Forson, a professor of American studies at the University of Maryland and the author of *Eating While Black*, said it is still common for people of a certain age to have reservations about eating watermelon—or, rather, to be *seen* eating watermelon. "I cite Black people who are absolutely, in some instances, adamant that they would not eat watermelon in public, unless it's cut up in cubes or unless it's served a very particular way," she told me.

On my latest visit to my parents' house in Illinois at the tail end of the watermelon season, we bought a big melon in Beardstown, and my father did yeoman's work cutting most of it into irregular cubes to stash in the refrigerator. The rest he cut into tiny wedges to eat right away. But even when presented with this, the most modest and daintiest wedge of rind-on watermelon, my mother will slice the flesh away with a knife and fork and cut it up before eating it. When I ask why she bothers, she just says that's how she likes to do it.

In Senegal, where I moved a decade ago, watermelons are a winter fruit, reaching peak ripeness in November or December when the weather cools, so I have started to associate them with the end of the year holidays. No Senegalese Christmas or New Year's celebration at my mother-in-law's house would be complete without one or two watermelons cut into manageable wedges so we can eat them directly from the rind.

I wonder about these small differences between my husband's family in Senegal where the watermelon is simply enjoyed, and my own family in the United States where the watermelon isn't just a luscious fruit, but also a symbol of violence, a metaphorical weapon whose cut still stings and sometimes burns.

After the Egyptian pharaoh Tutankhamun died suddenly in 1324 BCE, the royal staff had to race to prepare his elaborate grave. He came to power at the tender age of nine and had ruled for only about a decade, so maybe they hadn't expected his death quite so soon. While his body was mummified, a process that took a little over two months, they painted stories of his life and exploits on the walls; constructed his nesting wood-and-gold coffins and a quartzite and granite sarcophagus; fabricated 400 *shabtis*, figurines of servants who were meant to work for him in the shadow fields of the otherworld; and created the gold death mask that has now become iconic as the treasures of King Tut have been exhibited around the world. They were also tasked with assembling the food the young ruler might need in the afterlife: mummified meats for a mummified human, jars of wine and honey, hundreds of baskets stuffed with wheat, chickpeas, dates, and figs, as well as eleven baskets of seeds from the watermelon (*Citrullus lanatus*). Excavators opened the inner rooms of Tutankhamun's tomb more than 3,000 years later and found that some of the foods and seeds had been reclaimed by time, bacteria, and beetles, but the watermelon seeds that had been harvested, cleaned, and dried by unknown hands millennia ago were still in relatively good condition.

And now they had a new purpose: to help solve the mystery of where and why the watermelon grows.

If you pick up an old science textbook from even, say, thirty years ago, you'd probably read that the watermelon originated in southern Africa, maybe even in the Kalahari Desert, where Livingstone saw so many melons. Indeed, four other species of *Citrullus* (there are only seven total) are native to that region. But German botanist Susan Renner, who calls herself "a classically trained herbarium-based taxonomist," says that assumption was based on a misinterpretation of one specific specimen from South Africa that had been gathered in 1773 by Carl Peter Thunberg, a student of and successor to Linnaeus.

Renner's excitement bubbled over as she recounted the tale. Thunberg was familiar with cultivated watermelon, since it was grown in southern Europe, and Linnaeus had already described it in 1753, calling it *Cucurbita citrullus*. But this South African melon had green flesh, it was bitter, and the fruit was hairy, so he doubted that it could be closely related to cultivated watermelon. He gave it the name *Momordica lanata*—"lanata" means wooly. "But then, later in 1930, people looked at this specimen [in the herbarium]," said Renner, "and they thought it was the same as the cultivated watermelon that we eat, which is sweet and red." Thunberg's sample was the link, they believed, to an ancestor of the watermelon we know and love, and so they renamed the sweet watermelon *Citrullus lanatus*.

But Renner had her doubts as she looked through Thunberg's old journals and decided to dig deeper. She and her team asked for a sample of the DNA from the wooly melon that Thunberg collected, which is conserved in the herbarium at Uppsala University in Sweden. When they analyzed it, they found that not only was Thunberg's sample not sweet watermelon, but it was not even closely related to it. It was, in short, a taxonomy fail. But still, more mysteries about the sweet watermelon remained. "Where was it domesticated?" asked Renner. "To find this out, we needed to sample all over Africa."

And that's where Tutankhamun's seeds come in, as well as seeds from another ancient Egyptian tomb, and some from a Stone Age site in Libya that are about 6,000 years old. Renner and her colleagues analyzed the DNA of most of these ancient seeds, along with more contemporary samples from around the African continent. They were not able to get permission to extract DNA from King Tut's seeds but used micro-CT imaging of them. The sum of their analyses, DNA and otherwise, added up to a new conclusion: the progenitor of the cultivated watermelon came not from South Africa or even from Egypt or Libya, but from the Kordofan region of central Sudan, not far from Darfur.

Zhangjun Fei, the watermelon researcher in upstate New York, explained that knowing the direct progenitor of the cultivated watermelon will make it easier to use modern breeding techniques to select for traits like drought tolerance and disease resistance. Most wild species of watermelon are quite bitter, but the Kordofan watermelon has varietals that have a nice smell and a bland flavor. Fei hopes that will mean it will be easier to take the benefits of the ancient melon and leave behind the bitter flavor that ruins it for modern palates.

When I asked Fei if there were any cultural obstacles to raising watermelons in China, where he grew up, any stereotypes or negative associations with eating it, he thought for a moment but said he couldn't remember any. "Watermelon is an essential fruit," he said. It's cheap and accessible to the poor in China, but you can also find it at five-star hotels. Everyone eats it, without thinking twice. It's a fruit of the people.

Recently, when I asked my father about why he avoided watermelon as a young man, he denied ever telling me this. My father and I, the lawyer and the journalist, we rarely give each other answers, but volley questions back and forth like a game. I contended that he did, that I can remember how he tried to offer me comfort during a difficult time, didn't he remember? Always on the case, he asked me for proof, for corroborating witnesses. I said that no one else was there, or at least I didn't think they were. If my mother had been there, after all, she would have been the one to try to sympathize with me or cheer me up. But, suddenly, I started to doubt my own memory. Could I have pulled it from a book, a movie, someone else's story about racism?

My father's memory has always been a little slippery too—birthdays, names, everyday details of all kinds have always escaped him, maybe shoved away to make room for case law; he relies on my mother's penchant for remembering the minutiae of life. He said he always loved watermelon, that his uncle grew it on the family farm, that he ate it every chance he got. His life was his proof.

No matter his protestations, my father was—and still is—hyperaware of the stereotypes that the white people around us hold. He is a man who never wears light or bright suits, refuses to tip his baseball hat to the back or the side, and would never crank up his music loud, even when barbecuing or picnicking outside. Some months after my parents moved into their current house in a predominantly white subdivision, a neighbor told them that she was so glad that my father kept his yard so tidy, that she had been worried that a Black family would create a mess. Did she imagine a *Sanford and Son*–worthy junkyard? My dad tells the story with more good humor than I could muster, perhaps because he has spent his life trying to prove white stereotypes wrong.

In her poem "Salt," Vievee Francis recounts a time when her much younger sister is pleasantly surprised to be served fruit for dinner at a resort and exclaims, "*Watermelon!*" in a crowded dining room. Her pleasure is uncomplicated, but the weight of American history intervenes for Francis in the form of a "gentleman from Georgia" who sits with them and shares a knowing moment with her:

> . . . A whole history rides
> the vehicle, a mule train, the wagon, the dust
>
> track of my sister's outburst.

They laugh from what at first seems like the friendly complicity of an inside joke, but Francis reveals that her laughter hides a sudden urge to cry.

Francis's sentiment conveys something recognizable to me, even if it does not land on me the same way. I did not really grow up with these watermelon images, so I don't feel their full weight. I do know that every once in a while, they reemerge in the United States, an atavistic response to any kind of Black success. When Barack Obama was elected in 2008, the watermelon trope crept into not only right-wing memes but also mainstream newspapers and comics.

But the United States of America has more racist tools than nefarious stereotypes about delicious fruit. When I was younger, my battle was more likely to be with the servile figures of Uncle Ben and Aunt Jemima, staples of American kitchens and American advertising. In college, in Chicago, I remember finding a print of Murry DePillars's ink drawing of Aunt Jemima somewhere, on the street or in a thrift shop, one that transformed her from a mammy into a superhero as she broke free from her pancake-mix box. I put it up in my kitchen, hoping to channel this Jemima's force and passion for justice as she lifted her spatula like a weapon. She was reclaiming herself. Telling new stories.

When I spoke with botanist Susanne Renner, she asked me to look at an image related to the watermelon, an artwork. I knew from her scientific papers that she and other botanists often examined ancient artworks for clues, peering at images of watermelons in ancient Egyptian murals, classical frescoes from Greece, paintings in medieval Europe and Joseon Korea, so I expected something similar. But it was an image of a glittery mixed-media assemblage by artist and poet Vanessa German, a piece called *Glory*. On a sparkly background, the flat form of a Black woman is given relief by textural elements: a brush, a mirror, red birds taking flight from her heart, butterflies and flowers swirling about her legs, an appliqué of a watermelon womb full of fertile seeds, and a holy sign "to state the obvious & the invisible obvious, the submerged obviousness," she writes in the description. The figure has two legs, but six arms, "alla those arms cuz there's so much to carry." German performs a kind of alchemy with this figure, reaching through time to transmute the past and return the watermelon's original symbolic meaning to us.

Back in metro Beardstown, on the side of a hill, I looked west to the setting sun, squinting across fields of corn in the hopes of seeing the Illinois River. But it was just out of view.

Mike Powell was harvesting now and walked through the field thumping watermelons with the back end of his field knife. "This one's kind of dead sounding I call it," he said of one promising-looking melon. It was not ripe yet, or maybe it was overripe. But a few paces later, another melon sounded more promising. "This one has a ping to it," he said, a higher tone resonating in the water of its body. He cut one open to check, to make sure his ear was calibrated just right so that he could pick ones that were ripe but not too ripe. The first one had just slipped into the first blush of the mushy place of no return. The next one, though, looked a bit better. He asked me, "Would you like to try it?" I hesitated for a moment. I thought about whether I should. I felt an ever-so-slight twinge about me in this Black body in a white man's field and all that has ever meant. But it was hot, and I was thirsty, and the field was beautiful in its chaos. All this flitted through my mind, and then I said simply, "Sure." He cut a long chunk from the heart. I took it with my fingers, and I ate.

Taste the Feeling

FROM T: *The New York Times Style Magazine*

A JELLYFISH TASTES of nothing. Maybe a little salt—a trace of the sea, or of how the creature is packed, once wrested from its natural habitat, for preservation (not of its life but of its viability as food). When its bell is prepared as a raw salad, it tastes only of the ingredients it absorbs: a sluice of soy sauce, sesame oil and black vinegar, scattered garlic, a pinch of sugar. What makes it coveted as a dish in some cultures is the texture, which is nothing like jelly at all. The flesh wobbles but doesn't deliquesce; instead, it resists, crunching under the teeth, because a jellyfish is almost half made of collagen, the connective tissue whose braided strands run through skin and bone.

This is a different crunch than you get from sinking your teeth into walnuts, say, or lacy rounds of lotus root tumbled in a wok, or the golden tips of a croissant, or sugar torched into a glassine pane atop crème brûlée. And yet an English speaker must flounder for words to delineate these textures, beyond "crunchy" (which some etymologists date back to the late nineteenth century) and "crispy" (from "crisp," which originally meant "curly" but came to signify "brittle" in the sixteenth century). Other languages are more bountiful. The British food writer Fuchsia Dunlop has written about the Chinese distinction between *cui*, a crispness that "offers resistance to the teeth but finally yields, cleanly, with a pleasant snappy feeling" (e.g., scalded goose intestines, stalks of celery), and *su*, "dry, fragile, fall-apart crispness" (e.g., deep-fried duck skin). A 2008 report in the *Journal of Texture Studies* lists 144 Chinese terms for food texture, including even finer gradations of crunchy and crispy: *cui nen*, crisp but tender, like young bamboo shoots and spears of asparagus in spring; *su song*, crisp and loose, like the tangled tendrils of rousong (pork simmered, shredded and dried until sucked of all moisture); *su ruan*, brittle, then soft, like pastry that dissolves at the touch.

In Japan, such terms number more than 400. "Too many," a team of Japanese scientists demurred in a paper presented at the 2016 International Conference on Knowledge-Based and Intelligent Information and Engineering Systems, noting that these descriptions are inconsistently used even among native speakers, making translation difficult. Onomatopoeia rules the day: A ruffly strip of well-seethed bacon delivers a clean crack that in Japan is called *kari kari*, as opposed to *shaki shaki* (a gushy bite, as of an apple right off the tree), *saku saku* (a fracture cushioned by richness, as found in buttery cookies and chicharrón—pork skins dropped in hot oil, where they expand like clouds), *gari gari* (a hard crunch, like ice, that taxes the jaw), *bari bari* (the kind of delicate shattering epitomized by a rice cracker), and *pari pari* (the even more evanescent shattering achieved by the sheerest-cut potato chips).

And this is merely crunch. What of the coy half-surrender that the Italians venerate in pasta as "al dente" and the Taiwanese in noodles and boba as "Q" (or "QQ," if the food in question is exceptionally springy); the restive yolk threatening to slither off a six-minute egg; the seraphic weight of a chiffon cake; the heavy melt of fat off a slab of pork belly, slowly liquefying itself? What of goo, foam, dust, air? What of the worlds that lie between slime and velvet, collapse and refusal, succulence and desiccation?

Not only does English lack a robust vocabulary for food textures but, whether as corollary or coincidence, English speakers also tend to value a narrower range of textures. There have always been differences in what people of different regions eat, based on the flora and fauna supported by local climate and geography. Europe, to which the majority of Americans trace their heritage, is far less biodiverse than Asia, Africa, and South America, where what many Americans consider more challenging textures are celebrated, from the viscosity of soups thickened with ogbono (bush mango seeds) in Nigeria to the sponginess of ubre asada (grilled cow udder) in Chile. In a survey by the American sensory scientist Jeannine F. Delwiche conducted at Ohio State University in 2002, respondents considered texture significantly less important than taste and scent in its impact on flavor. Flavor is often conflated with taste, but where taste is quantifiable—corresponding to messages sent to the brain by receptor cells on the tongue when they detect specific chemical components in food—flavor is nebulous: an aesthetic judgment. It is often defined as a confluence of taste, scent, and memory, yet other senses intrude. Studies have shown that diners have difficulty identifying flavors when foods are dyed different colors, for example. The eyes lead them astray.

Sound plays a role, too—as a marker of texture. In a 2004 study by the Italian cognitive neuroscientist Massimiliano Zampini and the British experimental psychologist Charles Spence, participants rated the same potato chips as crisper when the frequencies of their splintering were amplified. The louder the splintering—the more it echoes in the skull—the crisper and better we think the potato chip is, the truer to its destiny. After all, a potato chip's entire purpose in life is to be crisp. Here, as with the jellyfish, taste is an afterthought. Texture is all.

When we call a food crunchy or creamy—arguably the two most craved textures in the United States—we are identifying in part its mechanical properties: how it responds to and deforms itself under an application of force, whether it opposes or capitulates. Crunch registers as a small act of destruction. We feel the teeth breaking through the apple's flesh. Exactly which teeth are engaged may make the difference between gari gari and pari pari; food scientists have posited that crunchiness, which implies density, requires gnashing of the molars at the back of the mouth, whereas the higher pitch of crispness is caused by biting at the front with the incisors.

Liking crunch may have bestowed an evolutionary advantage on early humans, as a marker of freshness in food, showing that it was safe to eat. (If sogginess in a potato chip is failure and disgrace, in other foods it can signal rot and danger.) Our ancestors initially relied on a diet of crunchy raw plants and insects and, when they learned to wrangle fire and cook—which, because it made food easier to digest, led to greater caloric intake with less investment of time and a corresponding increase in brain size—those who were drawn to the crisping and browning that takes place when food is introduced to heat (with the chemical reactions of amino acids and sugars) were "more likely to keep on cooking, thus accruing long-term benefits over evolutionary time," the American anthropologist John S. Allen writes in "The Omnivorous Mind" (2012).

Perhaps our love of crunch is an artifact of our primal selves. The sound of demolition reaffirms that we are animals, with jaws engineered to tear things apart. There's something decisive about how easily certain foods fracture—how quickly we reduce them to rubble. Creaminess we experience more passively, as a weight on the tongue or a state of flow, judged by speed: how slowly a substance moves, how closely it clings to the spoon. (One factor in this is a particular enzyme in the saliva that breaks down starches; the more enzyme is present, the quicker the breakdown, which may explain why the same spoonful might be creamy to one person and runny to another.) For our ancestors, such richness may have served as testament to the presence of necessary nutrients and fats. For us, it's a proxy for luxury.

We could go further and read the dominance of crunchy and creamy in American diners' preferences as metaphor: a sly enactment of the dynamic of conquest and submission, historically a favored American mode of interacting with the other. But sometimes a potato chip is just a potato chip. You can enjoy a good crunch without channeling imperialism. And imperial ambitions have hardly been confined to America. Should we interpret a culture's insistence on devouring every texture as another form of proclaiming dominion, reducing all nonhuman life—everything that is not *us*—to potential food?

The more interesting question is why textures beloved by many cultures came to be shunned by so many Americans: the prolonged chewiness of tripe; the tendon turned to jelly in a bowl of pho; the thick slickness of okra, leaking its mineral-rich mucilage. These were once common elements of most people's diets; until relatively recently in human history, our ancestors could not afford to be so choosy. Eating was simply a matter of survival, and a group of people living in the same area, with access to the same resources, ate pretty much the same food. As the British social anthropologist Jack Goody has written, the notion of cuisine only arises when members of a group begin to hoard more of those resources and restrict access to them; when hierarchy takes hold.

Traditionally, those at the top of the hierarchy had the most wide-ranging diets, including ingredients that were difficult to procure, sometimes from the ends of empire, and thus expensive and a way to telegraph status. Then industrialization, beginning in England in the mid-eighteenth century, changed the relationship between diners and the sources of their food. In 1820, farm workers were reported to make up around 72 percent of the American labor force; today, according to the US Department of Agriculture, they represent just over 1 percent. An estrangement set in, and with it a dwindling. In the wake of the Second World War, prepackaged, processed food became the standard in many American homes—food stripped of both fuss and complexity, of anything to wrestle with, like a recalcitrant chicken heart or the stretchy, gluey splendor of natto (fermented soybeans). This was food that simply obliged. Gone were the textures of resistance, if you will; the messy ones that call to mind a body's murky interior, that remind us where our food comes from.

Yet today Americans are gravitating away from complacency, toward more dramatic sensations in food, from nigh lethally sour candy and the funk of fermentation to ever fiercer chiles and hot sauces. This could be a manifestation of a general social trend toward extremes. Or is it a desire for more—to feel more, know more, be more? Could the tide be turning? The counterculture of the 1960s focused in part on an idea that is now almost mainstream: the need to retreat from the commercialization and corporatization of life, including what we put on our tables and how we nourish each other. In the past decade, the homey meal cooked from scratch has triumphed as an ideal (if not always an achievable one for people with limited resources).

At the same time, knowledge of other cuisines has become a kind of cultural capital. Globalization, while threatening to erase difference by turning everywhere into a market for the same products, has given Americans the boon of greater exposure to foods from around the world. Sometimes these foods have been mocked, as on the television game show *Fear Factor*, which initially ran from 2001 to 2006 (when the now hugely influential podcaster Joe Rogan was its host) and involved forcing contestants to eat the likes of silk moth pupae (a street snack in parts of Asia), the eyeballs of various animals (often reserved for honored guests in other cultures), and buffalo testicles (actually home-grown American cowboy fare, which, when cooked properly, can be wondrously tender).

To be sure, none of these foods have gained a place in the mainstream American diet. But consider that Americans were lured into sushi bars half a century ago by the compromise of the California roll, with its affable mixture of imitation crab and avocado slaked in mayonnaise—essentially evoking a tuna salad sandwich, reconfigured with rice and seaweed—and today clamor for the silkiness of raw fish and the cool, briny custard of sea urchin. What was once a dare is now just a night out. Go ahead and look a little farther down the menu, or submit to the chef's will. Maybe you will receive a gift: a little plate of what looks like chubby curls of dough, creamy beans, or larvae huddled together for warmth. This is shirako, the sperm sacs of cod, soft and milky as oysters. Let them slip on the tongue.

My Catalina

FROM *12th Street*

KNIFE-CUT CHUNKS OF iceberg lettuce, wedges of pale scarlet tomato, cucumber rounds with insolent seeds glaring from their centers, mean slivers of green bell peppers, thin slices of red radishes. The radishes were bitter, as was my mother. The iceberg lettuce showed her dislike of cooking, the tomatoes represented something sweet, yet rarely expressed. The angled slivers of green pepper were an artistic touch, resembling tiny armed soldiers who might leap right out of the bowl unless quickly skewered by a fork. The cucumber slices were her perseverance as a single mother raising a child alone.

She cut these ingredients with a cheap dull knife on the kitchen counter, then threw them into a blue Corelle bowl. From the dining table she took a clear plastic bottle, which always held the exact same thing. This was her culinary magical potion, her secret ingredient. Truthfully, it was far from secret, and any cook could use it. She made a perfect circle around the edges of the salad with this potion, which was so thick and viscous it almost glowed, then with slotted stainless steel spoons she carefully mixed everything together. While doing so, she imagined herself as a gourmet. She'd ruined any potential credibility as a true gourmet the moment she placed her hands on that bottle, but she didn't know that.

Catalina, to me, is not the beautiful island off the coast of California. Nor is it the woman known as Saint Catalina of Palma. It's just a salad dressing, a condiment. And it's a pretty weird one, if you think about it—which I do.

Catalina, when poured over a salad, clings to the ingredients in an incredibly sticky way because of its high sugar content. The orange color is disturbing, like something from a science fiction story. The smell is tangy, ripe. The flavor is sweet and sour, sharp, tomatoey, and fat with umami. Kind of awful and kind of great. Salad with Catalina dressing was the only salad my mother ever made, and she made it quite often. This was my Catalina, her Catalina. Was it our Catalina? I don't know, and she's not here anymore to ask.

Catalina happens to be my food culture. My birthright, one might say, though it doesn't have the kind of authenticity or tradition others claim for their respective food cultures. My mother had no food culture of her own to draw upon—nothing in her childhood was reminiscent of delicious times past. Her mother was a maker of burnt roast meats and tuna sandwiches on white bread with butter. Her father served up watery split pea soups that nobody wanted to eat. Surely his soup didn't resemble the traditional one he knew as a child on the Swedish island of Gotland. Turning to my father's side of the family is no use, as he's always been nonexistent in my life.

A quick online search shows that Catalina is a "bright-orange to red and sickly sweet French dressing" and offers the information that Kraft Foods trademarked the "Catalina" name in 1962. Due to the lack of a solidly framed history for Catalina, they say it has a "murky past." Catalina might be considered a love child born in the twentieth century, when a product called "French dressing" grew up to meet contemporary consumer tastes. Catalina is used in different ways, as we learn that "On the Mississippi Gulf Coast, it is a common practice to dip pizza in Catalina French Dressing." In the more formal food culture sources I looked at, such as *The Penguin Companion to Food*, *The Oxford Companion to Food*, or *The Encyclopedia of Food and Culture*, Catalina does not exist.

Should I reveal at this point that the base of Catalina is ketchup? That stuff that gives American french fries their lifeblood? This actually works for me. I fully accept the label of "American Mutt." If we are what we eat, then the soil that's grown me—the food that makes my mouth water at times, while at other times makes me want to hide my head in shame—is this food that lives somewhere in the triangulation of white trash, lower-middle class, and solid-middle class. This condiment would never enter the realm of the well-to-do, or at least not without a hell of a lot of reeducation.

As I write this, my tastebuds pucker, saliva gathers greedily at the inside corners of my cheeks. In my mind, I see the almost hysterical orange-red color, the slightly greasy surface of Catalina as it oozes out of the little round hole in the white plastic bottle cap. Catalina is a gift my mother gave me before I left home to raise myself at thirteen years old and, though it may seem strange, I don't regret this gift. Longing for the past—even if for a past that may have never really existed—is like that. Some of us take what we can get.

A single bite of a certain food can carry a person away to a different time. It can conjure people and places, aromas, the colors and textures of clothing, bits of conversations, the edge of a smile, a glance of quick anger. The foods of your culture will fascinate some people and alienate others. Nobody can escape this phenomenon. Merely looking at a food, even without tasting it, can reveal your family's background, a specific region of a faraway country, and whether your family had money or lacked it.

As an adult, I've lived in the world of fine dining as an executive chef, a lover of fine food, a gourmet, a gourmand, a foodie. Catalina is persona non grata in these social circles. But during the pandemic, as everyone on Instagram created wildly decorated layer cakes and learned to bake bread, all I could think about was Catalina. I finally gave in and bought some for the Thanksgiving dinner I was planning, along with the salad ingredients I remembered from my childhood.

The bottle was smaller than I remembered, the color an even more hallucinogenic orange. I made the salad exactly as my mother did, even imitating the cut of the little green pepper soldiers. God, it made me hungry! Lacking a Corelle bowl, I used a glass Pyrex one. I tossed it, using the exact same spoons she'd used, one of the few things she unexpectedly left me when she died alone, in a far-distant place. But the hands gripping them were different. Hers: elegant, light, with long, tapered fingers that ended in perfectly oval, unpainted nails. Mine: workmanlike, solid, with short, square fingers, round, solid palms. How did this quiet and angry woman have such an outgoing, exuberant, gregarious child like me? She disliked even the thought of cooking—it was "women's work," which made it unimportant. She wanted to do bigger things, important things. But I liked—maybe even loved— food and cooking, regardless of its stature in human enterprise.

There was one essential difference between her recipe and

mine. The bitterness of her version was gone, replaced by my own retrospective longing. Once upon a time there was a mother; she belonged to me. I called her Mom and I was her only child. She wasn't like the other mothers, and I knew that. They knew it too. They probably didn't know how little she talked to me, or how, when I was small and alone after school, she'd finally come home from work and sit in her spot on the royal blue couch next to a black enamel table that held a tarnished, round, brass zodiac ashtray, a cup of instant black coffee in its white china cup with saucer and faux-gold spoon, silently staring in front of her until my need to reach her would bring me right up next to her on the couch, then right up onto her lap. Her beautiful hands lay on the couch, inanimate. I'd throw my arms around her neck, pushing her hair out of the way, then I'd hug her and give her a kiss right on the tip of her nose and she'd laugh a light little noncommittal laugh as her blue eyes shifted to some other point in the room. I'd give her a few more kisses then roll off her lap and go to my room to read. This is what my retrospective longing was for, the one I called Mom, sitting there in her spot on the couch.

I was mesmerized by the salad as it sat on the table among the other holiday foods. My eyes were drawn to it, as if someone new was at the table who might need extra attention. I waited to see if anyone would say anything about it, and finally somebody did: "What is this salad?" I responded, nervously, "Something my mother used to make. Do you like it?" I was slightly taken aback when everyone said they loved it.

Things got weird following that dinner. Every day, I woke up hungry for that salad. I coveted that Catalina taste. For a few weeks I made the salad daily. I went through one bottle, two bottles, then three bottles of Catalina. I'd make it at random times of the day then sit around and shovel it into my mouth in overloaded forkfuls as fast as I could, as if I actually needed it to survive.

I wasn't really starving for the salad, of course. I was starving for times past, and Catalina was a strong memory that felt singularly good. This salad dressing may only be an industrial-complex condiment on the low end of the food spectrum, but at thirteen years old it was one of the only consistent and true things in my life. In it, I recognized home.

Back then, my mother and I silently ate dinner together, kitty-corner at the table from each other. I always sat on her left. She'd stare at the pale-yellow pat of cold, hard butter she'd placed atop the lukewarm canned green beans on our plates. I'd stare at whatever open book I'd brought to the table with me that night. I surmised, years later, that Catalina spoke for her. "I'm trying. I'm doing the best I can. I'm not sure I can do this," it said, its tone unwilling, terse, and proud.

A condiment poured over a salad—no matter how religiously—just can't make everything better. A day came when I sat next to my mom at a scratched-up table in family court. I'd been arrested for hitchhiking. Is there a way to easily explain how that happened? Probably not. She'd given me permission to go to a weekend rock festival some miles away. I was going alone. She was going somewhere else that weekend, leaving me at home to manage myself, which she believed was a good thing. It was the summer of my thirteenth year. She didn't ask how I was getting to the festival or how I'd get back home. By this point in time my mother was in many ways simply "missing in action" where I was concerned. I went to the festival, taking a bus with my saved allowance money, the festival turned into more of a drug festival, I met some people I liked there who liked me. At the end of the weekend, rather than go home to where there was nobody to even talk to, I left with them. We hitchhiked our way to their home together. Who were they? This was the early seventies. They were nice, fun, intelligent people in their early twenties—they were hippies. We all got arrested in Delaware, a state that's not even a real place, to my mind. The cops didn't believe I was who my fake ID said I was, a twenty-six-year-old girl who looked entirely different from me. Eventually, I told them who I was, and they called my mother to come get me.

In family court that day, we sat together. We were a family as far as I knew, mother and daughter, a tiny circle of two. As I sat next to her I stared at her hands, motionless on the heavy wood table. A woman with tight white curls cut close to her head sat across from us, then opened a file, looked at my mother, and asked if she was capable of keeping me at home with her. If she could promise to care for me. If she could keep me out of trouble. I didn't understand when she answered no to those questions. I saw her nod yes when the woman told her I'd be placed in juvenile detention within the next few days, to be followed by foster care—if a foster family could be found.

We returned home together that day. She headed to her corner of the couch. I retreated to my room with my cat and my books, closing the door behind me. The next morning my mother left for work. I packed a duffel bag with as many clothes as I could carry, a few books, and my Raggedy Ann doll. I pried the rubber stopper off the bottom of my piggy bank, which actually was a pink ceramic pig, and took out all the money inside. I said goodbye to my cat, shoved a curly brunette wig over my easily identifiable strawberry-blond hair and set off for the Greyhound bus station. I believed that was the end of my Catalina. I didn't think of it, or my mother, for a long time.

After that Thanksgiving during the pandemic, my Catalina binge ended around a month after it began. I sat in the exhaustion of the holiday season that day, skewering yet another chunk of orange-glazed iceberg lettuce onto my fork. The foghorns in the harbor outside my window sounded endlessly on; people rushed by in heavy coats, their faces glittering in the holiday lights. The fork holding the lettuce chunk slowed as it approached my mouth. I wondered what I was doing. The salad suddenly tasted horrible. The flavor, the texture, the color, the overwhelmingly sweet, acrid smell—all of it disgusted me. I realized I'd eaten more than enough of this stuff and threw it all in the trash.

My desire to taste Catalina came about through my desire to travel backward in time. I wanted to see myself as I'd once been; a child with a home she'd never thought to question. I was also curious about my mother—not the mother who decided she didn't want to be my mother anymore, but the other one, the nurturing one. I wasn't sure she ever actually existed for more than a few moments at a time, but the game I played with myself worked. I found her in that store-bought condiment.

We add meanings to what we eat and how we eat it, as we gather, create, write, and rewrite our stories. Someone makes the rules of measurement for insiders or outsiders, for high or low culture. The ruling class have always been the arbiters of taste, shaping the cultural measurements of our times based on exclusivity. In places where class shifts, we have etiquette books, finishing schools, and of course cookbooks, which teach how to cook high to impress or low to go slumming.

The potato saved the Irish from starving and it remains on the spectrum of poor people's food as a sufficient answer to hunger.

Yet it changes identity when dolled up with caviar and sour cream. Where do you get your coffee—from Devoción or Dunkin' Donuts? Offal vs. tenderloin, vegan vs. BBQ, rainbow carrots vs. regular orange plastic-bagged carrots. It's never only about how it tastes, it's about everything that goes along with it.

Isn't it odd that a condiment—or any other food—would be thought capable of defining who a human being may be? Although we may be what we eat, we're also so much more. I have no problem with this food being a part of who I am. In making this salad with my estranged mother's recipe, I explored the contours of my broken family. The taste of Catalina filled me with questions. Why did things happen the way they did? Why did she abandon me? How do we go on after betrayals to become a different person, yet the same? Am I "less than" because of my strange food culture? Eating Catalina over and over, day after day, so many years later, didn't answer most of my questions.

Yet something transpired during the course of these Catalina salad days, a phenomenon more valuable than finding answers to the same never-ending questions I'd had for years, answers that could never truly be verified. As I chewed my way through these salads as if my life depended on it, something was pushing at the edges of my consciousness where Catalina hovered, still not sure if it was welcome. It has a murky past, after all. Yet so do I. During this Catalina experiment, a dream pushed its way into my mind, hinted at, waiting to be fully known, wanting to enter and stay. A dream of the rare evanescent moment in life when the taste of something almost forgotten suffuses both body and soul with the feeling of being safe and loved, of being one with the world right here and now, even if not in the past.

ALEXANDER SAMMON

Forbidden Fruit

FROM *Harper's*

PHONE SERVICE WAS down—a fuse had blown in the cell tower during a recent storm—and even though my arrival had been cleared with the government of Cherán in advance, the armed guard manning the highway checkpoint, decked out in full fatigues, the wrong shade to pass for Mexican military, refused to wave me through. My guide, Uli Escamilla, assured him that we had an appointment, and that we could prove it if only we could call or text our envoy. The officer gripped his rifle with both hands and peered into the windows of our rental car. We tried to explain ourselves: we were journalists writing about the town's war with the avocado and had plans to meet with the local council. We finally managed to recall the first name of our point person on the council—Marcos— and after repeating it a number of times, we were let through.

To reach Cherán's militarized outskirts, we had driven for hours on the two-lane highway that laces through the cool, mountainous highlands of Michoacán, in south-central Mexico. We passed through clumps of pine, rows of corn, and patches of raspberry bushes. But mostly we saw avocado trees: squat and stocky, with rust-flecked leaves, sagging beneath the weight of their dark fruit and studding the hillsides right up to the edge of the road. In the small towns along the way, there too were avocados: painted on concrete walls and road signs, atop storefronts, and on advertisements for distributors, seeds, and fertilizers.

Michoacán, where around four in five of all avocados consumed in the United States are grown, is the most important avocado-producing region in the world, accounting for nearly a third of the global supply. This cultivation requires a huge quantity of land, much of it found beneath native pine forests, and an even more startling quantity of water. It is often said that it takes about twelve times as much water to grow an avocado as it does a tomato. Recently, competition for control of the avocado, and of the resources needed to produce it, has grown increasingly violent, often at the hands of cartels. A few years ago, in nearby Uruapan, nineteen people were found hanging from an overpass, piled beneath a pedestrian bridge, or dumped on the roadside in various states of undress and dismemberment—a particularly gory incident that some experts believe emerged from cartel clashes over the multibillion-dollar trade.

In Cherán, however, there was no such violence. Nor were there any avocados. Twelve years ago, the town's residents prevented corrupt officials and a local cartel from illegally cutting down native forests to make way for the crop. A group of locals took loggers hostage while others incinerated their trucks. Soon, townspeople had kicked out the police and local government, canceled elections, and locked down the whole area. A revolutionary experiment was under way. Months later, Cherán reopened with an entirely new state apparatus in place. Political parties were banned, and a governing council had been elected; a reforestation campaign was undertaken to replenish the barren hills; a military force was chartered to protect the trees and the town's water supply; some of the country's most advanced water-filtration and recycling programs were created. And the avocado was outlawed.

Citing the Mexican constitution, which guarantees indigenous communities the right to autonomy, Cherán petitioned the state for independence. In 2014, the courts recognized the municipality, and it now receives millions of dollars a year in state funding. Today, it is an independent zone where the purples and yellows of the Purépecha flag, representing the indigenous nation in the region, is as common as the Mexican standard. What started as a public safety initiative has become a radical oddity, a small arcadia governed by militant environmentalism in the heart of avocado country.

But the environmental threats posed by the fruit have grown only more pressing since then. In the United States, avocado consumption has roughly doubled, while domestic production—mostly confined to drought-stricken corners of central and southern California—has begun to collapse. The resulting cost increases have encouraged further expansion in Mexico, attracting upstarts that are sometimes backed by cartels, whose members tear up fields and burn down native trees to make way for lucrative new groves. Some landholders and corporations are getting very rich. I had come to Cherán to see whether this breakaway eco-democracy could endure in the face of a booming industry.

As we drove into the center of town, home to some twenty thousand people, the narrow streets hummed with activity. Colorful murals commemorated various anniversaries of the uprising. Exhortations to protect the earth adorned white stucco walls. Vendors sold mushrooms, vegetables, and grilled corn. Stray dogs traipsed through the plaza. We parked in a gravel lot down a side street and began asking around for Marcos. Eventually, a diminutive man wearing a parka emerged from a nearby building. As we shook hands, Uli joked about our holdup at the checkpoint, but Marcos didn't laugh. He scanned the square suspiciously, as though worried we'd been tailed.

Marcos led us into the town hall, and I followed him up a staircase and came face-to-face with a floor-to-ceiling portrait of Emiliano Zapata, the Mexican revolutionary and champion of land reform. Above the doorways of offices hung photos of Cherán's own armed *comuneros* next to photos of pine saplings. In the modest legislative chamber, I took a seat in front of a U-shaped banquet table, where the elected council meets. Half of its dozen members were seated, attending to paperwork. When they saw me, they began a second interrogation, asking what my motivations were and what exactly I was there to see. They squinted at the business card in a plastic sleeve that I was passing off as a press credential, handing it back and forth. Another life-size portrait of Zapata frowned at me from the wall.

I understood their suspicion. Just weeks prior, the neighboring state of Jalisco had sent its first-ever shipment of avocados to the United States. Violence in the sector was increasing, with reports of drone-bombed fields. A few months earlier, inspectors from the US Department of Agriculture, which verifies the fruit's quality for export, had received threatening messages. And there were plenty of reasons for avocado groups to size up Cherán: its fertile soil, its abundant water. Besides, what revolutionary regime isn't a little paranoid?

But the council eventually agreed to show me the full sweep of its operations. I was told to report by 7 a.m. for rounds with the

patrol unit that surveys the region and wards off threats. Together
we would head to the front lines.

The avocado has been grown and eaten in Mexico for centuries.
The glyph representing the Mayan calendar's fourteenth month
features the fruit, and Aztec nobles often received it as tribute.
"Looks like an orange, and when it is ready for eating turns yellowish," observed the Spanish colonizer Martín Fernández de Enciso
in 1519. "So good and pleasing to the palate."

Some four hundred years later, the fruit was rediscovered by
California's real estate industry. The state was in the midst of a
speculative land frenzy that was always threatening to go bust. The
citrus craze, an advertising hit that had helped sell the southern
California promise of certain riches from backyard harvests, had
started to sour, and land developers were desperate for a new marketing ploy. "The lichee, the loquat, the kumquat, the cherimoya,
the feijoa, and the sapote," writes the historian Jeff Charles, "were
all announced with great fanfare as potential moneymakers for
anyone who could plant a tree." Out of this haze of hucksterism
emerged the avocado. Soon the peculiar stone fruit was being used
to upsell wide-eyed buyers on overpriced mortgages, pledging that
just two or three trees would bear enough fruit to pay them off. A
1935 *BusinessWeek* article marveled at the "chance at independent
incomes with enormous profits from a few acres of land suitable
for avocados."

For the better part of the twentieth century, however, the fruit
failed to catch on. Among the challenges faced by marketers were
the fruit's many names: alligator pear, aguacate, avocado, Calavo—
the last a portmanteau of California and avocado. (The name in
Nahuatl, an indigenous language, *ahuacatl,* is slang for testicle, and
was never really an option.) Money was poured into advertising to
fix the problem, and the state funded research on farming techniques, though these still didn't solve for the novel taste. Growing
ranks of producers, and the small consumer base, led to ruinous
drops in price while costs kept increasing. Water and land got
more expensive as new housing developments demanded more
and more.

By the late sixties, only farms that produced more than five
thousand pounds of the fruit per acre each year were profitable;
just five growers in San Diego, the industry's epicenter, depended

on avocados for their entire income. Agribusiness began to look south of the border in the seventies. The California Avocado Society, a collective founded by growers, deployed multiple research missions to Michoacán, where envoys made careful note of the region's plentiful water. "In this area, water is free," marveled their report from a trip in 1970. Local avocado growers' only concern was "how to divert the water into channels on their property and to get the water to the trees." At that point, imports of fresh avocados from Mexico to the United States were prohibited by federal regulation (established in 1914 to protect California farmers), but the large avocado firms began investing in the region anyway, with designs on selling the fruit elsewhere.

The North American Free Trade Agreement, when it went into effect in 1994, largely kept the ban in place, but crippling droughts and exorbitant land and water costs eventually pushed California's industries into accepting a slow repeal of protections. Many small domestic growers were facing bankruptcy; the larger firms that weren't had already invested in Mexico. After decades of malaise, the avocado became a surprise winner, and a cipher of the promise of free trade—"NAFTA's shining star," as one consultant later put it. Hill+Knowlton Strategies, the advertising firm best known for its role in goading the United States into the first Gulf War on behalf of the Kuwaiti government, helped rebrand the fruit. After achieving notoriety as one of the most spectacular commercial food failures of the twentieth century—as salad centerpiece, Mediterranean delicacy, and tropical delight—the avocado finally entered the mainstream. Guacamole and avocado toast became two of the most successful gustatory trends of the twenty-first century, pushed with prime-time Super Bowl ads. Michoacán's avocado production went from around 800,000 metric tons in 2003 to more than 1.8 million metric tons in 2022. Over the same period, America's avocado consumption quadrupled.

Today, groundwater in Michoacán is disappearing, and its bodies of water are drying up. Lake Zirahuén is polluted by agricultural runoff. Nearly 85 percent of the country was experiencing a drought in 2021, and experts project that the state's Lake Cuitzeo, the second largest in all of Mexico, could disappear within a decade. In part because of the conversion from pine to avocado trees, the rainy season has shrunk from around six months to three. So profound is the drain on the region's aquifers that small earthquakes have newly become commonplace. The one-hundred-mile avocado corridor has, in effect, become the only live theater of what is often referred to as "California's water wars."

It's unclear whether the avocado can survive this changing climate. But in Michoacán, the more pressing question is whether its residents can survive the avocado.

At 6:45 the next morning, Uli and I reported to the town jail, where we'd been told we would find the *ronda tradicional communal*, the community police. The detail—by some counts the town's largest agency, and the only one for which jobs do not rotate every three years—is tasked with all security, manning the checkpoints, guarding against poachers, and even punishing public drunkenness. Through the darkness I could make out a commander meting out orders to officers wearing flak jackets, helmets, and fatigues. It was almost time for a shift change. An unfamiliar truck by the sand mine would need to be investigated; everyone was reminded to keep their weapons on them at all times.

The *ronda* is most heavily armed while guarding the forest. The job is to monitor the entire 27,000-hectare region of Cherán, ensuring that there is no illegal logging, no burning, and no planting of avocado trees. I was assigned to join a unit of four people, each carrying a rifle and handgun. We piled into a white Mitsubishi pickup, emblazoned with the word GUARDABOSQUE, two of the members perched in the bed. I squeezed into the back seat, where an AR-15 was wedged between the driver's seat and console. A toy rifle hung from the rearview mirror.

We were headed to the northeast border, where a new avocado grove had recently appeared. But thirty minutes into our drive, an order came through redirecting us to the town's nursery. We parked before a sign reading THE PLANTING OF AVOCADOS IS STRICTLY PROHIBITED. After some back-and-forth with local farmers and nursery workers, we learned that some loggers were laying claim to a patch of forest near Capácuaro, a town to Cherán's southwest. The *ronda* would have to intervene and try to forge some sort of agreement that would protect the trees.

The confrontation sounded tame enough, I thought, but the crew felt differently. Any group of local loggers could be backed by monied avocado interests, or cartels, and it didn't take much for bullets to start flying. Our safety couldn't be ensured, they said, and our seats in the truck would be needed to transport reinforcements. They deposited us back at the jail, where we waited to be assigned to another patrol group.

After a few hours, a second pickup arrived, manned by a team of three. We loaded back in and headed out of town on a sunken dirt road, up into the mountains. As the truck lurched over potholes, we passed spindly pines—some replanted, others old-growth—as well as another sign, this one in red: THE COMMUNITY IN GENERAL IS PROHIBITED FROM PLANTING AVOCADOS.

The truck's driver, Edgar, had spent eight years in the *ronda*, enlisting not long after the uprising. He'd done construction work in South Carolina before getting deported. I asked if he'd encountered illegal avocados in Cherán. He said he had. Everyone knows the rules, he told me, "But there is still tension here, even now." When avocados are discovered, patrols dig up the trees and destroy them. The offending planter will be sent to the town jail, where he'll be forced to issue a formal apology and pay a fee. A repeat offender can have his land requisitioned by the government.

We drove until the road ran out, then parked above a sweeping hillside. A barbed-wire fence ran along a dirt trench, marking the division with the neighboring municipality of Zacapu. At our backs were a wall of pines; in front of us, rows of juvenile avocados. The trees grew right to the edge of the muddy border. All of this had been old-growth forest until four years ago, Edgar told me. He pointed to a barren hillside in the distance. Eight months prior it had been full of pines, but it had recently been clear-cut, marking the next stage of the forward march. Soon, it too would be covered with avocados.

There was something else Edgar wanted me to see if I was willing to venture with him into the woods. We returned to the truck and drove cautiously through deeper and deeper puddles until the trail was completely washed out. We parked, left some nonessentials, and began our trek with three militants in full protective gear.

As we passed into denser forest, the patrolmen sometimes paused to rustle the pine needles blanketing the forest floor, exposing the mushrooms that grow naturally in the area. On occasion, one of them would find a bright orange lobster mushroom, which I was told tasted just like pork. Those were pocketed for dinner. Finally, we emerged into a blackened clearing, which abruptly gave way to a ravine. All around us, the trees and shrubs were charred.

A few months earlier, Edgar explained, this area had combusted. Loggers had been fast at work clear-cutting the forest, in anticipation, I was told, of avocados. To expedite the process, they set fire to some stumps, which can be especially flammable in the dry season. The blaze quickly jumped the town line of pine trees and took off in Cherán's forest. Edgar, along with volunteers and dozens of members of the *ronda*—eighty people in all—attempted to quell the conflagration.

They dug a perimeter right below where we stood. Having no ready water source, they tossed dirt onto the flames with shovels. Edgar spent three days and two nights on the fire line, long enough for the containment effort to succeed. But the losses continued to mount, as many of the rescued trees succumbed to blight in the weeks that followed. Eventually, the sickly trees were cleared. Four hectares of pines were lost.

Wildfires are a major concern in the region, and an estimated 40 percent of them are now purposefully set to clear the way for avocado groves, at a rate of some twenty thousand hectares of wild forest each year. Forests are set ablaze or leveled by chainsaws, quickly and indiscriminately; planters then suture avocado saplings onto the barren earth. Reforestation has since become a critical component of Cherán's economic strategy. In only a decade, the town has managed to reforest much of the town's twenty thousand hectares with native pines. It underwrites these efforts by selling juvenile pines, bred in a nursery, to nearby landscapers and farmers, and by harvesting pine resin that is used in everything from turpentine to oil to chewing gum. At the town's mill, dead and diseased trees are turned into two-by-fours for construction or fitted into wood pallets to be sold to trucking companies.

The reforestation campaign is also a water policy. Recent studies have suggested that the vapors released by pine trees can help seed clouds, substantiating in some sense the folksier notion—which I heard repeatedly—that trees bring rain. The deeper root structure of tall pines also helps convert precipitation into groundwater, providing a pathway for rain to travel to the water table during the rainy season. Avocado trees, short and appetent, are a drain on the water table throughout the entire year. A mature avocado tree demands as much water as fourteen adult pines. The forestry strategy, I was told by Edgar and others, was one of the chief reasons that Cherán had been able to escape the water problems that afflict the rest of the region. "You see, the clouds are only in our town," Edgar half-joked as the afternoon sky darkened.

While we drove back to town, Edgar asked me if I'd like to stop by the spring in Cherán where the revolution began. Twelve years earlier, the loggers turned their saws on the large pines growing on the ridge above; the imminent threat to the water source was what spurred the town to action. It was no longer the only water source, but its importance remained.

We stopped in front of a red metal archway. A hundred yards beyond the gate sat two long, concrete basins full of water, one feeding into the other. Above them, protected by a low chain-link fence and shrouded in branches, was a small mossy cave. We clambered over the fence to get a better look at the source. A few drops of water beaded up and fell silent onto the dark stones in front of us.

"I've never seen it that low," Edgar said, shaking his head. The conditions were dire enough to necessitate an official report. We rode back to town in silence.

Cherán's uprising became an inspiration, leading to a wave of copycat outbursts across Michoacán in what became known as the *autodefensas* movement. Vigilante groups took up arms and notched a number of victories, succeeding where the state had proven inept or corrupt. Community policing initiatives followed. For a time, this approach even enjoyed the tacit support of then-president Enrique Peña Nieto.

But the movement quickly dissolved. Many *autodefensa* organizations were infiltrated by former cartel members; some began selling drugs to raise money for weapons. Others were bankrolled by wealthy avocado interests sick of paying bribes or seeing shipments robbed. By 2018, the *autodefensa* system had, in many ways, become indistinguishable from cartel control.

Take one especially perverse example: in 2020, a group of avocado farmers formed a group called Pueblos Unidos, claiming to be protecting their livelihood against cartel extortion. The group's membership ballooned to around three thousand in a short amount of time, even scoring some international media coverage for their attempts to clean up the avocado supply chain. They lacked Cherán's environmental commitments from the get-go, and were soon linked to the Knights Templar Cartel. On the day I left Michoacán, they were involved in a standoff with authorities that resulted in the kidnapping of national guardsmen, the torching of a car, and over one hundred arrests. According to Mexican officials, it was one of the biggest cartel busts ever.

The Cherán council told me that dozens of other localities in Michoacán have adopted its model of governance, forming an archipelago of radical environmental resistance. While each town has its own method of implementation, the charter remains basically the same: a democratically elected council, a militarized commitment to environmental protection, and no political parties or avocados.

Twenty minutes from Cherán is the town of Arantepacua, which achieved official independence in 2018. When we drove over, a small team of laborers was at work building a checkpoint. No one stopped our car for questioning.

The town square was flanked by a crumbling church and a peach-colored municipal building. We parked alongside a Chevy Silverado pickup, with police lights mounted atop the cab. I was trying to get in touch with the mayor, Alberto Martinez, but he wasn't responding on WhatsApp. I asked a woman if she knew where I might find him. "He's right there," she pointed, "the small one in the green."

Standing on the corner was an excitable man, his hair neatly combed, wearing a pressed polo shirt tucked into khakis. He shook my hand vigorously before I'd even spit out an introduction, and pulled me into the administrative building behind him, where a portrait of Zapata again loomed above the entrance.

Sitting at one of the two desks in Alberto's corner office, bottle-feeding her four-month-old child, was Maria Elena Soria Morales, a thirty-three-year-old schoolteacher who is currently serving a two-year term as the head of security, elected alongside another woman. She oversees the *kuariches*, the town's version of Cherán's *ronda*.

But Arantepacua's adoption of the Cherán model, Maria told me, had little to do with environmental despoliation, at least at first. On April 5, 2017, Michoacán state troopers came to retrieve what they said were stolen vehicles. The town had had a long-standing feud with the state government because of territorial disputes and what I was told was overzealous policing.

Officers with shotguns kicked down the door of the house that Maria had taken shelter in, she told me, one shooting at her and another pointing a gun at her sister. A helicopter circled overhead. A terrified schoolboy in a red sweater, running toward the forest, was shot, his body flying through the air "like a kite," Maria said, fighting tears. Four people were killed.

The next day, the town set up a makeshift checkpoint at its highway exit to prevent the police from returning. Then they began to overhaul the government. "After that, we got organized to elect our own authorities," she told me. "If we don't organize ourselves, this will never stop. We have to do it like Cherán."

Arantepacua's new government made environmental protection a priority, and outlawed avocado cultivation on communal forest land. "It harms the soil," Maria told me. "When we drive on the road to Uruapan, we can feel the chemicals in the air and we know how bad it is. So we don't allow it."

Now one of her top concerns is the water supply. In recent years, the water level in the town's well has sunk lower and lower, while the neighboring town of Capácuaro cuts down its forests, and nearby Turícuaro expands its avocado operation. "We hear that they're doing it on the top of the mountains," she said. Still, she told me, the town was doing its best. Her baby burst into tears, and she whisked him away for a nap.

I wanted to see what life was like in the thick of the avocado corridor, a stretch of fertile soil and clement weather that yields an astonishing year-round harvest. At one end is the town of Tancítaro, where one of the avocado-themed statues depicts the earth as a pit. At the other end is Uruapan, home to a professional soccer team called the Aguacateros. Uruapan hosts an annual avocado festival; while I was there, Tancítaro held a world record for plating an 8,351.1-pound serving of guacamole. (This would be surpassed by a 10,961-pound serving in a nearby community a few months later.) Each town claims to be the avocado capital of the world.

They are, in less vaunted terms, the urban centers where avocados are packed and processed; the fruit is grown in the surrounding countryside. I made plans to head to the outskirts of Yoricostio, to a farming hamlet full of avocado orchards that are neither dangerous nor difficult to access. I pulled into a parking lot in front of a church where two farmers were leaning against a pickup truck.

They took me on a tour of the groves, which, by every indication, made them a handsome profit, and then to the home of Ernesto, a local avocado farmer who was hosting a number of his neighbors. Avocados weren't the only thing being farmed on Ernesto's holdings; there were also pepper plants, beans, and pumpkins.

Three decades ago, he didn't grow avocados at all. "I remember thirty-one years ago when Ernesto planted the first tree," Marilu, his wife, told me. "His father told us there was no point." But the decision paid off, and they had expanded their footprint steadily. Now they were selling avocados for export to the United States and had hired additional workers to harvest the crop. Theirs was a midsize operation, and the money seemed to be good enough—their pickup truck was new and their two-story home beautiful. They had plans for renovations. But there were problems of late. The year prior, for the first time, they had to dig retaining ponds and set up rain barrels to secure enough water for a desiccated avocado harvest. The other crops, too, needed to be watered by hand. "The climate has changed," Marilu told me. "It's hotter, drier. We used to water all our plants just with the rain. Not anymore."

Above the town was a small dam, and a reservoir to draw from in case of drought. That winter a work crew, armed with expensive heavy machinery, had begun laying a pipe at the foot of the dam. They claimed to be acting on behalf of the local water authority, but their story kept changing. Some of the farmers complained to the local government, to no avail. Others alleged corruption.

"You don't have to be very smart to figure out where the water is going," said Noemi Mondragon, a local farmer. The unfinished pipeline seemed to be pointed toward a new two-hundred-hectare avocado grove. "People say that the avocado is the devil," Noemi told me. "That isn't true. There are ways to raise it sustainably." As she saw it, the biggest problem with the avocado was that "it brought greed, which brings ambition, which brings scarcity." Water levels at the dam had already reached new lows. "Look at the size of the pipe," she added. "If they get that water, the dam will be empty in two weeks."

The farmers told me that they had scared off the construction crew the day before Christmas, with a shovel-wielding Marilu at the lead. Staring down a menacing foreman and a line of tractors, she told me, she'd filled in the basin where the pipe was being laid. Noemi and other neighbors joined, shoulder to shoulder, until the group grew large enough to drive the workers away.

Given the exceptional amount of avocado-related violence in the region, the story struck me as surprisingly tame. Earlier that year, a prominent anti-avocado activist had been kidnapped and beaten in another part of the state. Months later, I expressed some confusion about the account, and found out that the farmers had also been stockpiling guns, many of which were illegal. They'd left that detail out.

Still, the situation reminded me of Cherán's path: the alleged municipal corruption, the threatened water supply, the uprising. It seemed like the town might be open to a radical environmental overhaul, to save their community and some elements of their way of life. It wasn't hard to envision a near future in which that was one of very few viable outcomes. But when I mentioned Cherán, no one praised it as an inspiration; no one seemed to know what it was at all. And there were critical differences. Cherán had been a relatively poor, indigenous community, cut off from the green-gold rush. The farmers of Yoricostio had managed to tap into a global flow of water and wealth. Was there a way forward for these farmers that wasn't also a step down? If the climate or the industry abandoned them, which way would they point their guns?

Later that afternoon, the farmers gathered around a grill, where Ernesto was scaring carne asada. They placed a big bowl of guacamole at the center of a long picnic table and passed around a jug of mezcal, encouraging me to pour myself a drink, and then another. The clouds gathered overhead, and light rain began to fall. Then it stopped.

ADAM SELLA

In the West Bank, Palestinians Preserve Grapes and Tradition

FROM *Eater*

JAMIL SARRAS, A Palestinian viticulturist, is typically put to-gether and well-spoken by 6 a.m. I met him early one morning in September to pick grapes before the heat set in. He has a day job as a medical lab specialist at a hospital in Bethlehem, but before clocking in for work, he manages the Sarras Family Vine-yard forty minutes away in the hills near Hebron, known as Al-Khalil in Arabic, a city in the occupied West Bank. Starting in late August each year, the family and staff pick grapes for a month or two, before Sarras sells their haul to Palestinian wineries and arak distillers.

Grapes, after olives, are the second-most cultivated fruit crop in Palestine, where there are three different grape harvests. The first is in early spring, when farmers pick the leaves. Stuffed for waraq dawali, the leaves sell for five times the price of grapes themselves. A couple of months later, unripe grapes, still hard and green, are picked to make hosrum, a sour condiment used in Palestinian cooking to give a pungent, sour taste to dishes.

In late summer, the grapes themselves are finally picked. In ad-dition to being eaten raw as a dessert, they are also used to make wine, arak, vinegar, and raisins, and other treats like dibs, a winter-time grape molasses that's mixed with tahini and scooped up with bread for what Palestinian food writer Reem Kassis describes as the "Middle Eastern version of a peanut butter and jelly sandwich" in her cookbook *The Palestinian Table*.

With just a few clusters left to pick, Sarras took me to a vantage point so I could see the whole property. The view is quite different from European and American vineyards. Instead of trellises, Palestinian grape growers plant vines around metal stakes stuck deep into the ground. The plants form thick stems around the stakes, and leafy canopies grow over the fruit. This actually allows the farmers to control ripening: if demand is high, the farmer can cut back the canopy, exposing the grapes to the sun and causing them to ripen faster.

Another sight not common on European vineyards, white walls of an Israeli settlement hover over Sarras's property from a nearby hill. The Sarras vineyard is in a region known by Israel as Gush Etzion, one of a number of areas where the Israeli government has explicitly helped and implicitly allowed the incursion of Israeli settlers. Israeli settlements are illegal under international law, and the UN describes the Etzion settlement bloc as "one of the main settlement areas in the West Bank." In 2020, the Washington Institute for Near East Policy estimated that Gush Etzion was home to around 100,000 settlers, and that number has grown since.

As settlers have expanded, they've increasingly come into violent conflict with nearby Palestinians; according to the UN, violence by settlers against Palestinians spiked throughout the first half of 2023, resulting in casualties, property damage, and displacement. To get to his vineyard, Sarras has to pass through an intersection that was previously a hotbed of violence. The vineyard itself, set beneath the Gush Etzion settlement, has long seemed to exist in the shadow of a looming threat. In recent weeks, that abstract fear has become an existential threat for the family and the vineyard.

"We are locked down in our house," Sarras told me on October 16. "Every single street that connects us with the outside world is closed as some kind of collective punishment."

On October 7, Hamas, the Palestinian militant group that controls the Gaza Strip, launched a surprise attack on Israel, killing more than 1,400 people, most of whom were civilians, and taking hundreds of hostages. In response, Israel declared war against Hamas, began a weeks-long aerial bombardment of Gaza that has claimed the lives of 8,000 Palestinians according to the Gaza Health Ministry, and tightened the borders around the territory, making it difficult for humanitarian aid to reach people within and for news to make it out. On October 27, the Israel Defense Force expanded its ground assault into Gaza, and Israeli Prime

Minister Benjamin Netanyahu predicted a "long and difficult" war to come. Today, Israeli troops attacked Gaza City.

Increased violence has spread to the West Bank as well, leading to fears that the fighting centered on Gaza will spread into a wider regional conflict. Clashes between Israeli forces and Palestinians in the West Bank, combined with violence by armed settlers, has resulted in the most deadly weeks for West Bank Palestinians in fifteen years. Though the area is controlled by the Palestinian Authority, not Hamas, Israeli forces have launched raids and an airstrike (the latter is historically rare for the West Bank) targeting militants from Hamas and the Palestinian Islamic Jihad, another militant group. Israeli forces have also severely restricted travel within the West Bank, making it difficult for aid workers, or anyone, to move freely.

After some back and forth, Israeli forces eventually agreed to allow Sarras to visit his farm to feed his animals, provided he doesn't go down into the vineyard, which he suspects is "because they don't want anybody anywhere near the settlements."

Sarras and his family have been cultivating their land for generations. The area around Gush Etzion—which Palestinians call Al-Shefa, which means a healing spa—is home to 85 percent of Palestine's vineyards. It's the most fertile land in the Palestinian territories, serving as the breadbasket for Bethlehem and Hebron. Now Sarras has been left without access to his grapes, and there's no clear path out of the spiraling escalation of conflict.

"What's left of our grapes are still on the vines and will go bad very soon because we cannot get to our vineyard," he said.

Like the rich soil Sarras showed me as we walked through the fields that September morning, it could all slip through his fingers.

Sarras was picking dabouki grapes the day I visited the vineyard in September. Before grapes were available in supermarkets all year round, Palestinians would look forward to dabouki, the first grapes of the season, for their slightly sweet, slightly sour taste, or fateer in Arabic, meaning not completely ripe.

The dabouki grape is no longer quite a strong selling point, Sarras said that day, "but it's perfect for malban." The traditional Palestinian dried fruit leather, preserved like a fruit roll-up, is made from grapes, nuts, and spices. It's enjoyed as a snack, something sweet and healthy between meals.

During the Second Intifada, the Palestinian uprising against Israeli occupation in the early 2000s, the economy took a downturn, making it hard for Sarras to sell his production grapes. In response, he decided to make large batches of malban with the unsold grapes. The family found that customers loved it, and they've made malban ever since, attracting customers with their distinct use of nigella seeds from Hebron. The batch we were going to make together, he said, was already sold out from preorders.

Products like malban and dibs are time-consuming and expensive to make, but in an ever-changing landscape of political conflict, they are also methods of preserving the Sarras family's food traditions. At the same time, grapes, like other crops, are at the center of the area's violent history.

Much of the conflict between settlers and Palestinians in the West Bank has centered on agriculture. The UN Office for Coordination of Humanitarian Affairs has noted that agricultural communities, especially herders, have been particularly vulnerable to attack. Palestinian farmers have experienced loss of land, destruction of their crops, and physical threats. On October 28th, during a surge of attacks by settlers since Israel's war with Hamas began, settlers killed a Palestinian farmer harvesting olives.

Palestinians have caused injuries and fatalities against settlers in the West Bank as well: The *New York Times* reports, via UN records, that an outbreak of violence in early 2022 resulted in casualties and injuries "roughly comparable" between Palestinians and settlers. But consequences have rarely been equal; as violence has risen over the last six years, especially during harvest seasons, rights groups have accused the Israeli military of failing to intervene during settler attacks and failing to punish Israeli perpetrators, even while prosecuting Palestinians.

"Settlers regularly burn groves of olives and grapes," Kassis told me on August 21, adding that land that has been cultivated by Palestinians for generations "is overtaken illegally by settlers and [Palestinian] farmers are no longer allowed access [to their land]."

Farmers will likely lose more land if the Israeli government annexes the occupied territory. In 2019, Netanyahu vowed to annex sections of the West Bank; the plan gained steam after Israel received backing from the US in Donald Trump's 2020 peace plan and again when the Netanyahu government limited the power of the supreme court (the body that usually checks the executive branch) in July 2023. Following the declaration of war, it's unclear if or how annexation would play out. Though the exact territory to be annexed could take several forms, according to Machsom Watch, a group of Israeli women who monitor human rights abuses in the West Bank, Israel will likely demand "to annex the Gush Etzion region in a permanent agreement with the Palestinians." Even in the most restrained version of annexation, the settlement bloc would likely be engulfed by Israel.

Given the large concentration of Palestinian vineyards in the area, annexation would decimate the Palestinian grape industry, as well as downstream companies such as wineries, distilleries, vinegar producers, and raisin-makers.

"For agro-businesses like myself that depend on the grape as the main product for my project, I don't know what we're going to do," Nader Muaddi, a Palestinian distiller at Arak Muaddi in Beit Jala, told me in August. Muaddi uses Sarras's grapes to make arak, a traditional, anise-flavored spirit commonly found in the Levant. "I could try sourcing grapes from other areas like Jenin, but then the shipping will cost as much as the grapes themselves."

Given the presence of right-wing settlers like Bezalel Smotrich and Itamar Ben-Gvir in high ministerial positions, it's difficult to make plans for the future when annexation could completely redraw the map of the West Bank.

"It's very unpredictable," Muaddi said. "It's not sustainable or stable at all."

Most restaurants have remained closed since the most recent war between Israel and Hamas began, but Palestinian grapes had long been a critical component for both Palestinian and Israeli chefs in all sorts of dishes before October 7. Asaf Doktor, an Israeli chef with several hyperlocal restaurants in Tel Aviv—Dok, Ha'Achim, and Abie—preferred to source fruit from Palestinian farmers, including grapes.

At the flagship Dok—which temporarily closed for regular business on October 8 and just reopened for standard service yesterday—the chef had served a take on Palestinian musakhan; traditionally, roasted chicken and onion are served atop a taboon flatbread, but at Dok, quail replaced the chicken, house-made Khorasan wheat pasta was swapped in for the taboon, and a pasta sauce featured wine and plump raisins made by Philokalia, a skin-contact winery in Bethlehem. Doktor would also reach for Palestinian grape molasses to sweeten vinaigrettes or other sauces.

"Dibs is one of my favorite molasses that we use. It is very old-school," he told me in August. "Acid is also very important to our cuisine," he added, "and we try to choose acid components according to the season." Lemons are a winter fruit, so come summertime, Doktor's restaurants usually switch to hosrum, the sour grape condiment. "Hosrum reacts better on proteins [like Doktor's carpaccio and sashimi] because it doesn't cure the meat or fish like lemon would."

Habib Daoud, the chef and owner of two Palestinian restaurants in Israel serving Galilean cuisine—Kabakeh in Jaffa and Ezba in Rameh—cited the idea of baladi, common among Palestinian farmers, in explaining the quality of the agriculture.

"Baladi refers to a place, a smell, a method of cultivating crops—overall an attitude," he said in September. For Daoud, this approach is characterized by a small plot of land next to the house of the fellahin (farmer), who can maintain a close connection to the land. Because output is small, people rely on their neighbors, sharing when they have extra and coming together for celebratory meals. It's what gives Palestinian grapes, and Palestinian cuisine more broadly, its flavor, Daoud explained.

It's also why chefs like Doktor and Daoud tended to buy produce from nearby Palestinian farms. There are echoes of baladi in the Slow Food movement, which promotes local agriculture, and the farming principle produces excellent local, seasonal ingredients.

"Through my visits to the markets in the West Bank," Daoud said, "I notice the [difference] in flavor of Israeli produce and Palestinian farms, especially in the fruit department."

As the vineyard heated up on that September morning, Sarras took me to his home, where the rest of the family was preparing to process the grapes to make malban. I was greeted at the door by Carlos Sarras, Jamil's father. Carlos, now in his eighties, has been growing grapes all his life.

The first step in making malban is extracting the juice from the grapes. In the old days, the family would stomp on the grapes, Carlos explained, but they use a machine today to make the process easier. After straining out the seeds and skins a couple times, they let the juice boil down in a big pot, which can take a while. As we waited, the family invited me in for a breakfast of stewed tomatoes, hard-boiled eggs, olive oil, and za'atar.

At breakfast, I learned more about the family and their history. Carlos was raised near Bethlehem, but his mother was a Palestinian born in Chile. Like many Palestinian families, the Sarrases have family living in the diaspora across the world.

In recent years, Palestinians in the diaspora have gained visibility through new restaurants and cookbooks. As part of this wave, a new generation of Palestinian chefs are modernizing Palestinian cuisine to great acclaim. While stuffed grape leaves can be found at most of these restaurants, grapes and grape products from Palestine itself rarely make it out of the territories. You can find Arak Muaddi and Philokalia wine at select liquor shops and restaurants in the US, but products like malban and dibs are harder to come by.

That international culinary recognition is also a fraction of what it could be. For Kassis, one existential threat to Palestinian food culture is "the false marketing of many of our foods abroad as Israeli, instead of Palestinian, which was a conscious effort to remove any mention of our existence," she told me. When she first moved to the US, Kassis explained in the *Washington Post*, she was frustrated to see iconic dishes from her childhood served at Israeli restaurants without any mention of their Palestinian origins. Despite leading Israeli food scholars acknowledging that Israeli chefs first gleaned hummus and falafel from Palestinians, the erasure continues.

"We the Palestinians have been caretakers for these grapes, preserving them and keeping them alive for so long," Muaddi said, pointing out that the community has maintained twenty-three unique, heirloom grape varieties for thousands of years. "It would be a shame to lose this element of viticulture, because viticulture is very much a part of Palestinian culture."

This is just one of the many ways Palestinians are trying to preserve their food culture and traditions under the active threat of violence and annexation. The Palestinian Heirloom Seed Library in Battir, just across the valley from the Sarras family home, preserves a variety of seeds and distributes them to Palestinian farmers. Today, seeds from the library are available for purchase in the US, allowing Palestinians in the diaspora to sow the seeds of Palestine in their own backyard.

As we finished our breakfast in the Sarras home, and the grape juice finally boiled down sufficiently, we added nuts and seeds to the malban, which lend the fruit leather the perfect combination of chew and crunch. We also added spices like aniseed, turmeric, and sesame seeds that subtly enhance the natural grape flavor. Finally, we added a mixture of flour and well water to thicken it.

The final step of the day was to pour out the mixture onto heatproof plastic and spread it into a thin layer to dry out for a week. In the past, Carlos told me, they would pour the mixture onto bedsheets, but they've switched to plastic. "The sheets were a mess," he said.

Saying my farewells, I made plans to return at the end of the harvest to make dibs. But the war broke out, and I have not made it back to the Sarras home.

"The situation is bad, and we hope for the best," Sarras told me on October 16. "Escalation leads to escalation and more radicalization of both parties. Enough people have died."

The wait for malban to set or grapes to ripen is incomparable to the generations-long wait for peace. But the process of juicing, cooking, and drying grapes reveals a sliver of the paradoxical yet irresistible work the Sarras family and the Palestinian community do to preserve their traditions from total erasure. That work will have to continue. For now, many grapes remain on the vines.

Meet America's Godmother of Tofu

FROM *Atlas Obscura*

IN THE SUMMER of 1918, the kitchen on the top floor of 641 Washington Street in New York City was filled with buckets of cream-colored slurry. Pails sat next to the stove; jars and bottles of the liquid lined the shelves. It looked as if someone had just milked a herd of cows.

But this "milk" did not come from any animal. All of it was soy milk.

"I might talk to you until doomsday about the manifold uses of soybeans, but you wouldn't understand," Dr. Kin Yamei told a reporter for the *St. Louis Post-Dispatch* visiting her laboratory, which was operated by the United States Department of Agriculture. She had just returned from a six-month mission to China on behalf of the US government.

The American government feared World War I would deprive soldiers and the American public of constitution-fortifying meat. They tasked Kin with researching the soybean's varied applications in China as an alternative. Kin was well aware of this little legume's potential. She knew that, if you curdled its milk long enough, it would clot into a protein-rich cushion called tofu.

The word "tofu" hadn't yet entered American vernacular. Kin often described it as a "vegetable cheese" to a public that considered soybeans inedible pebbles. In the early twentieth century, said public held deep prejudice toward both Chinese cooking and Chinese people. The American government at the time still rigorously enforced the Chinese Exclusion Act of 1882, which barred Chinese-born laborers from entering the country.

To Kin, the soybean was a nutritional miracle, possessing the benefits of meat and milk without its drawbacks. But despite her passion, Kin's efforts just didn't take. Those predicted wartime shortages didn't come to pass, and American attitudes toward Chinese people also muffled her message. She died in China, in 1934, without seeing the fruits of her advocacy blossom in America.

Only in the last five years has Kin gained greater attention, with features in the *New York Times* and *America's Test Kitchen* presenting her as a woman ahead of her time. A century later, America has finally started to embrace her message.

Kin spent her life torn between two countries. Born in the Chinese city of Ningbo in 1864, she was only two when she lost her biological parents to a cholera epidemic. A pair of white American Protestant medical missionaries adopted her, raising her between China, America, and Japan. Around 1880, she began medical school at the Women's Medical College of the New York Infirmary at age sixteen. She enrolled there as Y. May King, likely to conceal her racial origins. This was two years before the passage of the Chinese Exclusion Act. The senator who introduced the law called Chinese people a "degraded and inferior race," while others who supported it referred to them as "rats," "beasts," and "swine."

This climate of intolerance infected Kin's day-to-day life. Workmen would pelt her with insults when she walked outside. Her classmates treated her with antagonism. While in school, Kin boarded with a fellow immigrant from India whose religious credo forbade her from eating meat. The writer Jaroslav Průšek, a Czech Sinologist and translator, befriended Kin later in life. In his 1940 autobiography, he wrote that Kin told him that her roommate eventually died of starvation. Kin knew from an early age that the United States was unfriendly to vegetarians.

Kin's graduation from university reportedly made her the first Chinese woman to obtain a medical degree in the United States, a rebuke of the racism of the era. But discrimination dogged her in the years that followed. She encountered venomous anti-Chinese sentiment as a medical missionary in China from her peers, while her advisor declined to provide lodging because she was a woman.

Dejected, she sought refuge in Japan, where she practiced medicine for several years. There, she met a mustachioed musician named Hippolytus Laesola Amador Eça da Silva and married him in 1894. Though their marriage soured and eventually led to divorce, she doted on their son, Alexander.

In the early 1900s, Kin reinvented herself. Traveling across the United States, she became a celebrity of the speaking circuit, enthralling crowds with lectures about Chinese culture. She often wore Chinese fashions while speaking, while her flawless elocution and commanding mien dispelled any racist presumptions from her audiences. Reporters often didn't know what to make of Kin, this being who toggled so fluidly between cultures with her "puzzling blend of eastern looks and western speech," as one journalist for the *Leader*, a newspaper in Canada (now the *Regina Leader-Post*), put it.

On occasion, her speeches turned to the beauty of China's food. She regaled her audiences with cooking demonstrations for chop suey, the riot of meat, vegetables, and sauce most commonly associated with Chinese cooking in America at that point. She also spoke of what she called bean cake—tofu—and described how it was cooked in China.

Even if few Americans knew of tofu at that point, its place within Chinese cooking tradition was well-established, stretching back centuries, if not millennia. There are competing theories about tofu's origins. One legend even attributes its invention to the ancient philosopher-prince Liu An, who ruled a kingdom in northern China starting in 164 BC. The first written mention of *dòufu* (豆腐, or bean curd) dates to the year 965, when a document called it the "vice mayor's mutton," relating how a poor vice mayor who could not afford meat had to make do with tofu instead.

The food spread to Japan not long after (the exact date of its migration is, again, a matter of dispute). Tofu was first mentioned in Japanese writing in 1182, and the Japanese pronunciation for the food was one of many that Americans used during Kin's lifetime, alongside "bean curd," "soybean curd," and "soy cheese."

As Kin continued delivering these addresses, the world around her was changing. In 1911, the Qing Dynasty collapsed, and in 1912, China became a republic. In 1917, the United States entered World War I. It was then that the USDA identified Kin as an ideal evangelist for the soybean, due to her fame and spellbinding lectures. Kin embarked for China in the spring of 1917, roaming around the country and collecting soybean samples for the USDA.

Kin underwent this grueling journey despite being denied

American citizenship. Nevertheless, she felt a patriotic pull toward the United States, especially since her son was fighting in the war on America's behalf. "My boy is at the front doing his bit," she told one reporter. "I want to do mine, too."

On her return to New York, she set up shop at the USDA's Washington Street lab and experimented with various treatments of tofu. Others from nearby laboratories would pop their heads in, jonesing for a taste of "soy bean cheese." One of them fried it with the same gravy in which he'd cooked fish; the curd crisped up so convincingly that he couldn't distinguish the animal from the bean. "It has a way of absorbing the flavor of whatever it's cooked with," the dazzled man told the *St. Louis Post-Dispatch* journalist. Kin would invite reporters over to her nearby apartment, too, where a hired Chinese cook would chop tofu up and mix it with onions, celery, and chicken stock before cramming it into green peppers. Unsuspecting diners were delighted: They just couldn't believe that what they were eating wasn't meat.

For Kin, cooking was a source of wonder and an outlet for creativity. But she believed American cuisine was in dire need of both. "American women, you must admit, are lacking in artistic sense," she said bluntly to that *St. Louis Post-Dispatch* reporter. "That is because the country is so young. When the process of refinement is farther advanced they will not regard household work, especially cooking, as drudgery. It really is art." She felt that tofu's adoption amongst Americans could break the monotony of a staid plate of pork and beans.

Kin wasn't vegetarian herself, but she found joy in not consuming "what was once a palpitating little animal, filled with the joy of life," she continued to the *St. Louis Post-Dispatch*. China has a long tradition of vegetable-forward dining, and she told American cooks how tofu could mix nicely with beef, chicken, or ham. But Kin also knew that tofu could completely replace animal products if home cooks so desired. "It has all the advantages and none of the faults of animal cheese," Kin said to another paper.

Prior to Kin, "mainstream American awareness of tofu was pretty nonexistent," says Matthew D. Roth, author of *Magic Bean: The Rise of Soy in America*. Those who consumed it lived on the fringes. Some small shops frequented by Asian American communities made it fresh, while home economists and Seventh-day Adventists who'd gone to Asia on missions were clearly aware of it. But American incuriosity, particularly when it came to Chinese cooking, was stubborn.

To work against that ingrained disinterest, Kin poured her energies into proselytizing tofu through as many avenues as possible. She corralled the press into her laboratory and kitchen to show them the wonders of tofu. She traveled up and down the East Coast, holding demonstrations and lectures along the way. But her crusade was constantly met with indifference and logistical roadblocks. She tried to persuade the National Canners Association, a trade group, to offer soybean dishes to sell on the American market. According to Roth's book, there's no sign that the organization ever responded to that plea. Kin also wanted to arrange large-scale tofu meals for soldiers in nearby camps, only to find that shipping soybeans in bulk from the nearest farm that grew them, in North Carolina, was far too cumbersome.

Ultimately, Kin's project failed. Convincing Americans to embrace tofu at the dawn of the Jazz Age may have been too big an ask, Roth says, though xenophobia isn't the sole factor that felled her efforts. "I would say that it's fair to assess her attempt as a failure," Roth says. "There were several reasons that the time wasn't ripe. A big factor was that soybeans were not yet a widespread American crop." In addition to Kin's trouble with sourcing soybeans, Roth clarifies that wartime rationing ended up being brief. In the end, meat remained cheap and easy to come by.

Funding for her project soon got slashed, and personal tragedy struck Kin just before the war's end: Her son died while fighting in France. Kin couldn't make sense of this loss. "What did he die for?" she later asked Průšek, the Czech Sinologist. "What did we have to do with that sickening war?" In the wake of this catastrophe, Kin lost faith in the American project and left for the comforts of China.

Though she dabbled in food—she contributed recipes to community cookbooks in China, for example—Kin's years in Beijing were spent as a high-society matriarch, often hosting younger people like Průšek for dinner parties. A bout with pneumonia killed her in early 1934, when she was seventy. She asked that her body be buried on a farm in Haidian, in northwest Beijing. "Here my dust will blend with soil," she said to Průšek. "And after the pile of clay they will place upon my grave has crumbled as well, I will become a field, a fertile field."

*

In the decades that followed, the cultural tide began to shift. The passage of the Magnuson Act in 1943 effectively repealed the Chinese Exclusion Act, establishing quotas for the entry of Chinese immigrants to America. Subsequent immigration laws after World War II—namely 1965's Hart-Celler Act, which did away with mandates about national origins—helped soften public hostility to Chinese immigrants and, in turn, their food.

By the 1960s, Roth says, American soybeans were widely available for anyone who wanted to make their own tofu. Meanwhile, demand for tofu amongst growing Asian American communities, particularly in California, led to factories who produced it purely for those markets. Tofu also began to appear in grocery stores across the state.

Chinese cookbooks from major publishing houses, such as 1962's *The Pleasures of Chinese Cooking* by Grace Zia Chu, helped demolish the stereotypes that had defined Chinese cooking in America. But it was the work of other cookbooks that really shepherded tofu beyond Asian American communities. The groundbreaking 1971 publication of Frances Moore Lappé's *Diet for a Small Planet* advocated for plant-based eating as both an individual and public good. It also contained recipes such as tofu sautéed with spinach.

If you grew up with hippie parents (or were a hippie yourself), this might not sound terribly surprising. "Tofu was never an important food in America until the hippies came along," says William Shurtleff. Shurtleff and his former wife Akiko Aoyagi are the founders of the Soy Info Center, which bills itself as the world's foremost repository of soybean knowledge. He and Aoyagi bear as much responsibility for ushering tofu to a wider audience in the later twentieth century as Lappé: They co-wrote *The Book of Tofu*, a 1975 introduction to this food.

Word got around that eating tofu could lower cholesterol, giving it a health-food shine. (More recent studies show that it can, marginally.) Yet that promise, along with tofu's vegan ingredients, made it appealing to younger Americans in the 1970s. "Many people during that period were vegetarians, and some were even vegans," Shurtleff says. "And so it fit nicely into desires for foods that people had, and met those desires in a nice way. As this demand grew, the number of tofu companies grew."

Tofu was especially alluring to political progressives during the era of civil rights activism and anti-Vietnam War demonstrations, Roth adds. "The counterculture embraced tofu for a number of reasons: many were exploring Buddhism, non-violence, and vegetarianism, and tofu—replacing blood with water, so to speak—appealed to these sensibilities," Roth says. "From an anti-war perspective, eating Asian food demonstrated solidarity with the Vietnamese and others being killed and bombed in an American imperialist war."

But as tofu inched into the mainstream diet, it gained a grim reputation as tasteless health food. Many non-Asian cooks had no idea how to cook it. A century since Kin's work, tofu still faces a struggle for respect from casual American cooks who might misread it as a lifeless, waterlogged pillow. These are prejudices that Hetty McKinnon, the author of *Tenderheart: A Cookbook About Vegetables and Unbreakable Family Bonds*, finds herself running up against. "Growing up in a Cantonese household, tofu was an everyday food, as foundational to my mother's cooking as meat or vegetables," the Australian-born McKinnon says. Her mother would steam tofu and serve it with cilantro and mushroom gravy, whose flavors spotlighted tofu's innate creaminess and silkiness.

McKinnon has occasionally been frustrated by what she calls the "whitewashed" mainstreaming of tofu. "In the West, the concept of tofu is still quite narrow and I still often encounter the 'bland' and 'tasteless' stereotypes," McKinnon says. She also hears grousing about its so-called "rubbery" texture. "My response to this is clear and emphatic," she says. "If you have eaten tofu that is bland, tasteless, or rubbery, it is because it wasn't cooked properly." McKinnon also wonders if the distorted impression of tofu as a mere protein might limit it in the American culinary mind. "In Chinese cooking, we don't think of tofu or meat as 'protein,' but rather as textural elements that add to the final dish," she says.

These are words one can imagine Dr. Kin Yamei would've said herself a century ago, when she wanted Americans to honor tofu in all its forms and uses: as a meat replacement for cooks who wanted to be gentler to their bodies and the planet, as well as an ingredient for eaters who wanted to expand their palates and their minds. "I shouldn't be surprised if the soy bean will save the lives of many American animals," Kin said to the *St. Louis Post-Dispatch*. Tofu, Kin knew, could do anything.

The Butchering

FROM *Emergence*

I RATTLED WITH the truck as my family and I drove a short way to the corral to get the sheep. It had been donated to us to help feed the many who were scheduled to show up later in the day in celebration and reverence for a relative who was reaching a pinnacle in her/their life: the Kinaałda, or what has been loosely translated as the Diné puberty ceremony. An intense and refreshing four days of family, song, and food. The ceremony is a moment when beauty of the beyond and beauty of the world come together as we sit around a fire and grind corn, tell stories, and prepare food.

As we rolled up to the corral, my mom was worrying because there was no one to do the butchering. Butchering for ceremony takes a tremendous amount of labor and often requires several people. She had called everyone in our family, even distant family, and I had posted on social media asking for anyone who might happen to be free. But no one responded. There is no blame here. Times change, pressures build. We are often pulled in so many directions. I told my mom we had to do it ourselves. Uncertain, she agreed, and I would do it.

My role in these ceremonies has slowly begun to shift. I'm no longer a child who simply witnesses but an adult who must participate, and as such it's important to enter the space with the proper mindset. We don't think negatively or with anxiety during the next four days. We don't hesitate or feel unsure about our roles and duties. We enter the space with a lean toward what is beautiful in the world, what is right and balanced. Even writing this essay, I feel compelled to focus on what is working rather than what is not working, because you don't pair a ceremony like this with more negative assumptions. It is beauty way. It is hope. Some might call it a naïve, optimistic hope, but I call it a critical hope.

As a child, I remember these kinds of ceremonies often being well attended; many of our distant relatives would travel to our home and we to theirs. My aunts and grandmothers from all across our family tree would work together to butcher. We would help wherever we could, learning what we could and participating in the continuation of our culture. However, time brought us forward, and now my parents are grandparents and families are growing distant, meandering through the thickets of existence in the what-might-be end times. Much of Navajo consciousness has been focused on the idea of language and culture loss, with each generation finding less to hold on to. I remember first hearing about language revitalization and cultural integration as a child in elementary school. How do we sustain our Diné way of life? Of course, we don't think about that or comment on such things during this ceremony. We offer only prayer and critical hope for the future. When my mom worried that not enough people would show up or there wouldn't be enough food, I reminded her of this. We don't worry about those things so as to not pass on those anxieties to the younger ones.

This ceremony is about bravery, and I was hoping my instinct to take on the butchering would pay off. This ceremony is also about showing yourself to the world for the first time. So I was hoping to emulate that in any way I could; to be an example, an uncle, no longer a child.

In college, I joined the Diné of UNM, a group devoted entirely to celebrating and exploring Diné culture. Every spring semester, we traveled to To'Hajiilee, New Mexico, a small town just west of Albuquerque—the closest piece of reservation we had—to learn how to butcher a sheep. We camped, told stories, and taught each other how to butcher from start to finish. The ones who knew how to butcher taught those who did not know, and we each went around sharing what we had been told, what we knew from family stories. No one was ever wrong in these circles. *Food sovereignty*. A group of kids experimenting with instinct, story, and a deep respect for land and nature.

Sheep represent so much more than food, so food sovereignty itself represents the inherent right of peoples to their own ways of living. "Sheep is life," as the saying goes. Sheep offer nourishment, clothing, and tools. No part of the sheep is wasted. However, to get this harvest you must tend to the sheep, waking up early every day to ensure their survival. This shepherding gives way to a circle of care and attention that births a way of life. A way of life we have an inherent right to. This is food sovereignty.

I come from a lineage of people who had sophisticated approaches to nourishment, corn being the prime example of what Native science could engineer. But despite our long history of relationship with food, the government built a system of dependency, introducing families to commodity foods. This practice diminished the validity of Native science and agricultural engineering altogether. The Consumer Protection Act of 1973 established the Food Distribution Program on Indian Reservations, which sought to increase the livelihood of Native people. As children, we tore through white boxes with black text that read "Corn Flakes Cereal," pried open canned pineapple juice, fruit cocktail, and powdered eggs. For quick lunches, we would put "commodity cheese" on tortillas or bread. The cheese is a household treasure where I'm from. It's a delicacy. But the flavors we savored in childhood became a detriment to our health. In my research into the program, I found many articles that explored the link between commodity food and obesity rates on reservations. Eating dinner from cans and boxes as kids often leads to eating dinner from cans and boxes as adults. I've called it comfort food.

At the only convenience store in Tsaile, Arizona, I saw a mother buying groceries. In her cart, she had the staples: Hamburger Helper, ground beef, Spam, potatoes, bread, cereal, chips, bologna, American cheese, and snacks like cookies and ramen noodles for her kids. She also had *The Holy Trinity*: lard, Blue Bird flour, and baking soda. Filling your stomach on the reservation is a tale of processed foods. Humans need food, so we go out and buy food. There shouldn't be any shame in that. But this system that creates food deserts and marginalizes communities can make you feel at fault for not finding nourishment, even though the structures in place limit access to quality foods.

I traveled into Rock Point, Arizona, with my partner and his sister because she was training to run for Miss Navajo Nation. The pageant had created a new traditional foods competition, so my partner and his sister turned to the one person they knew who would be able to teach them: their grandmother. I was scared because their family is fluent in the Diné language and have a strong knowledge of ceremonial ways, and I felt like I didn't know enough or even belong at all. I was a child again, watching and trying to learn. The teaching moved quickly and went on into the night. Their grandmother told a few stories then showed my partner's sister how to make the dish—only once. From there, it was trial and error. She took charge and carefully moved through the motions. Her grandmother only offered small words and phrases of correction. They showed no hesitation. I think I was the only one feeling it, because this environment felt foreign to me.

Looking back, I now realize that this kind of education is crucial to surviving and there is no room for hesitation. This experience might have spurred a kind of loose confidence in myself that drove me to take charge in the butchering. It also showed me a kind of pedagogy that exists in our communities. There are no grades in these moments, only stories and sometimes another pair of hands to guide your way. My partner tells me often that his upbringing shaped a way of interacting with the world. I felt it when I was there, watching them in utter wonder.

Their house had no electricity, so the light grew dimmer as we sat around the fire and ate the fruits of their labor, their offering. Soon, it was night, and we were still sitting outside in the pitch darkness with only a partial moon for light. No sound for miles. Just us and the cosmos. Each star a story. Each rock formation, another. Each memory folding into a story. And each ingredient of the food we enjoyed folding into even more stories, each food carrying a story of its own. *Food sovereignty.*

My partner's sister ended up winning the title of Miss Navajo Nation, and we believe it's in part due to the rare traditional dish she created and the story behind it. While serving in the role of Miss Navajo Nation, she kept the traditional foods category in the competition, and it continues to this day. Another Miss Navajo Nation titleholder even helped produce *Cooking with Miss Navajo Nation*, a bilingual cooking show where she demonstrated ways to make traditional foods. The first episode featured chiiłchin, or sumac berry mush, which is a storied dish, famous across all of Navajo.

During the latter part of the pandemic, my partner and I decided we would visit as much of the rez as possible. So we drove with some friends to Page, Arizona. Woven through the ridge lines, meadows, and open fields were the stories we told about our past, about times we did things or said things. We talked about our families. We grew hungry. In a small town, we pulled into a local flea market. An older woman, grandmother-age, was selling chiiłchin. We stopped and bought some to enjoy on the road. One of my friends had never eaten it before, and this opened up many stories about chiiłchin, and those stories unfolded into even more, carrying us to our destination. It was as if no time had gone by. In a flash, we were driving into Page.

Stories have a unique ability to collapse time. Food does too. Stories move through time differently than we do. They can move between times, slow time, or even stop time. Food operates similarly, carrying metaphors, images, and memories. Which is why so much of our culture involves gathering around a table for a nice sit-down dinner or hunching over a barstool on the roadside to devour street tacos. Each culture carries traditions around food. Native and Indigenous foods also carry certain traditions. They are able to navigate the past, present, and future.

Blue corn, for example—a staple dish for Navajo people—embodies the past, finds innovative representations in the present, and acts as a metaphor for a future where Native people can express sovereignty. In a trendy brewery in the Wells Park area of Albuquerque, New Mexico, called Bow & Arrow, I had an American pilsner made with blue corn. Bow & Arrow is sharing with the world unique ways to use Native ingredients to create an experience. Each experience at the brewery is different, and the brews themselves change with the seasons, because the ingredients are versatile and can create stunning concoctions that represent an entirely new way to tell a story through food. This is an example of reclaiming the stories that exist within our foods and the power that can be felt when enjoying their flavors. It's more than food, it's a lifestyle.

Diné farmers are also beginning to see the ways in which farming and food can help sustain a very sacred Diné way of life. Graham Biyáál started Biyáál Trading Post, which sells seeds, teas, and other materials needed to make traditional foods, like the Tąąniil & Blue Corn Pancake Kit and Gad Bit'eesh, juniper ash, which is needed to make blue corn mush. In my cabinet right now are blue corn seeds from Biyáál's farm. I visited his farm and homestead after a series of storms had changed the landscape of the area in 2021. He texted me about the potential of getting stuck in the mud, but I was determined to get my hands on those seeds. I haven't found time to plant them, but I am hoping to continue the story of these seeds, the seeds in my cabinet. Their legacy transcends families, borders, and timeliness, each carrier committing to their survival; each adding their own stories to the collected voices already ingrained in the seeds themselves. The seeds are the start of a cycle: the tilling, the plowing, the planting, the watering, the tending, the harvesting, the preparing, the cooking, the nourishing, and the sharing. After harvesting the fruits of the labor, we digest that history and allow it to nourish our bodies. That is how food is supposed to operate, as part of story.

There is no way to explain this to my doctor at our check-ins. It's not easy to talk about this history in such a short period of time. Through no fault of her own, my doctor sees me through numbers: this is high, that is normal, this is a little high, that is a little low. The mechanisms of my body are as complex as the universe it seems. Too much of one thing throws it off its axis. Each food makes its journey known through your body, and we exhibit that journey through our emotions, our energies, our physicality, our actions. My body is telling me that I need to take time away from my work and make time for myself and those stories.

But for myself and others like me, time is not an easy thing to come by. I can't even imagine the families back home on Navajo, the way time is more fluid there and easily evaporates into nothing. Growing up, my mother commuted from Vanderwagen, New Mexico, to Window Rock, Arizona, across state lines for work. Both of my parents worked full-time. It's the same today, finding time is difficult. It's almost as if "being healthy" is altogether unsustainable.

The answer to this predicament is easy: a return to our own agricultural histories. That return can be both literal and figurative. We can quite literally return to our own ancestral foods. However, figurative returning can mean allowing foods to travel through time, to be timeless, or rather to be timeful. They are artifacts that hold within them all the stories and traditions and generate more and more each time they are prepared. An artifact to hold with it all the stories and traditions that can generate more and more each time it is made.

The term "agricultural history" implies that history exists in the past tense. However, history is an active presence and can be a tool for futuritive imagination: for example, blue corn reimagined into contemporary dishes and Miss Navajo Nation teaching how to make blue corn mush. The past, present, and future exist simultaneously. There are movements toward a transformation in our relationships with food—more intentional relationships and less reactionary ones. I make small steps in that direction as well. However, it's not as easy to determine how to disengage from the agricultural and consumerist practices that are draining resources from the earth. How do we stand against that machine?

I hope for more moments where I can lean into the sovereignty of food to reclaim a way of life stolen from me. I hope for a healthier way of living that's sustainable and that addresses the needs of my own complex body and the world around me. I hope for language that can best articulate this complex history and these complex wishes for a future. I hope that I might help others move through their own health journeys, but not like social influencers who market health through lecturing and shaming rather than discussing. I hope to tell well-rounded stories, both with language and without. This hope is a radical one; both optimistic and critical. It is a revolutionary act.

In what I have learned from Diné ways of living, the morning time symbolizes this kind of ambition. Each morning is another opportunity for beauty, each sunrise a promise, each day a blessing. It's never just another morning and another day. Still, pressures build, dams give way, and there's another mild breakdown in the middle of a kitchen when the stew burns, dishes pile up, or food runs out. But in all that undoing, another day is about to break.

The butchering started like any other: the sheep faced east per protocol. My mom and uncle were telling me what I needed to do to properly cut into the neck. We don't think of suffering at times like this, we think of nourishment; we don't think of sacrifice, we think of offering. The sheep had been looked after for years. Each morning, someone ventured to the corral to let it out to graze. Each day, it was given food and water. Each spring, a new haircut. Generations of sheepdogs, one litter after another, had been trained to care for the sheep. Offerings were made, money passed, to sustain the land, the corral, and the health of the herd. My own family cared for a herd of sheep and goats, so I know this well. My aunts made a slow walk to the corral every morning, just like their mother and her mother and her mother. My grandmother even tied me to a highchair once and dragged my mom to the corral to care for the herd.

Each sheep represents life. Each sheep represents living with nature. So I cut into the sheep's neck with care and precision, despite my own worries, because we were gathering to celebrate life. One of the things I learned during our trips to To'Hajiilee was to let the knife guide you, because guiding the knife could lead to forcing the knife into the meat or bone. This could lead to even more mistakes. You should trust the knife and trust the instinct. The very first act, the severing, must be done in an exact spot to minimize suffering.

I hesitated and asked my mom for help. My older cousin, without hesitation, grabbed my hands and guided me toward the spot. "Like this," she said. My younger cousin took over from there, again without hesitation. In that moment, I felt safe. I didn't feel shame. I felt safe.

And from there, my mom and sisters got to skinning. Each one teaching the other, everyone learning, leaning into instinct, into generations of knowledge, coming together, just like when I was a kid, helping out, wide-eyed to it all. And for a moment, I was a child all over again. I listened and helped when I could. I kept thinking, if only I had listened when I was a child. If I had listened just a bit more, I might've been able to butcher two sheep that day. Maybe even three. My mom wouldn't worry so much, and I would be able to carry for my family a tangible skill, unlike writing poetry, for example. As an uncle, I wanted to contribute in a way an uncle should. And in that moment I realized I had help and I should contribute in any way I can. My older cousins were there, and they knew how to do it. And even more salvation was on the way.

From the corner of our eyes, we saw the glint of a windshield making its way down the road toward us. My mom had put a call out to my father's side of the family, a lineage of strong women who come from strong women who come from even stronger women. Each one a vessel of laughter and lesson, open and tough love. They were coming to help.

We all shared our gratitude as they walked up, joking that

someone had put into the wind that we were needing a pair of butchers. It was my aunt and a grandmother from my dad's side of the family, one I hadn't met before—because being Diné means having family you know nothing about until it's time to gather for a ceremony and then you meet them and share a connection deeper than time. So much history entangled and detangled with a simple acknowledgment that we were connected through blood, through story, through commitment, through gatherings.

My aunt was getting older, and my grandmother was older as well. They could not do the butchering on their own, so we all continued to help, and they taught us all over again. Guiding where we cut or how to follow protocols. Each lesson a story, each story a lesson. The butchering was never about the ending of a life for personal gain but a deep relationship between elements of nature. Hope is the thing with wool, after all.

The sheep was not as large as we thought. There wasn't enough sheep fat to create achii', or sheep fat wrapped with intestines and grilled, a dish that is considered a delicacy. It's best enjoyed with naneeskadi or Navajo tortillas. My aunt wasn't worried, however. She showed me a way to make a medley of intestines, sheep heart, and liver with onions. "This was your dad's favorite when he was young," she shared, as we enjoyed them over an open fire. And in that moment I was connected with my family in a way I had never been before, with their history, with their youth, their comfort foods, their upbringings. The power of it all held in my hands and devoured with some salt. So we sat around the fire some more and we made more food and told more stories. My parents and aunts and uncles unlocked new relatives and new connections. They shared wisdom that helped squash all the anxieties my mother was feeling. We stayed around the fire into the evening, and right before we started to clean, there was a moment of silence. A sigh of relief. One long exhale. The sound of worries let go, troubles melted down, and pressures unsealed. A family sitting around a fire telling stories and eating them too. It was a great way to wind down from a butchering, which shouldn't be called "butchering" at all, but gathering, sharing, opening. A way through. A way back. A way forward. Filled with memory and future. Best served right off the grill. A flavor of hope.

The next time I butcher I'll have my own story to tell, my own memory to share, knowledge to offer. One more voice to add to the chorus on those nights when you're out in the desert under the night sky, no sound for miles, just the moon and the ground beneath you, reminding you it's all real. That and your full stomach. Generations heard through wind, the air, the stirring gleaming stars. All that knowledge, all that story, all that beauty.

From Blackout to Bakhmut

FROM *Cake Zine*

AT THE BEGINNING of December 2022, Illia and Slava got up at dawn as they had done every day. It was time to fire up the deck ovens to bake bread at their small Odesa-based bakery, DOU, nestled in a side room at the front of a produce store where old men were said to go for illicit breakfast vodka. Only this morning, something was different. The night before, Russian cruise missiles and Iranian Shahed kamikaze drones had slammed into the electricity plant and power lines that kept Odesa warm and lit. Everyone heard it; the explosions had been enormous. Too loud to sleep through, even if most of the city's residents had become so used to the wail of the air siren they barely turned over in bed. This night was different and so was the impact. More than a million people had no lights, and in the cold of winter, no heat. For many, there was no water supply—the city was shrouded in the eerie, inky darkness of blackout.

Illia and Slava founded the bakery a few months before the full-scale war began, intending to make good bread for local restaurants that were struggling to stay afloat without the usual tourism. But even in war, everyone needs to eat. So they baked beautiful loaves of crusty sourdough, some made with buckwheat and some with rye, some studded with dried fruit and hazelnuts, some emblazoned with the Ukrainian tryzub shield. The loaves were packed into bags for volunteers to deliver to people in need and dropped off down the road at the big aid-distribution hub— where people who'd fled homes now occupied by Russian forces came to get supplies for their temporary new lives, from winter clothes to baby food.

On the morning of December 10th, Illia and Slava couldn't fire

up the ovens, but the dough was over-proofing without a working fridge. Officials warned that the blackout could last as long as
three months. For days, they couldn't work. The bakery, which fed
refugees, pensioners, and people in frontline villages, stood idle.
They would need to raise the funds to buy a precious generator to
get it working again. It was awful thinking of all those people who
needed bread, while they had to throw away yet another batch of
spoiled dough. But they were determined not to give up. They
packed the fridge with bottles of ice to keep it cold and, in the
moments when power briefly sprang back to life, they turned the
oven on for a few minutes: just about long enough to bake cookies.
Delicious cookies they could sell to raise funds, cookies they would
sometimes press into your hands as a gift whenever you stopped
by: peanut butter ones, thick and fudgy with a pool of caramel in
the middle, and miso cookies which were almost savory, studded
with dark chocolate, because Slava liked them that way. And when
they had enough money for more ingredients, they made prune
and nut butter–packed energy bars, packed them solidly into card-
board boxes, and sent them east to soldiers fighting on the zero
line in Bakhmut.

The dense, sticky energy bars were for guys with wolf-head chev-
rons and tryzubs tattooed over their hearts, guys who sometimes
snatched sleep standing up, if they got any at all. For the guys
who still found the energy to keep on fighting, weighed down with
body armor, carefully eking out the ammunition for their Soviet-
era Kalashnikov guns, the Bakhmut bars were a popular gift, something homemade and "not army," sustaining and sweet. For Illia
and Slava, it was always an honor to help the defenders, even just
with cookies.

Back in Odesa, on the eve of the New Year, the new generator finally arrived. The bakery ovens cranked up and the fridge
came on, and Illia and Slava were able to bake their sourdough
loaves again. The whole city was filled with the hum of thousands
of diesel engines, the smell of benzine constantly drifting through
the air, as ubiquitous as the sound of air defense shooting down
Shahed drones while angry sirens sliced through dark skies. But it
helped the city to live, and to get back to work again.

Now, eighteen months into the full-scale war, the team at DOU
hauls open the shutters at dawn, like it has done every day without fail, and gets the big mixers going with their sourdough rye

starter. The air soon fills with the heady smell of baking bread, some for the local restaurants, some offered for free to people in need. And still, they bake cookies, lots of different cookies, because they love to create new recipes, and people love to try them. And when they have enough funds, they make their special energy bars for Ukrainian defenders, because the front is the only thing that matters.

BEN TAUB

The Titan Submersible Was "An Accident Waiting to Happen"

FROM *The New Yorker*

THE PRIMARY TASK of a submersible is to not implode. The second is to reach the surface, even if the pilot is unconscious, with oxygen to spare. The third is for the occupants to be able to open the hatch once they surface. The fourth is for the submersible to be easy to find, through redundant tracking and communications systems, in case rescue is required. Only the fifth task is what is ordinarily thought of as the primary one: to transport people into the dark, hostile deep.

At dawn four summers ago, the French submariner and *Titanic* expert Paul-Henri Nargeolet stood on the bow of an expedition vessel in the North Atlantic. The air was cool and thick with fog, the sea placid, the engine switched off, and the *Titanic* was some thirty-eight hundred meters below. The crew had gathered for a solemn ceremony, to pay tribute to the more than fifteen hundred people who had died in the most famous maritime disaster more than a hundred years ago. Rob McCallum, the expedition leader, gave a short speech, then handed a wreath to Nargeolet, the oldest man on the ship. As is tradition, the youngest—McCallum's nephew—was summoned to place his hand on the wreath, and he and Nargeolet let it fall into the sea.

Inside a hangar on the ship's stern sat a submersible known as the *Limiting Factor*. In the previous year, McCallum, Nargeolet, and others had taken it around the earth, as part of the Five Deeps Expedition, a journey to the deepest point in each ocean. The team had mapped unexplored trenches and collected scientific samples, and the *Limiting Factor*'s chief pilot, Victor Vescovo—a Texan hedge fund manager who had financed the entire operation—had set numerous diving records. But, to another member of the expedition team, Patrick Lahey, the CEO of Triton Submarines (which had designed and built the submersible), one record meant more than the rest: the marine-classification society DNV had certified the *Limiting Factor*'s "maximum permissible diving depth" as "unlimited." That process was far from theoretical; a DNV inspection engineer was involved in every stage of the submersible's creation, from design to sea trials and diving. He even sat in the passenger seat as Lahey piloted the *Limiting Factor* to the deepest point on earth.

After the wreath sank from view, Vescovo climbed down the submersible hatch, and the dive began. For some members of the crew, the site of the wreck was familiar. McCallum, who co-founded a company called EYOS Expeditions, had transported tourists to the *Titanic* in the two-thousands, using two Soviet submarines that had been rated to six thousand meters. Another crew member was a *Titanic* obsessive—his endless talk of davits and well decks still rattles in my head. But it was Paul-Henri Nargeolet whose life was most entwined with the *Titanic*. He had dived it more than thirty times, beginning shortly after its discovery, in 1985, and now served as the underwater-research director for the organization that owns salvaging rights to the wreck.

Nargeolet had also spent the past year as Vescovo's safety manager. "When I set out on the Five Deeps project, I told Patrick Lahey, 'Look, I don't know submarine technology—I need someone who works for me to independently validate whatever design you come up with, and its construction and operation,'" Vescovo recalled, this week. "He recommended P. H. Nargeolet, whom he had known for decades." Nargeolet, whose wife had recently died, was a former French naval commander—an underwater-explosives expert who had spent much of his life at sea. "He had a sterling reputation, the perfect résumé," Vescovo said. "And he was French. And I love the French."

When Vescovo reached the silty bottom at the *Titanic* site, he recalled his private preparations with Nargeolet. "He had very good knowledge of the currents and the wreck," Vescovo told me. "He briefed me on very specific tactical things: 'Stay away from this place on the stern'; 'Don't go here'; 'Try and maintain this distance at this part of the wreck.'" Vescovo surfaced about seven hours later, exhausted and rattled from the debris that he had encountered at the ship's ruins, which risk entangling submersibles that approach too close. But the *Limiting Factor* was completely fine. According to its certification from DNV, a "deep dive," for insurance and inspection purposes, was anything below four thousand meters. A journey to the *Titanic*, thirty-eight hundred meters down, didn't even count.

Nargeolet remained obsessed with the *Titanic*, and before long, he was invited to return. "To P. H., the *Titanic* was Ulysses' sirens—he could not resist it," Vescovo told me. A couple of weeks ago, Nargeolet climbed into a radically different submersible, owned by a company called OceanGate, which had spent years marketing to the general public that, for a fee of two hundred and fifty thousand dollars, it would bring people to the most famous shipwreck on earth. "People are so enthralled with *Titanic*," OceanGate's founder, Stockton Rush, told a BBC documentary crew last year. "I read an article that said there are three words in the English language that are known throughout the planet. And that's 'Coca-Cola,' 'God,' and '*Titanic*.'"

Nargeolet served as a guide to the wreck, Rush as the pilot. The other three occupants were tourists, including a father and son. But, before they reached the bottom, the submersible vanished, triggering an international search-and-rescue operation, with an accompanying media frenzy centered on counting down the hours until oxygen would run out.

McCallum, who was leading an expedition in Papua New Guinea at the time, knew the outcome almost instantly. "The report that I got immediately after the event—long before they were overdue—was that the sub was approaching thirty-five hundred meters," he told me, while the oxygen clock was still ticking. "It dropped weights"—meaning that the team had aborted the dive—"then it lost comms, and lost tracking, and an implosion was heard."

An investigation by the US Coast Guard is ongoing; some debris from the wreckage has been salvaged, but the implosion was so violent and comprehensive that the precise cause of the disaster may never be known.

Until June 18, a manned deep-ocean submersible had never imploded. But, to McCallum, Lahey, and other experts, the OceanGate disaster did not come as a surprise—they had been warning of the submersible's design flaws for more than five years, filing complaints to the US government and to OceanGate itself, and pleading with Rush to abandon his aspirations. As they mourned Nargeolet and the other passengers, they decided to reveal OceanGate's history of knowingly shoddy design and construction. "You can't cut corners in the deep," McCallum had told Rush. "It's not about being a disruptor. It's about the laws of physics."

Stockton Rush was named for two of his ancestors who signed the Declaration of Independence: Richard Stockton and Benjamin Rush. His maternal grandfather was an oil-and-shipping tycoon. As a teenager, Rush became an accomplished commercial jet pilot, and he studied aerospace engineering at Princeton, where he graduated in 1984.

Rush wanted to become a fighter pilot. But his eyesight wasn't perfect, and so he went to business school instead. Years later, he expressed a desire to travel to space, and he reportedly dreamed of becoming the first human to set foot on Mars. In 2004, Rush travelled to the Mojave Desert, where he watched the launch of the first privately funded aircraft to brush against the edge of space. The only occupant was the test pilot; nevertheless, as Rush used to tell it, Richard Branson stood on the wing and announced that a new era of space tourism had arrived. At that point, Rush "abruptly lost interest," according to a profile in *Smithsonian* magazine. "I didn't want to go up into space as a tourist," he said. "I wanted to be Captain Kirk on the *Enterprise*. I wanted to *explore.*"

Rush had grown up scuba diving in Tahiti, the Cayman Islands, and the Red Sea. In his mid-forties, he tinkered with a kit for a single-person mini-submersible, and piloted it around at shallow depths near Seattle, where he lived. A few years later, in 2009, he co-founded OceanGate, with a dream to bring tourists to the ocean world. "I had come across this business anomaly I couldn't explain," he recalled. "If three-quarters of the planet is water, how come you can't access it?"

OceanGate's first submersible wasn't made by the company itself; it was built in 1973, and Lahey later piloted it in the North Sea, while working in the oil-and-gas industry. In the nineties, he helped refit it into a tourist submersible, and in 2009, after it had been sold a few times, and renamed *Antipodes*, OceanGate bought it. "I didn't have any direct interaction with them at the time,"

Lahey recalled. "Stockton was one of these people that was buying these older subs and trying to repurpose them."

In 2015, OceanGate announced that it had built its first submersible, in collaboration with the University of Washington's Applied Physics Laboratory. In fact, it was mostly a cosmetic and electrical refit; Lahey and his partners had built the underlying vessel, called *Lula*, for a Portuguese marine research nonprofit almost two decades before. It had a pressure hull that was the shape of a capsule pill and made of steel, with a large acrylic viewport on one end. It was designed to go no deeper than five hundred meters—a comfortable cruising depth for military submarines. OceanGate now called it *Cyclops* I.

Most submersibles have duplicate control systems, running on separate batteries—that way, if one system fails, the other still works. But, during the refit, engineers at the University of Washington rigged the *Cyclops* I to run from a single PlayStation 3 controller. "Stockton is very interested in being able to quickly train pilots," Dave Dyer, a principal engineer, said, in a video published by his laboratory. Another engineer referred to it as "a combination steering wheel and gas pedal."

Around that time, Rush set his sights on the *Titanic*. OceanGate would have to design a new submersible. But Rush decided to keep most of the design elements of *Cyclops* I. Suddenly, the University of Washington was no longer involved in the project, although OceanGate's contract with the Applied Physics Laboratory was less than one-fifth complete; it is unclear what Dyer, who did not respond to an interview request, thought of Rush's plan to essentially reconstruct a craft that was designed for five hundred meters of pressure to withstand eight times that much. As the company planned *Cyclops* II, Rush reached out to McCallum for help.

"He wanted me to run his *Titanic* operation for him," McCallum recalled. "At the time, I was the only person he knew who had run commercial expedition trips to *Titanic*. Stockton's plan was to go a step further and build a vehicle specifically for this multi-passenger expedition." McCallum gave him some advice on marketing and logistics, and eventually visited the workshop, outside Seattle, where he examined the *Cyclops* I. He was disturbed by what he saw. "Everyone was drinking Kool-Aid and saying how cool they were with a Sony PlayStation," he told me. "And I said at the time, 'Does Sony know that it's been used for this application? Because, you know, this is not what it was designed for.' And now you have the hand controller talking to a Wi-Fi unit, which is talking to a black box, which is talking to the sub's thrusters. There were multiple points of failure." The system ran on Bluetooth, according to Rush. But, McCallum continued, "every sub in the world has hardwired controls for a reason—that if the signal drops out, you're not fucked."

One day, McCallum climbed into the *Cyclops* for a test dive at a marina. There, he met the chief pilot, David Lochridge, a Scotsman who had spent three decades as a submersible pilot and an engineer—first in the Royal Navy, then as a private contractor. Lochridge had worked all over the world: on offshore wind farms in the North Sea; on subsea-cables installations in the Atlantic, Indian, and Pacific oceans; on manned submarine trials with the Swedish Navy; on submarine-rescue operations for the navies of Britain and Singapore. But, during the harbor trial, the *Cyclops* got stuck in shallow water. "It was hilarious, because there were four very experienced operators in the sub, stuck at twenty or twenty-five feet, and we had to sit there for a few hours while they worked it out," McCallum recalled. He liked and trusted Lochridge. But, of the sub, he said, "This thing is a *mutt*."

Rush eventually decided that he would not attempt to have the *Titanic*-bound vehicle classed by a marine-certification agency such as DNV. He had no interest in welcoming into the project an external evaluator who would, as he saw it, "need to first be educated before being qualified to 'validate' any innovations."

That marked the end of McCallum's desire to be associated with the project. "The minute that I found out that he was not going to class the vehicle, that's when I said, 'I'm sorry, I just can't be involved,'" he told me. "I couldn't tell him anything about the Five Deeps project at that time. But I was able to say, 'Look, I am involved with other projects that are building classed subs'—of course, I was talking about the *Limiting Factor*—'and I can tell you that the class society has been nothing but supportive. They are actually *part* of our innovation process. We're using the brainpower of their engineers to feed into our design.

"Stockton didn't like that," McCallum continued. "He didn't like to be told that he was on the fringe." As word got out that Rush planned to take tourists to the *Titanic*, McCallum recalled, "People would ring me, and say, 'We've always wanted to go to

Titanic. What do you think?' And I would tell them, 'Never get in an unclassed sub. I wouldn't do it, and you shouldn't either.'"

In early 2018, McCallum heard that Lochridge had left Ocean-Gate. "I'd be keen to pick your brain if you have a few moments," McCallum emailed him. "I'm keen to get a handle on exactly how bad things are. I do get reports, but I don't know if they are accurate." Whatever his differences with Rush, McCallum wanted the venture to succeed; the submersible industry is small, and a single disaster could destroy it. But the only way forward without a catastrophic operational failure—which he had been told was "certain," he wrote—was for OceanGate to redesign the submersible in coordination with a classification society. "Stockton must be gutted," McCallum told Lochridge, of his departure. "You were the star player . . . and the only one that gave me a hint of confidence."

"I think you are going to [be] even more taken aback when I tell you what's happening," Lochridge replied. He added that he was afraid of retaliation from Rush—"We both know he has influence and money"—but would share his assessment with Mc-Callum, in private: "That sub is not safe to dive."

"Do you think the sub could be made safe to dive, or is it a complete lemon?" McCallum replied. "You will get a lot of support from people in the industry . . . everyone is watching and waiting and quietly shitting their pants."

"It's a lemon."

"Oh dear," McCallum replied. "Oh dear, oh dear."

Lochridge had been hired by OceanGate in May 2015 as its director of marine operations and chief submersible pilot. The company moved him and his family to Washington and helped him apply for a green card. But, before long, he was clashing with Rush and Tony Nissen, the company's director of engineering, on matters of design and safety.

Every aspect of submersible design and construction is a trade-off between strength and weight. In order for the craft to remain suspended underwater, without rising or falling, the buoyancy of each component must be offset against the others. Most deep-ocean submersibles use spherical titanium hulls and are counter-balanced in water by syntactic foam, a buoyant material made up of millions of hollow glass balls, which is attached to the external frame. But this adds bulk to the submersible. And the weight of titanium limits the practical size of the pressure hull, so that it can accommodate no more than two or three people. Spheres are "the best geometry for pressure, but not for occupation," as Rush put it.

The *Cyclops* II needed to fit as many passengers as possible. "You don't do the coolest thing you're ever going to do in your life by yourself," Rush told an audience at the GeekWire Summit last fall. "You take your wife, your son, your daughter, your best friend. You've got to have four people" besides the pilot. Rush planned to have room for a *Titanic* guide and three passengers. The *Cyclops* II could fit that many occupants only if it had a cylindrical midsection. But the size dictated the choice of materials. The steel hull of *Cyclops* I was too thin for *Titanic* depths—but a thicker steel hull would add too much weight. In December 2016, OceanGate announced that it had started construction on *Cyclops* II, and that its cylindrical midsection would be made of carbon fiber. The idea, Rush explained in interviews, was that carbon fiber was a strong material that was significantly lighter than traditional metals. "Carbon fiber is three times better than titanium on strength-to-buoyancy," he said.

A month later, OceanGate hired a company called Spencer Composites to build the carbon-fiber hull. "They basically said, 'This is the pressure we have to meet, this is the factor of safety, this is the basic envelope. Go design and build it,'" the founder, Brian Spencer, told *Composites World*, in the spring of 2017. He was given a deadline of six weeks.

Toward the end of that year, Lochridge became increasingly concerned. OceanGate would soon begin manned sea trials for *Cyclops* II in the Bahamas, and he believed that there was a chance that they would result in catastrophe. The consequences for Lochridge could extend beyond OceanGate's business and the trauma of losing colleagues; as director of marine operations, Lochridge had a contract specifying that he was ultimately responsible for "ensuring the safety of all crew and clients."

On the workshop floor, he raised questions about potential flaws in the design and build processes. But his concerns were dismissed. OceanGate's position was that such matters were outside the scope of his responsibilities; he was "not hired to provide engineering services, or to design or develop *Cyclops* II," the company later said, in a court filing. Nevertheless, before the handover of the submersible to the operations team, Rush directed Lochridge to carry out an inspection, because his job description also required him to sign off on the submersible's readiness for deployment.

On January 18, 2018, Lochridge studied each major component, and found several critical aspects to be defective or unproven. He drafted a detailed report, which has not previously been made public, and attached photographs of the elements of greatest concern. Glue was coming away from the seams of ballast bags, and mounting bolts threatened to rupture them; both sealing faces had errant plunge holes and O-ring grooves that deviated from standard design parameters. The exostructure and electrical pods used different metals, which could result in galvanic corrosion when exposed to seawater. The thruster cables posed "snagging hazards"; the iridium satellite beacon, to transmit the submersible's position after surfacing, was attached with zip ties. The flooring was highly flammable; the interior vinyl wrapping emitted "highly toxic gasses upon ignition."

To assess the carbon-fiber hull, Lochridge examined a small cross section of material. He found that it had "very visible signs of delamination and porosity"—it seemed possible that, after repeated dives, it would come apart. He shone a light at the sample from behind, and photographed beams streaming through splits in the midsection in a disturbing, irregular pattern. The only safe way to dive, Lochridge concluded, was to first carry out a full scan of the hull.

The next day, Lochridge sent his report to Rush, Nissen, and other members of the OceanGate leadership. "Verbal communication of the key items I have addressed in my attached document have been dismissed on several occasions, so I feel now I must make this report so there is an official record in place," he wrote. "Until suitable corrective actions are in place and closed out, *Cyclops* 2 (*Titan*) should not be manned during any of the upcoming trials."

Rush was furious; he called a meeting that afternoon, and recorded it on his phone. For the next two hours, the OceanGate leadership insisted that no hull testing was necessary—an acoustic monitoring system, to detect fraying fibers, would serve in its place. According to the company, the system would alert the pilot to the possibility of catastrophic failure "with enough time to arrest the descent and safely return to surface." But, in a court filing, Lochridge's lawyer wrote, "this type of acoustic analysis would only show when a component is about to fail—often milliseconds before an implosion—and would not detect any existing flaws prior to putting pressure onto the hull." A former senior employee who was present at the meeting told me, "We didn't even have a baseline. We didn't know what it would sound like if something went wrong."

OceanGate's lawyer wrote, "The parties found themselves at an impasse—Mr. Lochridge was not, and specifically stated that he could not be made comfortable with OceanGate's testing protocol, while Mr. Rush was unwilling to change the company's plans." The meeting ended in Lochridge's firing.

Soon afterward, Rush asked OceanGate's director of finance and administration whether she'd like to take over as chief submersible pilot. "It freaked me out that he would want me to be head pilot, since my background is in accounting," she told me. She added that several of the engineers were in their late teens and early twenties, and were at one point being paid fifteen dollars an hour. Without Lochridge around, "I could not work for Stockton," she said. "I did not trust him." As soon as she was able to line up a new job, she quit.

"I would consider myself pretty ballsy when it comes to doing things that are dangerous, but that sub is an accident waiting to happen," Lochridge wrote to McCallum, two weeks later. "There's no way on earth you could have paid me to dive the thing." Of Rush, he added, "I don't want to be seen as a Tattle tale but I'm so worried he kills himself and others in the quest to boost his ego."

McCallum forwarded the exchange to Patrick Lahey, the CEO of Triton Submarines, whose response was emphatic: if Lochridge "genuinely believes this submersible poses a threat to the occupants," then he had a moral obligation to inform the authorities. "To remain quiet makes him complicit," Lahey wrote. "I know that may sound ominous but it is true. History is full of horrific examples of accidents and tragedies that were a direct result of people's silence."

OceanGate claimed that *Cyclops* II had "the first pressure vessel of its kind in the world." But there's a reason that Triton and other manufacturers don't use carbon fiber in their hulls. Under compression, "it's a capricious fucking material, which is the last fucking thing you want to associate with a pressure boundary," Lahey told me.

"With titanium, there's a purpose to a pressure test that goes beyond just seeing whether it will survive," John Ramsay, the designer of the *Limiting Factor*, explained. The metal gradually strengthens under repeated exposure to incredible stresses. With carbon fiber, however, pressure testing slowly breaks the hull, fiber by tiny fiber. "If you're repeatedly nearing the threshold of the material, then there's just no way of knowing how many cycles it will survive," he said.

"It doesn't get more sensational than dead people in a sub on the way to *Titanic*," Lahey's business partner, the co-founder of Triton Submarines, wrote to his team, on March 1, 2018. Mc-Callum tried to reason with Rush directly. "You are wanting to use a prototype un-classed technology in a very hostile place," he emailed. "As much as I appreciate entrepreneurship and innovation, you are potentially putting an entire industry at risk."

Rush replied four days later, saying that he had "grown tired of industry players who try to use a safety argument to stop innovation and new entrants from entering their small existing market." He understood that his approach "flies in the face of the submersible orthodoxy, but that is the nature of innovation," he wrote. "We have heard the baseless cries of 'you are going to kill someone' way too often. I take this as a serious personal insult."

In response, McCallum listed a number of specific concerns, from his "humble perch" as an expedition leader. "In your race to *Titanic* you are mirroring that famous catch cry 'she is unsinkable,'" McCallum wrote. The correspondence ended soon afterward; Rush asked McCallum to work for him—then threatened him with a lawsuit, in an effort to silence him, when he declined. By now, McCallum had introduced Lochridge to Lahey. Lahey wrote him, "If OceanGate is unwilling to consider or investigate your concerns with you directly perhaps some other means of getting them to pay attention is required."

Lochridge replied that he had already contacted the United States Department of Labor, alleging to its Occupational Safety and Health Administration that he had been terminated in retaliation for raising safety concerns. He also sent the OSHA investigator Paul McDevitt a copy of his *Cyclops* II inspection report, hoping that the government might take actions that would "prevent the potential for harm to life."

A few weeks later, McDevitt contacted OceanGate, noting that he was looking into Lochridge's firing as a whistleblower-protection matter. OceanGate's lawyer Thomas Gilman soon issued Lochridge a court summons: he had ten days to withdraw his OSHA claim and pay OceanGate almost ten thousand dollars in legal expenses. Otherwise, Gilman wrote, OceanGate would sue him, take measures to destroy his professional reputation, and accuse him of immigration fraud. Gilman also reported to OSHA that Lochridge had orchestrated his own firing because he "wanted to leave his job and maintain his ability to collect unemployment benefits." (McDevitt, of OSHA, notified the Coast Guard of Lochridge's complaint. There is no evidence that the Coast Guard ever followed up.)

Lochridge received the summons while he was at his father's funeral. He and his wife hired a lawyer, but it quickly became clear that "he didn't have the money to fight this guy," Lahey told me. (Lochridge declined to be interviewed.) Lahey covered the rest of the expenses, but, after more than half a year of legal wrangling, and threats of deportation, Lochridge withdrew his whistleblower claim with OSHA so that he could go on with his life. Lahey was crestfallen. "He didn't consult me about that decision," Lahey recalled. "It's not that he had to—it was his fight, not mine. But I was underwriting the cost of it, because I believed in the idea that this inspection report, which he wouldn't share with anybody, needed to see the light of day."

A few weeks after Lochridge was fired, OceanGate announced that it was testing its new submersible in the marina of Everett, Washington, and would soon begin shallow-water trials in Puget Sound. To preempt any concerns about the carbon-fiber hull, the company touted the acoustic monitoring system, which was later patented in Rush's name. "Safety is our number one priority," Rush said, in an OceanGate press release. "We believe real-time health monitoring should be standard safety equipment on all manned-submersibles."

"He's spinning the fact that his sub requires a hull warning system into something positive," Jarl Stromer, Triton's regulatory and class-compliance manager, reported to Lahey. "He's making it sound like the *Cyclops* is more advanced because it has this system when the opposite is true: The submersible is so experimental, and the factor of safety completely unknown, that it requires a system to warn the pilot of impending collapse."

Like Lochridge, Triton's outside counsel, Brad Patrick, considered the risk to life to be so evident that the government should get involved. He drafted a letter to McDevitt, the OSHA investigator, urging the Department of Labor to take "immediate and decisive action to stop OceanGate" from taking passengers to the *Titanic* "before people die. It is that simple." He went on, "At the bottom of all of this is the inevitable tension betwixt greed and safety."

But Patrick's letter was never sent. Other people at Triton worried that the Department of Labor might perceive the letter as an attack on a business rival. By now, OceanGate had renamed *Cyclops* II "Titan," apparently to honor the *Titanic*. "I cannot tell you how much I fucking hated it when he changed the goddam name to *Titan*," Lahey told me. "That was *uncomfortably* close to our name."

"Stockton strategically structured everything to be out of US jurisdiction" for its *Titanic* pursuits, the former senior OceanGate employee told me. "It was deliberate." In a legal filing, the company reported that the submersible was "being developed and assembled in Washington, but will be owned by a Bahamian entity, will be registered in the Bahamas and will operate exclusively outside the territorial waters of the United States." Although it is illegal to transport passengers in an unclassed, experimental submersible, "under US regulations, you can kill crew," McCallum told me. "You do get in a little bit of trouble, in the eyes of the law. But, if you kill a passenger, you're in big trouble. And so everyone was classified as a 'mission specialist.' There were no passengers—the word 'passenger' was never used." No one bought tickets; they contributed an amount of money set by Rush to one of OceanGate's entities, to fund their own missions.

"It is truly hard to imagine the discernment it took for Stockton to string together each of the links in the chain," Patrick noted. "'How do I avoid liability in Washington State? How do I avoid liability with an offshore corporate structure? How do I keep the US Coast Guard from breathing down my neck?'"

But OceanGate had a retired Coast Guard rear admiral, John Lockwood, on its board of directors. "His experiences at the highest levels of the Coast Guard and in international maritime affairs will allow OceanGate to refine our client offerings," Rush announced with his appointment, in 2013. Lockwood said that he hoped "to help bring operational and regulatory expertise" to OceanGate's affairs. (Lockwood did not respond to a request for comment.) Still, Rush failed to win over the submersible industry. When he asked Don Walsh, a renowned oceanographer who reached the deepest point in the ocean in 1960, to consult on the *Titanic* venture, Walsh replied, "I am concerned that my affiliation with your program at this late date would appear to be nothing more than an endorsement of what you are already doing."

That spring, more than three dozen industry experts sent a letter to OceanGate, expressing their "unanimous concern" about its upcoming *Titanic* expedition—for which it had already sold places. Among the signers were Lahey, McCallum, Walsh, and a Coast Guard senior inspector. "OceanGate's anticipated dive schedule in the spring of 2018 meant that they were going to take people down, and we had a great deal of concern about them surviving that trip," Patrick told me. But sea trials were a disaster, owing to problems with the launch-and-recovery system, and OceanGate scuttled its *Titanic* operations for that year. Lochridge broke the news to Lahey. "Lives have been saved for a short while anyway," he wrote.

OceanGate kept selling tickets, but did not dive to the *Titanic* for the next three years. It appears that the company spent this period testing materials, and that it built several iterations of the carbon-fiber hull. But it is difficult to know what tests were done, exactly, and how many hulls were made, and by whom, because Rush's public statements are deeply unreliable. He claimed at various points to have design and testing partnerships with Boeing and NASA, and that at least one iteration of the hull would be built at the Marshall Space Flight Center in Huntsville, Alabama. But none of those things were true. Meanwhile, soon after Lochridge's departure, a college newspaper quoted a recent graduate as saying that he and his classmates had started working on the *Titan*'s electrical systems as interns, while they were still in school. "The whole electrical system," he said. "That was our design, we implemented it, and it works."

By the time that OceanGate finally began diving to the *Titanic*, in 2021, it had refined its pitch to its "mission specialists." The days of insinuating that *Titan* was safe had ended. Now Rush portrayed the submersible as existing at the very fringe of what was physically possible. Clients signed waivers and were informed that the submersible was experimental and unclassed. But the framing was that this was how pioneering exploration is done.

"We were all told—intimately informed—that this was a dangerous mission that could result in death," an OceanGate "mission specialist" told Fox News last week. "We were versed in how the sub operated. We were versed in various protocols. But there's a limit . . . it's not a safe operation, inherently. And that's part of research and development and exploration." He went on, "If the Wright brothers had crashed on their first flight, they would have still left the bonds of earth." Another "mission specialist" wrote in a blog post that, a month before the implosion, Rush had confessed that he'd "gotten the carbon fiber used to make the *Titan* at a big discount from Boeing because it was past its shelf-life for use in airplanes."

"Carbon fiber makes noise," Rush told David Pogue, a CBS News correspondent, last summer, during one of the *Titanic* expeditions. "It crackles. The first time you pressurize it, if you think about it—of those million fibers, a couple of 'em are sorta weak. They shouldn't have made the team." He spoke of signs of hull breakage as if it were perfectly routine. "The first time we took it to full pressure, it made a bunch of noise. The second time, it made very little noise."

Fibers do not regenerate between dives. Nevertheless, Rush seemed unconcerned. "It's a huge amount of pressure from the point where we'd say, 'Oh, the hull's not happy,' to when it implodes," he noted. "You just have to stop your descent."

It's not clear that Rush could always stop his descent. Once, as he piloted passengers to the wreck, a malfunction prevented Rush from dropping weights. Passengers calmly discussed sleeping on the bottom of the ocean, thirty-eight hundred meters down; after twenty-four hours, a drop-weight mechanism would dissolve in the seawater, allowing the submersible to surface. Eventually, Rush managed to release the weights manually, using a hydraulic pump. "This is why you want your pilot to be an engineer," a passenger said, smiling, as another "mission specialist" filmed her.

Last year, a BBC documentary crew joined the expedition. Rush stayed on the surface vessel while Scott Griffith, OceanGate's director of logistics and quality assurance, piloted a scientist and three other passengers down. (Griffith did not respond to a request for comment.) During the launch, a diver in the water noticed and reported to the surface vessel that something with a thruster seemed off. Nevertheless, the mission continued.

More than two hours passed; after *Titan* touched down in the silt, Griffith fired the thrusters and realized something was wrong. "I don't know what's going on," he said. As he fiddled with the PlayStation controller, a passenger looked out the viewport.

"Am I spinning?" Griffith asked.

"Yes."

"I am?"

"Looks like it," another passenger said.

"Oh, my God," Griffith muttered. One of the thrusters had been installed in the wrong direction. "The only thing I can do is a three-sixty," he said.

They were in the debris field, three hundred meters from the intact part of the wreck. One of the clients said that she had delayed buying a car, getting married, and having kids, all "because I wanted to go to *Titanic*," but they couldn't make their way over to its bow. Griffith relayed the situation to the ship. Rush's solution was to "remap the PS3 controller."

Rush couldn't remember where the buttons were, and it seems as though there was no spare controller on the ship. Someone loaded an image of a PlayStation 3 controller from the internet, and Rush worked out a new button routine. "Yeah left and right might be forward and back. Huh. I don't know," he said. "It might work."

"Right is forward," Griffith read off his screen, two and a half miles below. "Uh—I'm going to have to write this down."

"Right is forward," Rush said. "Great! Live with it."

Shipwrecks are notoriously difficult and dangerous to dive. Rusted cables drape the *Titanic*, moving with the currents; a broken crow's nest dangles over the deck. Griffith piloted the submersible over to the wreck, and passengers within feet of it, while teaching himself in real time to operate a Bluetooth controller whose buttons suddenly had different functions than those for which he had trained.

"If you're not breaking things, you're not innovating," Rush said, at the GeekWire Summit last fall. "If you're operating within a known environment, as most submersible manufacturers do—they don't break things. To me, the more stuff you've broken, the more innovative you've been."

The *Titan*'s viewport was made of acrylic and seven inches thick. "That's another thing where I broke the rules," Rush said to Pogue, the CBS News journalist. He went on to refer to a "very well-known" acrylic expert, Jerry D. Stachiw, who wrote an eleven-hundred-page manual called *Handbook of Acrylics for Submersibles, Hyperbaric Chambers, and Aquaria.* "It has safety factors that—they were so high, he didn't call 'em safety factors. He called 'em conversion factors," Rush said. "According to the rules," he added, his viewport was "not allowed."

It seemed as if Rush believed that acrylic's transparent quality would give him ample warning before failure. "You can see every surface," he said. "And if you've overstressed it, or you've even come close, it starts to get this crazing effect."

"And if that happened underwater . . ."

"You just stop and go to the surface."

"You would have time to get back up?" Pogue asked.

"Oh, yeah, yeah, yeah. It's way more warning than you need."

John Ramsay, who has designed several acrylic-hulled submersibles, was less sure. "You'll probably never be able to find out the source of failure" of the *Titan*, he told me, in a recent phone call from his cottage in southwest England. But it seems as though Rush did not understand how acrylic limits are calculated. "Where Stockton is talking about those things called conversion factors . . ."

Ramsay grabbed a copy of Stachiw's acrylic handbook from his spare bedroom. When Stachiw's team was doing its tests, "they would pressurize it really fast, the acrylic would implode, and then they would assign a conversion factor, to tabulate a safe diving depth," he explained. "So, let's say the sample imploded at twelve hundred meters. You apply a conversion factor of six, and you get a rating of two hundred meters." He paused, and spoke slowly, to make sure I understood the gravity of what followed. "It's specifically *not* called a safety factor, because the acrylic is *not safe* to twelve hundred meters," he said. "I've got a massive report on all of this, because we've just had to reverse engineer all of Jerry Statchiw's work to determine when our *own* acrylic will fail." The risk zone begins at about twice the depth rating.

According to David Lochridge's court filings from 2018, *Cyclops* II's viewport had a depth rating of only thirteen hundred meters, approximately one-third of *Titanic*'s depth. It is possible that this had changed by the time passengers finally dived. But, Lochridge's lawyer wrote, OceanGate "refused to pay for the manufacturer to build a viewport that would meet the required depth."

In May, Rush invited Victor Vescovo to join his *Titanic* expedition. "I turned him down," Vescovo told me. "I didn't even want the appearance that I was sanctioning his operation." But his friend—the British billionaire Hamish Harding, whom Vescovo had previously taken in the *Limiting Factor* to the bottom of the Mariana Trench—signed up to be a "mission specialist."

On the morning of June 18, Rush climbed inside the *Titan*, along with Harding, the British Pakistani businessman Shahzada Dawood, and his nineteen-year-old son, Suleman, who had reportedly told a relative that he was terrified of diving in a submersible but would do so anyway, because it was Father's Day. He carried with him a Rubik's Cube so that he could solve it in front of the *Titanic* wreck. The fifth diver was P. H. Nargeolet, the *Titanic* expert—Vescovo's former safety adviser, Lahey and McCallum's old shipmate and friend. He had been working with OceanGate for at least a year as a wreck navigator, historian, and guide.

The force of the implosion would have been so violent that everyone on board would have died before the water touched their bodies.

For the Five Deeps crew, Nargeolet's legacy is complicated by the circumstances of his final dives. "I had a conversation with P. H. just as recently as a few months ago," Lahey told me. "I kept giving him shit for going out there. I said, 'P. H., by you being out there, you legitimize what this guy's doing. It's a tacit endorsement. And, worse than that, I think he's using your involvement with the project, and your presence on the site, as a way to fucking lure people into it.'"

Nargeolet replied that he was getting old. He was a grieving widower, and, as he told people several times in recent years, "if you have to go, that would be a good way. Instant."

"I said, 'O.K., so you're ready to fucking die? Is that what it is, P. H.?'" Lahey recalled. "And he said, 'No, no, but I figure that, maybe if I'm out there, I can help them avoid a tragedy.' But instead he found himself right in the fucking center of a tragedy. And he didn't deserve to go that way."

"I loved P. H. Nargeolet," Lahey continued. He started choking up. "He was a brilliant human being and somebody that I had the privilege of knowing for almost twenty-five years, and I think it's a tremendously sad way for him to have ended his life."

Lahey dived the *Titanic* in the *Limiting Factor* during the Five Deeps expedition, back in 2019. I remember him climbing out of the submersible and being upset at the fact that we were even there. "It's a mess down there," he recalled, this week. "It's a tragic fucking place. And in some ways, you know, people paying all that money to go and fly around in a fucking graveyard . . ." He trailed off. But the loss of so much life, in 1912, set in motion new regulations and improvements for safety at sea. "And so I guess, on a positive note, you can look at that as having been a difficult and tragic lesson that probably has since saved hundreds of thousands of lives," he said.

OceanGate declined to comment. But, in 2021, Stockton Rush told an interviewer that he would "like to be remembered as an innovator. I think it was General MacArthur who said, 'You're remembered for the rules you break.' And I've broken some rules to make this." He was sitting in the *Titan*'s hull, docked in the port of St. John's, the nearest port to the site where he eventually died. "The carbon fiber and titanium? There's a rule you don't do that. Well, I did."

Unsafe Passage

FROM *The New Yorker*

WHEN THE WAR comes to Gaza, my wife and I do not want to leave. We want to be with our parents and brothers and sisters, and we know that to leave Gaza is to leave them. Even when the border with Egypt opens to people with foreign passports, like our three-year-old son, Mostafa, we stay. Our apartment in Beit Lahia, in northern Gaza, is on the third floor. My brothers live above and below us, and my parents live on the ground floor. My father cares for chickens and rabbits in the garden. I have a library filled with books that I love.

Then Israel drops flyers on our neighborhood, warning us to evacuate, and we crowd into a borrowed two-bedroom apartment in the Jabalia refugee camp. Soon, we learn that a bomb has destroyed our house. Air strikes also rain down on the camp, killing dozens of people within a hundred meters of our door. Over time, our parents stop telling us to stay.

When our apartment in the refugee camp is no longer a refuge, we move again, to a United Nations Relief and Works Agency (UNRWA) school. My wife, Maram, sleeps in a classroom with dozens of women and children. I sleep outside, with the men, exposed to the dew. Once, I hear a piece of shrapnel ring through the school, as though a teacup has fallen off a table.

Now, when Maram and I talk about leaving, we understand that the decision is not only about us. It is about our three children. In Gaza, a child is not really a child. Our eight-year-old son, Yazzan, has been talking about fetching his toys from the ruins of our house. He should be learning how to draw, how to play soccer, how to take a family photo. Instead, he is learning how to hide when bombs fall.

On November 4th, our names appear on an approved list of travelers at the Rafah border crossing, clearing us to leave Gaza. The next day, we set out on foot, joining a wave of Palestinians making the thirty-kilometer journey south. Those who can travel faster than us, on donkeys and tuktuks, soon come into view again, traveling toward us. We see a friend, who tells us that Israeli forces have set up a checkpoint on Salah al-Din Road, the north-south highway that is supposed to provide safe passage. He says that gunfire there convinced him to turn around. We return to the school.

Mostafa and Yaffa, our six-year-old daughter, are so sick with fever that they can barely walk. My sisters have also been asking us not to go. "Let's not leave them," Maram says. We want to stay for our family, and we want to leave for our family.

Then, on November 15th, I am on the third floor of the school, about to sip some tea, when I hear a blast followed by screams. A type of shell that we call a smoke bomb has gone off outside. People are trying to put out a fire by dousing it with sand.

Moments later, another smoke bomb explodes in the sky above us, spewing a white cloud of gas. We race inside, coughing, and shut the doors and windows. Maram hands out pieces of wet cloth and we hold them to our noses and mouths, trying to breathe.

That night, we hear bombs and tank shells, and I barely sleep. In the days that follow, my throat tastes of gas and I have diarrhea. I cannot find a clean toilet. There is no water to flush. I feel like vomiting.

I have been joking with my family that by my thirty-first birthday, on November 17th, we will have peace. When the day arrives, I am embarrassed. I ask my mother, "Where is my cake?" She says she will bake one when she moves back into our destroyed house.

On November 18th, Israeli tank shells wreck two classrooms at another school, where Maram's grandparents and paternal uncles are staying. My brother-in-law Ahmad learns that several members of his extended family are dead. My parents urge us not to leave our shelter. But, when we hear the news, we pretend to go to the bathroom and go looking for our relatives.

On the dusty road that leads to the school, a heartbreaking scene greets us. People are fleeing with gas cannisters, mattresses, and blankets. A group of donkeys and horses are bleeding. One horse's tail is nearly detached. When a young man tries to quench its thirst, the water dribbles out of a hole in its neck. He asks me whether I have a knife, to put it out of its misery.

We are relieved to find Maram's grandparents inside, sitting on the floor. As her uncles pack their things, one of them talks about fleeing to the south. Maram's grandparents are pleading with him not to go.

The next morning, I wake at five to an overcast sky. A storm is coming. While everyone is sleeping, I fill a bottle of water from an open bucket, wash, and pray the dawn prayer. Then, at around 6:30 a.m., Maram's uncle Nader comes to our room. He is preparing to leave for the south with his brothers. "If anyone wants to join, we will be at the gate of the hospital," he says.

This time, when I ask Maram whether she wants to go, she says yes. "All our bags are packed," she tells me.

Maram informs her parents of our decision. They cry as she hugs them. Then we both go to the third floor, where my parents are sitting in the corridor on a mattress. They are drinking their morning coffee with two of my sisters and their husbands. I squat, and in a low voice I tell my parents that we are going to try to leave Gaza.

My mother goes pale. She looks at my children, tears in her eyes.

I don't want to hug anyone, because I don't want to believe that I am leaving them. I kiss my parents and shake hands with my siblings, as though I am only going on a short trip. What I am feeling is not guilt but a sense of unfairness. Why can I leave and they cannot? We are lucky that Mostafa was born in the US. Does it make them less human, less worthy of protection, that their children were not? I think about how, when we go, I may not be able to call them, or even find out whether they are alive or dead. Every step we take will take us away from them.

Before Maram was my wife, she was my neighbor. In 2000, when I was eight, my father moved us out of my birthplace, Al-Shati refugee camp, and built us the house in Beit Lahia. Maram, a year younger than me, lived next door. I liked her enough that, each school year, I gave her my old textbooks so she wouldn't have to buy new ones.

One day, Maram saw me on the third floor of our family home, peering into the distance through a new pair of binoculars. From our window, I could see the border with Israel. She sent her younger sister to ask me whether I was looking for a girl.

I told Maram's sister that it was none of her business. After that, though, I knew Maram had feelings for me. We started to smuggle each other messages via our little sisters. In 2015, when I was twenty-two, we married.

On the morning that we set out for the south, Maram wears a jilbab and carries Yaffa's blanket, which has the head of a fox and two sleeves, so she can wear it like a cape. We have one liter of water. By the time we gather our things and walk to the hospital gate with Maram's youngest brother, Ibrahim, her uncles have already left.

I hail a teenager who is driving a donkey cart. "Going south?"

He has no idea which way is south. "How much will you pay me?" he asks.

I offer a hundred Israeli shekels, about twenty-seven US dollars. Another young man, whose mother uses a wheelchair, splits the cost with us.

Our donkey cart rolls past bombed-out houses and shops. The street is a river of people flowing south, many of them carrying white flags to identify themselves as civilians. Ibrahim jumps off the donkey cart, picks up a stick, and ties a white undershirt to it.

In the crowd, I see a man named Rami, who played soccer with me more than a decade ago. He cries out with joy and asks whether his seventy-year-old father can climb into our cart. We make some space and ride on.

About thirteen kilometers into our journey, we pass Al-Kuwait Square. An Israeli checkpoint looms in the distance. Soldiers are controlling the flow of foot traffic with a tank and a sand barrier. When the soldiers want to block the way, they roll the tank onto the road.

Hundreds of people, young and old, crowd the road in front of the tank. I can think of one other scene like this—the Nakba of 1948, when Zionist militias forced hundreds of thousands of Palestinians to leave their villages and towns. In photographs from that time, families flee on foot, balancing what remains of their belongings on their heads.

The children are scared. Mostafa asks me if he can go back north again to his grandmother Iman, who used to tuck him into bed. I don't know what to tell him. We are going to see her, I finally say. Be patient.

As we near the tank, I hold up our stack of travel documents, with Mostafa's blue American passport on top. One of the soldiers in the tank is shouting into a megaphone; another holds a machine gun. I have lived in Gaza for almost all my life, and these are the first Israeli soldiers I have seen. I am not afraid of them, but I will be soon.

We are overjoyed to spot, up ahead of us, Maram's uncles. Ibrahim shouts out. One of them, Amjad, grins and yells back, "You made it!"

The line crawls along. One of Maram's great-uncles, Fayez, is pushing a wheelchair carrying Maram's ninety-year-old great-grandmother. To my surprise, Fayez convinces the soldiers that elders should go through first, with one person to accompany them. But, when two people try to accompany one wheelchair, a soldier angrily orders them to stop. He fires his gun into the ground.

Children scream. Panic ripples through the line. A gust of wind blows, as if to rearrange the stage of the theatre. The tank rolls back onto the road, and about twenty minutes elapse before it backs up again.

We are about to pass the checkpoint when a soldier starts to call out, seemingly at random.

"The young man with the blue plastic bag and the yellow jacket, put everything down and come here."

"The man with white hair and a boy in his arms, leave everything and come!"

They're not going to pull me out of the line, I think. I am holding Mostafa and flashing his American passport. Then the soldier says, "The young man with the black backpack who is carrying a red-haired boy. Put the boy down and come my way." He is talking to me.

I make the sudden decision to try to show the soldiers our passports. Maram keeps my phone and her passport. "I will tell them about us, that we are going to the Rafah border crossing and that our son is an American citizen," I say. But I have taken only a few steps when a soldier orders me to freeze. I am so scared that I forget to look back at Mostafa. I can hear him crying.

I join a long queue of young men on their knees. A soldier is ordering two elderly women, who seem to be waiting for men who have been detained, to keep walking. "If you don't move, we will shoot you," the soldier says. Behind me, a young man is sobbing.

"Why have they picked me? I'm a farmer," he says. Don't worry, I tell him. They will question and then release us.

After half an hour, I hear my full name, twice: "Mosab Mostafa Hasan Abu Toha." I'm puzzled. I didn't show anyone my ID when I was pulled out of line. How do they know my name?

I walk toward an Israeli jeep. The barrel of a gun points at me. When I am asked for my ID number, I recite it as loud as I can.

"Okay, sit next to the others."

About ten of us are now kneeling in the sand. I can see piles of money, cigarettes, mobile phones, watches, and wallets. I recognize a man from my neighborhood, who is slightly younger than my father. "The most important thing is that they don't take us as human shields for their tanks," he says. This possibility never crossed my mind, and my terror grows.

We are led, two by two, to a clearing near a wall. A soldier with a megaphone tells us to undress; two others point guns at us. I strip down to my boxer shorts, and so does the young man next to me.

The soldier orders us to continue. We look at each other, shocked. I think I see movement from one of the armed soldiers, and fear for my life. We take off our boxer shorts.

"Turn around!"

This is the first time in my life that strangers have looked at me naked. They speak in Hebrew and seem cheerful. Are they joking about the hair on my body? Maybe they can see the scars where shrapnel sliced into my forehead and neck when I was sixteen. A soldier asks about my travel documents. "These are our passports," I say, shivering. "We are heading to the Rafah border crossing."

"Shut up, you son of a bitch."

I am allowed to put on my clothes, but not my jacket. They take my wallet and tie my hands behind my back with plastic handcuffs. One of the soldiers comments on my UNRWA employee card. "I'm a teacher," I tell him. He curses at me again.

The soldiers blindfold me and attach a numbered bracelet to one wrist. I wonder how Israelis would feel if they were known by a number. Then someone grabs the back of my neck and shoves me forward, as though we are sheep on our way to be slaughtered. I keep asking for someone to talk to, but no one responds. The earth is muddy and cold and strewn with rubble.

I am pushed onto my knees, and then made to stand, and then

ordered to kneel again. Soldiers keep asking in Arabic, "What's your name? What's your ID number?"

A man addresses me in English. "You are an activist. With Hamas, right?"

"Me? I swear, no. I stopped going to the mosque in 2010, when I started attending university. I spent the last four years in the United States and earned my MFA in creative writing from Syracuse University."

He seems surprised.

"Some Hamas members we arrested admitted you are a Hamas member."

"They are lying." I ask for proof.

He slaps me across the face. "*You* get me proof that you are not Hamas!"

Everything around me is dark and frightening. I ask myself, How can a person get proof of something that he is not? Then I am walked aggressively forward again. What did I do? Where will they take us?

I am told to remove my shoes, and a group of us are led somewhere else. Cold rain and wind strike our backs.

"You raped our girls," someone says. "You killed our kids." He slaps our necks and kicks our backs with heavy boots. In the distance, we can hear artillery fire slicing through the air.

One by one, we are forced into a truck. Someone who is not moving lands on my lap. I fear that a soldier has thrown a corpse onto me, as a form of torture, but I am scared to speak. I whisper, "Are you alive?"

"Yes, man," the person says, and I sigh with relief.

When the truck stops, we hear what sound like gunshots. I no longer feel my body. The soldiers give off a smell that reminds me of coffins. I find myself wishing that a heart attack would kill me.

At our next stop, we kneel outside again. I start to wonder whether the Israeli military is showing us off. When a young man next to me cries, "No Hamas, no Hamas!" I hear kicks until he falls silent.

Another man, maybe talking to himself, says quietly, "I need to be with my daughter and pregnant wife. Please."

My eyes fill with tears. I imagine Maram and our kids on the other side of the checkpoint. They don't have blankets or even enough clothes. I can hear female soldiers, chatting and laughing.

Suddenly, someone kicks me in the stomach. I fly back and hit the ground, breathless. I cry out in Arabic for my mother.

I am forced back onto my knees. There is no time to feel scared. A boot kicks me in the nose and mouth. I feel that I am almost finished, but the nightmare is not over.

Back in the truck, my body hurts so much that I wish I had no hands or shoulders. After what feels like ninety minutes of driving, we are taken off the truck and shoved down some stairs. A soldier cuts my plastic handcuffs. "Both hands on the fence," he says.

This time, the soldier ties my hands in the front. A sigh of relief. I am escorted about fifteen meters. Finally, someone speaks to me in what sounds like native Palestinian Arabic. He seems to be my father's age.

At first, I hate this man. I think he is a collaborator. But later I hear him described as a *shawish*—a detainee like us, with little choice but to work for his jailers. "Let me help you," he says.

The *shawish* dresses me in new clothes and walks me inside the fence. When I raise my blindfolded head, I get blurry glimpses of a corrugated metal roof. We are in some kind of detention center; soldiers walk around, watching us. The *shawish* unrolls what looks like a yoga mat and covers me with a thin blanket. I place my bound hands behind my head, as a pillow. My arms sear with pain, but my body slowly warms. This is the end of day one.

For years, I have dreamed of looking out the window of a plane and seeing my home from above. In my adult life, I have never seen a civilian flight over Gaza. I have seen only warplanes and drones. Israel bombed Gaza's international airport in the early two-thousands, during the second intifada, and it has not operated since.

Most of my friends have never left Gaza. But in recent years, as they have struggled to find jobs and feed families, they have asked, How long should I wait? Some have immigrated to Turkey, and then to Europe. Some envy my three trips to the US. Each time I have returned, with photos of unfamiliar cities and trees and snow, people have called me "the American," and asked me why I came back. There is nothing in Gaza, they say. I always tell them that I want to be with my family and my neighbors. I have my house and my teaching job and my books. I can play soccer with my friends and go out to eat. Why would I leave Gaza?

We wake to the sound of a soldier shouting into a megaphone.

The *shawish* makes sure everyone is kneeling on the floor. He has told us that we are in a place called Be'er Sheva, in the Negev Desert. This is my first time in Israel.

The youngest of us, whose voice I recognize from the line, suddenly screams out that he is innocent. "I need to see my mother," he says. My feet start to feel numb.

I hear shouting and beating. "Okay, Okay, I will shut up," he says. "But please send me back." More beating follows.

The person next to me asks the *shawish* for water. "No water yet," the *shawish* says. He sounds frustrated, and I sympathize with him. More than a hundred detainees depend on him. When he takes me to the toilet, for the first time since the previous morning, he has to help me open the door and position me to urinate. The stench is very strong.

Breakfast is a small piece of bread, some yogurt, and a slosh of water poured directly into our mouths. I am not hungry, not even for my mother's birthday cake. When I return to the toilet, around noon, the *shawish* tells me that there is no toilet paper or water to wash myself.

Later, a soldier tells the *shawish* that we will be going to see a doctor. I sense relief in the room.

"I will tell him about my diabetes."

"Yes, and I will tell him about my bladder problem."

I will tell him about the pain in my nose, upper jaw, and right ear, where I had surgery a few years ago. Since I was kicked in the face, my hearing is weaker than before.

We kneel outside, with our hands on the back of the person in front of us. Wind strikes us; stones dig into our knees. We are put in a bus and a soldier pushes my head down, even though I can't see anything. Maybe they don't want to look at our faces.

When we exit the truck and my name is called, I am temporarily given my ID card. I feel a prick of hope. Maybe they are going to release us.

Inside a building, my blindfold is pulled off. A soldier is aiming an M16 at my head. Another soldier, behind a computer, asks questions and takes a photo of me. Another numbered badge is fastened to my left arm. Then I see the doctor, who asks whether I suffer from chronic diseases or feel sick. He does not seem interested in my pain.

Back at the detention center, blindfolded again, we kneel painfully for hours. I try to sleep. A man moans nearby; another is hopeful that he will get to go back to the doctor. Late in the evening, a soldier calls my name. The *shawish* leads me to the gate, and a jeep comes to take me away.

I am tied to a chair in a small room. An Israeli officer, Captain T., comes in and asks, "*Marhaba, keefak?*" This is Arabic for "Hello, how are you?"

I am very sad because of everything that has been done to me, I tell him.

Don't be sad, he says. We will talk.

The captain leaves the room and comes back with coffee. A soldier unties my right arm, so I can hold my cup.

I will tell him everything about me, I say, including where I was on October 7th, but I want him to answer one question.

"Sure. I'm listening."

Will he release me if there is nothing on me?

He promises that he will.

He takes notes as I tell him about my trips to the US, my poetry book, and my English students. I tell him that on the morning of October 7th, when Hamas began to launch rockets at Israel, I was wearing some new clothes, and my wife was taking a photo of me. The sound of rockets made Yaffa cry, so I showed her some YouTube videos on my phone. My father and brothers were on different floors of the house, and we started to shout a conversation out the windows. What's happening? Is this some kind of test?

On Telegram, we started to find videos of Hamas fighters inside Israel with their jeeps and motorcycles, encircling houses and shooting Israeli soldiers. In the beginning, some Gazans seemed excited and happy about the attack. But many of us were perplexed and scared. Although Gaza has been devastated by the Israeli occupation, I could not justify the atrocities committed against Israeli civilians. There is no reason to kill anyone like that. I also knew Israel would respond. Hamas had never done something like this before, and I feared that Israeli retaliation would be unprecedented too.

Captain T. asks me two questions. First, do I know of any Hamas tunnels or plans for ambushes?

I spent most of the past four years in the United States, I say. I spend my time teaching, reading, writing, and playing soccer. I don't know these things, and I'm not involved with Hamas.

Then Captain T. asks me the names and ages of my family members. Before I leave, he tells me that he hails from a family of Moroccan Jews. There are many shared things between us, he says. I nod and smile, trying to believe that he means what he says.

I ask him what will happen to me. They will look into what I have told him, he says. It may take several days.

"And then?"

"We will either imprison or release you."

I am on a bed, shackled and waiting to go back to the detention center. Someone comes to take me away, but then stops and has a conversation with someone else. They leave me for a while, and I fall asleep to the sound of Hebrew music. I like the singer's voice.

When I wake, a soldier says something in English that I cannot believe.

"We are sorry about the mistake. You are going home."

"Are you serious?"

Silence.

"I will go back to Gaza and be with my family?"

"Why wouldn't I be serious?"

Another voice chimes in: "Isn't this the writer?"

Back at the detention center, as I fall asleep, I think about the words "We are sorry about the mistake." I wonder how many mistakes the Israeli Army has made, and whether they will say sorry to anyone else.

On Tuesday, about two days after I left the school, the man with the megaphone teaches us how to say good morning in Hebrew. "*Baker Tov*, Captain," we say in unison. Some new detainees have arrived in an enclosure nearby, and the soldiers overseeing them seem to be having fun. They sing part of an Arabic children's song "Oh, my sheep!" and order the detainees to say "Baa" in response.

About an hour later, a soldier calls out my name and orders me to stand near the gate. The *shawish* warns me that they might interrogate me and beat me again. "Be strong and don't lie," he says. I feel a surge of panic.

After an hour, some soldiers approach. One has my ID, and another drops a pair of slippers for me and tells me to walk. Then one of them says, "Release!"

I am so overjoyed that I thank him. I think about my wife and children. I hope that my parents and siblings are alive.

I spend about two hours at the place where I was interrogated, with the Hebrew music. I am given some food and water, but the soldiers never find my family's passports. I climb into a jeep, surrounded by soldiers. After two hours, I can see around my blindfold that we are getting close to Gaza.

The soldiers get out, smoke, and return fully armed, wearing their vests and helmets. I am thinking about the man I recognized in line, and what he said about human shields. I am starting to wish that I could go back to the detention center when they give me my ID card.

Standing against a wall, I tell the closest soldier that I am scared. "Do not feel scared. You will leave soon."

My handcuffs are cut, and the blindfold is removed. I see the place where I had to take my clothes off. When I see new detainees waiting there, sadness overwhelms me.

I walk fast. Back at the checkpoint, in a big pile of belongings, I find my handbag, but not Yazzan's backpack, where we stuffed our children's winter clothes. A soldier shouts angrily at me. "I was just released," I say.

Back on Salah al-Din Road, dozens of people are waiting. A crying mother asks if I have seen her son. "He was kidnapped on Monday," she says. It is Tuesday. I have not seen him.

I have no money and no phone, but a kind driver offers to drop me off in the southern city of Deir al-Balah. I know that my wife's relatives have taken refuge there, and Maram probably would have joined them with the kids. As the man drives, I keep asking where we are, and he recites the names of refugee camps: Al-Nuseirat, Al-Bureij, Al-Maghazi.

In Deir al-Balah, I ask some young people, who are standing outside a bank, using its Wi-Fi, whether they know anyone from my hometown. One of them points me toward a school.

I take off my slippers and start to run. Passersby are staring, but I don't care. Suddenly, I spot an old friend, Mahdi, who once was the goalkeeper on my soccer team. "Mahdi! I'm lost— help me."

"Mosab!" We hug each other.

"Your wife and kids are at the school next to the college," he says. "Just turn left and walk for about two hundred meters."

I cry as I run. Just when I start to worry that I have lost my way, I hear Yaffa's voice. "Daddy!" She is the first piece of my puzzle.

She seems healthy, and is eating an orange. When I ask where the rest of the family is, she takes my hand and pulls me as if I were a child.

Maram's uncle Sari rushes off to find Maram. He does not tell her that I have arrived, only that she should return to the school for dinner. When she sees me, she looks like she might collapse, and I run toward her.

I learn from Maram how lucky I was. She used my phone to inform friends around the world, who demanded my safe release. I think about the hundreds or thousands of Palestinians, many of them likely more talented than me, who were taken from the checkpoint. Their friends could not help them.

The next day, Wednesday, I go to the hospital to have my injuries examined and see patients and corpses everywhere—in the corridors, on the steps, on desks. I manage to get an X-ray, but there are no results: the doctor's computer isn't working. I leave with a prescription for painkillers.

That Friday, a temporary ceasefire begins. Two of my wife's uncles try to go north, only to return an hour later. They say that Israeli snipers have shot and killed two people. At the souk, clothing costs more than ever. I wait five hours at an UNRWA aid center in the hope of receiving some flour, without success. A line to refill gas cannisters seems about a kilometer long.

As soon as the ceasefire ends, about seven hundred Palestinians are killed in twenty-four hours. Until recently, the south has been comparatively safe, but now we hear bombs not far away.

Then the US embassy in Jerusalem calls, advising us to head to the Rafah border crossing.

I struggle to find us a ride. The journey is about twenty kilometers, and the first two drivers we ask are scared. Israeli forces have isolated Rafah from the nearby city of Khan Younis. After a few calls, Maram's cousin, a taxi driver, agrees to take us.

At the crossing, we wait with hundreds of Gazans for four hours. I have my ID, which lists my children's names, but only Maram has her passport. I worry that we don't have the right documents to get through the crossing. But, at 7 p.m., officials wave us through the gate, and we join a crowd of exhausted families in the Egyptian travelers' hall. I feel as though I have been cured. The American embassy gives us an emergency passport

for Mostafa, and the Palestinian embassy gives us single-use travel
documents. Then a minibus takes us to Cairo.

In "A State of Siege," the Palestinian poet Mahmoud Darwish
writes something that is difficult to translate. "We do what jobless
people do," he says. "We raise hope." The verb *nurabi*, meaning to
raise or to rear, is what a parent does for a child, or what a farmer
does for crops. "Hope" is a difficult word for Palestinians. It is not
something that others give us but something that we must cultivate
and care for on our own. We have to help hope grow.

I hope that when the war ends I can go back to Gaza, to help
rebuild my family home and fill it with books. That one day all
Israelis can see us as their equals—as people who need to live on
our own land, in safety and prosperity, and build a future. That
my dream of seeing Gaza from a plane can become a reality, and
that my home can grow many more dreams. It's true that there
are many things to criticize Palestinians for. We are divided. We
suffer from corruption. Many of our leaders do not represent us.
Some people are violent. But, in the end, we Palestinians share at
least one thing with Israelis. We must have our own country—or
live together in one country, in which Palestinians have full and
equal rights. We should have our own airport and seaport and
economy—what any other country has.

An Egyptian friend welcomes us to Cairo. She lives in the Zamalek
neighborhood, on an island in the Nile. When I visit her garden, I
see flowers that my parents grew in Beit Lahia. On her shelves, I see
books that I left behind, under the rubble. When I tell her that her
house reminds me of home, she begins to cry.

Later, I find an article in the Israeli newspaper *Haaretz* about
a detention center in Be'er Sheva. It describes the same conditions that I experienced and says that several detainees have died
in Israeli custody. When the Israeli Army is reached for comment
about my story, a spokesperson says, "Detainees are treated in line
with international standards, including necessary checks for con-
cealed weapons. The IDF prioritizes detainee dignity and will review any deviations from protocols." The spokesperson does not
comment on detainee deaths.

On Telegram, I find a video of Khalifa Bin Zayed Elementary,
an UNRWA school that Yazzan, Yaffa, and I all attended. Two of
Maram's uncles, Naseem and Ramadan, who were born deaf and

mute, have been sheltering there with their families. When the kids hear the video, they drop their toys and join me. "There is my classroom," Yaffa says. She started first grade a few weeks ago. Yazzan sees his classroom too. In the video, the school is on fire.

I learn from a relative that the men in the school were taken to a hospital, stripped, and interrogated by Israeli forces. Afterward, Naseem and Ramadan went looking for their children. My relative says that, near the entrance to the school, a sniper shot them both, killing Naseem.

Naseem's younger brother Sari, whom I saw only days ago, sends me a photo of Naseem, wearing a white doctor's uniform stained with his blood. "These were the only clothes they could find at the hospital," Sari tells me on WhatsApp. Maram sits next to me, weeping.

The next day, Maram is cooking *maqluba*, a dish of rice, meat, and vegetables, which I have not eaten for two months. I am savoring the smell of potatoes and tomatoes when I get a call from a private number.

"Hello, Mosab. How are you?"

It is my father-in-law, Jaleel. At the sound of his voice, Maram's eyes brim with tears. He tells us that everything is fine, even though we know that this can't possibly be true. Then her mother comes to the phone.

"I'm sorry for our loss, Mum," Maram says. I hear her mother sob.

"Mum, are you taking your medicine?"

"Don't worry about me," she says. We never stop worrying about them.

I do not know whether our journey will end in Egypt or continue to the United States. I only know that my children need to have a childhood. They need to travel, and be educated, and live a life that is different from mine.

I have come to Egypt with only one book, a worn-out copy of my poetry collection. Since I last read it, I have lived a lot of new poems, which I still have to write. After weeks of typing on my phone, in streets and in schools, I am not used to opening my laptop without worrying about when I can charge it. I am not used to being able to close the door. But one morning I sit at my friend's beautiful wooden desk, in a room full of light, and write a poem. It is addressed to my mother. I hope that the next time we speak I can read it to her.

Numinous Strangers

FROM *Harper's*

AT THE YMCA Blue Ridge Assembly, in the mountains outside of Asheville, North Carolina, pilgrims gathered. It was the beginning of April 2022, and in the way of that country, the days were warm and the nights were cool, and the morning fog that blanketed the valley below glowed blue. The camp conjured certain romantic and suspect associations, with its historic lodges wrapped in wide porches, their tall, white pillars smudged with the traces of a century of wear. An amalgam of cultural products signaling "the South" seemed to float in on the fog: corsets and crumbling antebellum mansions, or whatever.

The occasion at hand was tradition of an altogether different phylum: The Annual Gathering of American Pilgrims on the Camino—as in the Camino de Santiago, an ancient network of paths taken by pilgrims that ends in Galicia. Hundreds of thousands of pilgrims make the journey each year, departing from various locations in Europe, following big yellow arrows through the north of Spain to the tomb of St. James, and some onward to the coast. The website of the American Pilgrims on the Camino says that the gathering gives Camino veterans and aspirants alike the opportunity to "share experiences" and to "learn more." But I had not come to trade intelligence on headlamps or blister care. I had come to meet the pilgrims. Really, I'd come to meet a particular pilgrim. Ann Sieben went on her first pilgrimage over fifteen years ago, and has been walking ever since. She abandoned a lucrative engineering career in nuclear remediation and gave away all her belongings, devoting herself to the life of the pilgrim.

Ann is not one to follow big yellow arrows, and she feels the Camino has largely become a "touristic" venture, in which one is

nudged along a track like an "economic widget." But she is a devoted servant of her God (Catholic), and part of her God-given
task on earth is to teach the world about the virtues of pilgrimage.
Since her friend Christine insisted on paying for her to attend the
gathering, she has decided to use this opportunity to test-drive a
set of six inspirational tales from her travels in front of a sympa-
thetic audience.

On the second night of the conference, about a dozen people had
congregated near the hearth in the main lodge to hear her speak.
We'd just come from a performance of a one-woman show titled
"Crying on the Camino," written and performed by a retired speech
pathologist. An hour and a half of bawdy jokes, musical numbers, and
a recurrent direct address—"Blessed are you, pilgrim"—culminated
in a tearful audience and a standing ovation. But just now, everyone
looked sleepy. One silver-haired gentleman slackened in his chair,
snoring.

Ann was standing before the hearth with her hands folded,
monkish. She is small, just over five feet tall. Her hair is a short,
white floof, buoyant as dandelion down, her eyes a blue so pale
they shine like ice. She was dressed in her pilgrim best: leather
walking boots, a hiking skirt, and a black, medieval-looking tunic
she refers to as "the hoodie." When she's on a pilgrimage, this
uniform is supplemented by a small backpack and a Day-Glo green
top of some technical material. I learned that the tunic was pat-
terned, in part, on a Lord of the Rings costume, and was "evening
wear" reserved for places of rest such as monasteries, or dinner
parties hosted by village mayors.

Ann introduced herself as a consecrated pilgrim who had re-
nounced worldly possessions. "I travel with no money," she said,
"which means, every night when I get to my destination . . . I ask
people for hospitality." Throughout fifteen years, fifty-six different
countries, and more than forty-five thousand miles, she told us, "I
have never *not* found hospitality."

Ann's talk wove together some of her greatest hits, subdivided into
related "couplets." A story about two men who leveled rifles at her in
the Western Desert of Egypt was paired with one about a crew of men
who appeared to be narco-traffickers confronting her with machine
guns while she "hoofed it" through the Chihuahuan Desert.

In the first case, Ann was walking across North Africa to Jerusalem, on a pilgrimage dedicated to "J.C. and the Boys." She was the

stranger in that story, the enemy "invader of their peaceful oasis."
She defused the situation by asking the men for water. By expressing an elemental need, she explains, the stranger made herself
familiar.

The alleged narcotraffickers confronted her while she walked
from Denver to Mexico City. "I am a pilgrim headed to Guada-
lupe," she told their ringleader. "My pilgrimage will either end
there, at the Basilica, or in Heaven with God. For me, it's equal.
You decide." In her telling, the men lowered their weapons. Some
crossed themselves and wrote down prayers for their grandmothers
and children, which Ann promised to deliver to "Our Lady." In this
case, the men were the strangers, and their love of family taught
Ann to love, in turn, "thy enemy."

Every encounter with the stranger is an opportunity to create
rapport. Ann's raison d'être is building trust, because trust is the
foundation of peace. Though she walks alone, pilgrimage is para-
doxically a social project. "It is personal," Ann told the crowd. "But
it is *not* private."

And a pilgrim never knows what gifts her needs will bestow upon
her host. Take, for example, a snowy night in Romania, when an
elderly peasant couple insisted that Ann sleep in their bed while
they bunked with the goats. She spent the night tossing and turning with guilt. But in the morning, the couple emerged from the
goathouse as flushed and giddy as naughty teenagers. The moral?
"More pilgrims, more love."

Someone must have tapped the dreaming man on the shoulder. By the time Ann finished the second couplet, the whole audience had leaned in, roused by allusion to eros and automatic
weapons. Later I asked how she thought it went. Did she get
much feedback?

"Just all the wows," she replied. "With the silence afterwards . . .
Spellbound. Speechless. Digesting."

I first encountered Ann in 2014. I'd had a difficult spring and
felt that my life had become, as they say in twelve-step, "unman-
ageable." I thought it might help to take a walk. A friend who was
living rough on the Rio Chama told me about a little shrine in the
Sangre de Cristo Mountains that people sometimes journeyed to,
hoping for a miracle.

I'm not religious, and my understanding of pilgrims involved

bonnets and the *Mayflower*, but I have been known to pray to in-
determinate forces in my foxhole. And I suppose I do believe in
a version of divine intercession, though I have no name for what
intervenes (nor any evidence to support such a belief).

All the same, I sent an email to the Santuario de Chimayó
requesting guidance. A few days later, I received a rigorous reply
from "Ann Sieben, Pilgrim-in-Residence," detailing seasonal con-
siderations, varieties of terrain, gear requirements, and optimal
points of departure. One route began, aptly, in a town called
Purgatory.

I clicked a link to a Blogspot embedded in her email signature
and spent some hours reading her "Winter Pilgrim" archive of
adventures. Some entries detailed touching encounters with "the
people of the world." Others railed against the hypocrisy of stingy
priests and nuns. Each resolved in the neat moral didacticism of
an Aesopian fable. "People are good" was one of her most frequent conclusions, along with, "The world needs more pilgrims."

While I doubted that I would sow world peace by walking, I
did hope to disarm the warring factions within me. Maybe that's
why I detected an alluring subtext in Ann's fables on the psycho-
biological, necromantic power of subjecting oneself to pilgrimage.
The pilgrim externalizes a dilemma—projecting divine resolution
upon the shrine or sacred relic she journeys toward—then she
works through that dilemma, step by literal step, all the while getting juiced on endorphins. Though the wanderer may not be
"lost," her narrative lacks a satisfying structure. Having a destination anchors the pilgrim's journey, providing a fixed point that
both mitigates the anxiety of the unknown and, ideally, delivers
catharsis on arrival.

Structure appealed to me. Up to that point, I'd lived much of
my life wandering without a tether. Typically, that meant taking a
dead-end food-service job, accumulating a thousand bucks—then
quitting, breaking up with whoever, stuffing my meager belongings into a backpack, and skipping town. I wandered all over and
had my share of fun and dicey adventures, and took my licks with
reasonable courage: parasites in Guatemala, dysentery in Myan-
mar, menacing dudes on the cross-country Greyhound. People
frequently warned me that it couldn't last, that eventually I would
be made to pay for my freedom, and at terrible cost. Most likely
I'd pay with my ass, though possibly with my life. At the very least I

would one day crave stability, and then I would finally understand that I was not, in fact, free to do whatever I wanted. Not at all.

This part of the prophecy came true. As touring musicians, backpackers, Casanovas, and other itinerants will tell you: eventually you dream of collecting cookware, or developing an exercise practice, or raincoat-free coitus uninhibited by the threat of STDs. In this imagined life, you will host dinner parties for friends who don't leave town in the morning. You will paint your walls a friendly color and hang on them your travel-gathered treasures. For my part, I imagined a child toddling at my feet while I baked goods and prepared whatever it is you prepare in Ball jars.

I hoped Ann Sieben would guide me out of Purgatory, but alas, our schedules did not align, and she soon vanished into her next adventure. Her blog posts petered out, then stopped altogether. Years passed.

Eventually, I cleaned up my act, moved, married, gave birth. It was the spring of 2020, so I held the baby up to the window while his relatives stood on the porch waving through the glass. I helped him learn to crawl, then walk, in the same square footage we'd been stewing in, day after rigidly structured day. (Feed, play, bathe, diaper, rock to sleep, repeat.) It was as total and protracted a confinement as I'd ever experienced, save perhaps for my own immobilized infancy. Like everyone else, I idled in the purgatory between onset and ending.

I had presumed, at the age of thirty-seven—the age, incidentally, at which my father was made a grandfather by my teenage sister—that I had fucked off more than enough to fulfill my lifetime's freedom quota. I was either ready to trade it in for stability and security or I would never be. I purchased a rolling pin, and used it to make an apple pie that my real-life toddler grasped after, repeating his grunt that means "I want." Thanks to that child— who is desire embodied, grunting after whatever *objet petit a* dangles beyond his reach—I saw into a mirror. And from its double vision came a painful clarity: there is no such thing as "enough" freedom. There will never be enough. You do not get used to not having it. You can make no lasting accommodation for its absence.

I began to wonder about the pilgrim again. Was she still out there, walking somewhere? And if so, could I join her?

*

As I've learned from Ann, pilgrims are not especially uncommon, but you'd be hard-pressed to find another like her. To wit: some pilgrims visit shrines by bus, and Ann calls these "bus pilgrims." The conference attendees were for the most part "walking pilgrims," though some will sleep in nice inns and pay to have their luggage portered, and these are known as "posh pilgrims." "Touristic pilgrims" is a general category that covers all those who use money to grease the skids of their travel, believing that they are entitled to whatever they pay for. The "penitent pilgrim" may wear a shirt of hair, or crawl for miles on his hands and knees, or shoulder a heavy cross, or flagellate himself as he walks, whipping away his sins as steadily as the horse's tail disperses flies. Ann is a "mendicant pilgrim," a designation for those who walk with few worldly possessions, surviving on charity alone. In my view, the mendicant pilgrim is the most hardcore. Penance, by definition, is payable and therefore finite. Soreness subsides in time. Scraped-up hands and knees scab over, lacerations mend, and shirts may be removed. But Ann's austerity is never ending.

In general, mendicancy means *begging*, surviving by asking alms. The early Franciscans lived as wandering street preachers and were allowed to work or beg for food, but were not permitted to accept money in any amount, even as alms. But as Ann explains it, the Franciscan reason for being, their charism, is *to love.* The Dominican charism is *to teach.* The Jesuit charism is *to learn.* "St. Ignatius was a pilgrim," she said, "St. Dominic was a pilgrim, St. Francis was a pilgrim—but that was a transitory situation until they transformed and figured out their charism. For me, the pilgrimage *is* the charism." Because there was no official designation in the Church for what Ann was doing, and because she didn't want to "feel like some whack-a-doodle out there walking," she worked with the judicial vicar of the Archdiocese of Denver to found the Society of Servant Pilgrims under canon laws 731 and 298, the latter of which relates to "associations of the Christian faithful."

Papist bookkeeping aside, in practice, Ann's life works like this: she hitches a ride to a point of origin, or someone donates a plane or a bus ticket, then she walks. She prefers winter but has walked in all seasons, in all kinds of weather, and over all sorts of terrain, averaging twenty-six miles a day when walking alone. At the end of each day, she arrives at a farmhouse, or a hut, or a village square, or a monastery, or a general store, and throws herself at the mercy of whoever answers the (sometimes proverbial) door. She has been offered shelter by the very wealthy and the very poor. She has slept on church pews, in a crypt, in mansions, and in a henhouse. She has been turned away by Benedictine priests avowed to greet each stranger as if Christ Himself. And she's been taken in by a great number of poor people living in tiny shacks. While it may be technically true that she has "never *not* found hospitality," neither did she enter every shelter willingly. For example, after she crossed into Panama illegally from Colombia via the Darién Gap, she was passed through a series of military encampments in the jungle, then spent eleven nights in a Panama City detention center. She once slept in an unmarked van as it sped through a conflict zone to the Egyptian border. (This was under orders from both the US embassy and the transitional Libyan government. She would have strongly preferred to walk.)

I found Ann again in May 2021. We would meet once a week over Zoom, where she would fill me in on her life. The pandemic had interrupted her most recent pilgrimage, in early 2020, in South Dakota to honor Nicholas Black Elk. She passed four months in "hermitage," moving into a sparsely furnished cave in the mountains of New Mexico. Every evening, she would heat stones on her wood-burning stove, then tuck them into her bedding for warmth. Once a week she hiked a mile to a friend's house to fill up jugs with water, and would haul them back in her knapsack over several trips. One night soon after she arrived, a wicked storm blew through and flooded the cave. It sounded pretty much biblical. She scrambled to rescue her notebooks from the water, but some pages bled. Even so, she said, life in the cave was "a lot of fun!"

By the time we started talking, she was staying with her friend Eileen in Denver, where she eagerly awaited her return to pilgrim life: the first of five eighty-eight-day walks dedicated to St. Martin, slated to begin in France that August. Eileen had helped Ann design and sew her many custom garments over the years, including the hiking skirt, the hoodie, and a pair of bespoke wool gaiters. Now they were at work on an anorak to keep Ann dry during the journey.

I was impressed by her ingenuity—by the cave and the custom gear—and told her so.

"I assessed the resources," she said breezily. "With duct tape and a sledgehammer, I can do a lot."

"Ann," I said, "you're like MacGyver."

This confused her. "Is that a television program?"

As spring gave way to summer, I began to plan an "assignment" that would justify taking leave of my domestic cloister. Ann was reluctant to participate at first. "On the one hand, a silent pilgrim does the world no good," she told me early on. "However, I also feel strongly that *who I am* is unimportant. What I *do* has to be radiated, but *who* I am isn't the thing of it."

I asked her what "the thing of it" might be.

"Shrouding myself in the shadow of my insignificance in order to arrive wherever the Holy Spirit directs me—is kind of the thing of it."

The abrupt appearance and disappearance of the mendicant pilgrim is part of her power. She emerges from a dense wood, in the dark of night, in a snowstorm; or she appears on the horizon in a remote desert; or she's on your doorstep, with her white hair and glacial eyes, asking for water. Because the experience is singular, it is preserved in the memories of those she meets, never to be dissipated by quotidian updates. Anonymity allows her to become an archetype. The archetype burns in the mind, numinous, and the encounter goes on unfolding after she leaves. That was the hope, anyway.

A pilgrimage begins in the heart, Ann says. You must first desire to make a sacred journey, then you must commit to your destination, "because it's gonna get tough. You have to need to get there." Cultivating an "openness to uncertainty" is the third component. A pilgrimage can't be planned to the minute; you have to get out of the way and make room for divine intercession.

I desired to make a sacred journey. But I didn't have a destination in mind, and I was having trouble getting my head around the childcare component. Ann was planning to guide a group along the Danube soon, and at first this seemed like a decent possibility. But it wasn't long before I realized that the cost of the trip—both in terms of cash and in time away from my toddler—made it impossible.

When I mentioned my concerns, Ann said, "He's welcome along. I would think a stroller would be not inappropriate. We're not on hiking trails, we're on wheelable surfaces."

For a moment, I indulged a vision of me and my son strolling along the riverbank, lunching on baguette and cheese—before I flashed on the last "vacation" we attempted as a family, a short trip to the Oregon coast where it poured rain for three days. Because I am an amateur, and did not so much as scan the rental listing for the phrase "child friendly," we spent those housebound hours body blocking the toddler as he lunged at precious shells, pottery, and glassware displayed on low shelves while gleefully screaming, "I want danger!"

Scapegoating one's child is a parent's favorite pastime. But even if my kid were a placid companion, walking with a group of retirees along a well-trodden path was not the transformative passage I had in mind. I wanted a pilgrimage as defined by the *Century Dictionary and Cyclopedia*: "A traveling on through a strange country . . . [to] obtain some spiritual or miraculous benefit." At first glance, the miracle might seem to be the objective. But it's the dislocation from the known, the *traveling on through* that strange terrain beyond the numbing repetition and habits of ordinary life that catalyzes transformation.

In my daydreams, I became the numinous stranger. A highway specter upon whom no one's well-being depended. Alone in the hands of the Gods, open to divine intercession, crossing paths with the Other for a moment of brief intensity before moving on. Like most fantasies, mine were not fashioned from pure imagination, but from scraps of formative experience—a version of my dissolute youth, its considerable physical discomforts and mental angst edited out. At first, I'd been drawn to Ann's discipline and purpose. Now, suffocated by purpose, I coveted her freedom—in both cases making her an avatar of the inaccessible. I longed for the kind of unmitigated connection to metaphysical forces that a life like hers made possible. Beyond freedom of movement, Ann possessed an existential freedom afforded not just by her faith, but by fearlessness in the face of death. (In fact, she once told me that she *hoped* to be martyred. Apparently, martyrs need proof of only one miracle, not two, to become saints.)

At present, I did not have freedom of movement or of mind. One of the strangest experiences of becoming someone's mother is that I have never cared so little about my own life, and at the same time, I have never been so afraid to die. Daily, I fantasize about stepping into the path of an active shooter, of using my body as a barricade between my child and a texting driver. Keeping myself alive is of paramount importance, but only in order to serve the single function of keeping him alive. I had to ask myself, What was this all about? Was I hoping to be transformed by an unscripted journey, or was I fleeing my responsibilities? Because the former was not achievable without accepting certain risks. You might even say the risks of such a journey are inextricable from its rewards.

Ann was no help on this front. She has little patience for the handwringing of those denizens of a fear-based reality. Courage comes through doing, not fretting. People are constantly asking her, *Aren't you afraid?* After an encounter with a particularly concerned Kansan couple, Ann wrote, "My standard answer, fully from the heart, is that fear and experience seem to me to occupy the same place in the soul. The more experience one has, the less room there is for fear; yet in the absence of experience—even borrowed experience—fear expands to fill the void. It can become paralyzing."

If experience is the source of Ann's fearlessness, it is an experience that she cultivated over the course of her life. She was born in 1963 on the Jersey shore, the middle of five children. Her mother was a librarian, her father a professor of English. She describes her family as "somewhat competitive." When the siblings played Scrabble, they competed for seven-letter words. On Sundays, they filled out the *New York Times* crossword "with a pen," she said, "because what kind of loser uses a pencil?"

Though her family was Irish Catholic, Ann cites two secular sources when asked what might have predicted her future as a mendicant pilgrim. On summer breaks, her father conscripted his children in renovating and flipping houses. If the children needed to learn how to repair something, they cracked open a book. The other decisive influence came through membership in the High Adventure Explorer Scouts, a co-ed program run by the Boy Scouts specializing in rugged backcountry trips, wherein she attained skills like orienteering, snow camping, and mountaineering. A life motto began to emerge: *Just figure it out.*

After high school, an interest in geology drew her out West. She moved to Denver to attend the Colorado School of Mines, where she studied geological engineering. In the late eighties, she entered the nascent field of nuclear and radioactive remediation, eventually running maintenance and clean-up crews at weapons depots and nuclear power plants, figuring it out as she went along. By her early forties, she had "ticked all her boxes." She was living in Europe, stacking coin, and driving a company Jag—but something was missing.

Like many pilgrims, Ann was introduced to pilgrim life by walking a leg of the Camino. A few weeks later, she walked the Via Francigena from Canterbury to Rome—less a proper route than a list of towns from the itinerary of a tenth-century archbishop named Sigeric—which she considers her first pilgrimage. Ann started from the cathedral in Canterbury on December 17, 2007, with plans to arrive in Rome for Easter. That meant walking over the Alps in the middle of winter. She had Sigeric's list and plotted the rest as she went along using "excellent 1:100,000 scale maps" purchased from local bookstores. "Few women had walked it alone, if any at that time," she later wrote, and people were "generally aghast, often to the point of scolding me like a child for my obvious unawareness—so they thought—of the inherent dangers of a woman alone and in winter."

She began to learn the ropes of mendicancy, resting her feet in churches and reading up on the lives of the saints. She quickly figured out that "candles in an enclosed chapel put out noticeable and cherished heat." In France, village mayors often held keys to designated pilgrim accommodations. "As a matter of pride, the towns have to host credentialed pilgrims—at least a lone woman in winter." The accommodation could be a room in a community center or a cabin in the forest. These little towns had been in the business of hosting pilgrims for centuries. "Always bunkbeds, a shower, an equipped kitchen with a stocked cupboard—pasta, soup, cans of tuna, coffee, tea . . . Who knew?"

Having made it to Santiago and Rome, Ann hoped to complete her personal trifecta and walk to Jerusalem. She looked for accounts from others who'd made the trip and learned that most had traveled around the Mediterranean—through Turkey, Syria, and Lebanon—and used boats. "Not even St. Francis or St. Ignatius had actually made it by foot," she wrote. "They hadn't attempted it, it seems."

For Ann, the potential to become the first in history to blaze a path only sweetened the deal. But there were travel restrictions in the region that would have made it nearly impossible for an American to complete the trek on foot—legally, at least. It seemed likely that she'd have to sneak across borders, and though Ann does not always defer to the authorities, she does tend to observe their laws. It wasn't the right time to complete the trifecta, but neither was she ready to return to her old life. Uncertain about where to go next, Ann did what she always did when she reached a crossroads: she assessed her resources and consulted the literature.

According to various Christian texts, when Jesus told the apostles to go to the ends of the earth and spread the Gospel, James apparently took this instruction literally and went to Galicia, to the coast where the known world collapsed into the sea at Cape Finisterre (from the Latin *finis terrae*: "the end of the earth"). And so we have the Camino de Santiago, or "the way of St. James." Meanwhile, Peter went to Rome, where he was crucified, the story goes, upside down at his own request. Thomas, Jude, and Simon went to Persia. John to Anatolia. But Andrew? Andrew went to Scythia, traveling through what is now Russia, Romania, and Ukraine. He might have journeyed for months or decades, no one knows for sure, but it's believed that he eventually wound up in Patras, Greece.

"Well, *there's* a guy!" Ann thought. "Brother Peter goes to the largest city of the Roman Empire," and Andrew goes on an adventure. It was a badass move, and thus appealed to her.

She would mount a pilgrimage in honor of St. Andrew, she decided, beginning in Kyiv and ending in Patras. Sure, there would be challenges. For example, she didn't speak Ukrainian or Russian, or Romanian, or Bulgarian, or Turkish, or Greek. Five languages, five countries, five months.

Ann returned to Denver to prepare, reaching out to the local Ukrainian Catholic Church, the Greek Orthodox Metropolis, and to a Turkish group at the Colorado Muslim Society, in search of language partners. The Ukrainian priest and his elderly parishioners were particularly helpful, eager to put Ann in touch with relatives back home. He prepared a letter of introduction, written in Ukrainian. A reverend at the Greek Orthodox Metropolis was less helpful, according to Ann. He refused to provide a letter, warning that she'd be received as a heretic, "raped, robbed, or worse," and adding that if, by some miracle, she made it out of Romania alive, she would undoubtedly be trafficked in Turkey.

This man did not frighten Ann, but he did annoy her. "St. Andrew no doubt faced the same challenges and then some," she wrote, cheerfully. "It's amazing how much confidence can come from other people's experiences, even if separated by 2,000 years. He did it; I can do it."

Ann bought a journal with accordion paper, decorated the cover with an image of the medieval pilgrim medallion, then coated it in boot wax. She cut another medallion from a tin can, punched a hole through it, and strung it on a ribbon to be worn around her neck. She tucked away twenty dollars to purchase a visa at the Turkish border and bought a one-way plane ticket to Kyiv. It had been two years since she'd earned a paycheck and she was nearly out of money.

On Monday, November 16, 2009, Ann walked out of Kyiv and into the countryside. She'd acquired a Russian military map that showed a Roman Catholic monastery within a day's walk. Every so often, she would ask for help from one of the many people foraging for mushrooms along the path, and they would point the way, though she came to realize that they'd been directing her to a Russian Orthodox monastery—not the Catholic one. It was too late to change course. The pivotal moment had arrived. Would she be denounced as a heretic?

Ann would later credit the events of that day with severing an "invisible tether." The Orthodox monks welcomed her warmly, as did the majority of people she met over the next five months. The families who took her in were mostly very poor, sleeping together on the floor under common blankets for warmth. It was extremely cold, and as she tells it, these families sometimes directed her to "sleep next to Grandmother, she's very fat and will keep you warm all night!" She slept with many people's grandmothers.

"I understood firsthand everyone has something to give," she reflected, "even something as fundamental as body heat, and everybody cherishes the opportunity to give to those less fortunate. In my case, I was seen as having the genuine and grave misfortune of insufficient body fat to endure subfreezing temperatures."

Her homemade pilgrim credential wound up serving her well. Hosts wrote the date, their names, and their towns in her book. Often, they'd include encouraging messages that would be read by her hosts down the road. Adults and children alike were fascinated by the "various languages and symbols." One priest would recognize the name of another and accept her more readily.

In a sense, Ann was learning to engineer her own vulnerability. By laying herself open to lethal temperatures, to unknown landscapes and languages, she occasioned the goodness of others. And the people she met were good, she maintained. "I saw this, because I put myself in the situation to see it."

Contrary to the warning from the reverend, she was not raped or robbed. And after 137 days and 2,748 miles, Ann finally arrived at the Cathedral of St. Andrew. "With the first step out of Kyiv, I became a pilgrim of faith," she later wrote. "Anywhere I faced was my future."

Pilgrimage is not inherently moral. It may be undertaken in good or bad faith, or with no faith at all. That said, certain motivations recur. Pilgrims have always walked in the hopes of being delivered; whether from evil or illness, from a guilty conscience, from the pain of loss, or the pain of paled belief. And there have always been those who used pilgrimage as a pretense to throw off obligations: debt, bad marriages, the burden of children. In the Middle Ages, opportunists on the Camino de Santiago disguised themselves as pilgrims and set about freely sowing oats, or robbing other pilgrims on the road. Then as now, their hosts could never be sure who walked in earnest and who in bad faith. In 1600, this prompted a vigorous condemnation from a subprior in Roncesvalles:

> To cover up their wicked lives they toss on a traveler's tunic
> and a shoulder cape, sling a messenger bag to one side, a
> gourd canteen on the other, staff in hand and a floozie for
> a fake wife, swarming all over Spain on their endless cycle of
> "pilgrimages."

But ulterior motives were not always so cynical. For serfs who walked the Camino in the Middle Ages, the perilous journey was often their single opportunity to escape a pattern of cradle-to-grave labor, to encounter the world, to touch the mountains and the sea—ecstatic experiences in their own right. Any freedom afforded by the journey came at the risk of mortal danger. Wolves, wild dogs, bears, and robbers haunted the way, which was already shadowed by the swords of plague, exposure, thirst, and starvation. Many did not survive the trip.

Like her forebears, Ann has navigated her share of hazards: savage dogs in the Greek countryside, crocodiles in Chiapas, a tornado in Kansas, vampire bats in Peru. When she was finally able to begin her walk to Jerusalem in 2011—thanks to a brief window of border fluidity opened by the Arab Spring—nearly every country she passed through was experiencing some level of conflict. But if you're betting on pilgrim mortality, smart money is on the workaday risks: infection, illness, dehydration, getting hit by a car, slipping on some rocks in a moment of lapsed vigilance. Ann's policy is to eat whatever her hosts eat (except for pickles!) and to drink whatever they drink, no matter where she is in the world. This has included boiled swamp water, and much meat of questionable age and derivation. She once sipped a bottle of tainted water in Morocco and for the next three days pissed "jet-black pee." When I asked if she'd picked up any parasites, she said that she'd rather not know. "I'm sure there's a lot of zoology that's not standard for a Denverite, but we're in harmony," she said, patting her abdomen. "I worked in nuclear. That was kind of our thing. On a need-to-know basis . . . Why start worrying, *oh I'm carrying some parasite that might come bursting through the soles of my feet one day*. I'll deal with that when it happens."

The truest believer eschews all parachutes. If you consult the Society of Servant Pilgrims' website—Ann is both its founder and its only dedicated member—you'll learn that this extends to money, because money burdens the pilgrim with "the need to protect it" and prevents engagement with those she'd otherwise seek out for alms. Moreover, if someone is tempted to steal from you, "the sin is owned by the pilgrim" and "sorrows await he who does the tempting." As for cameras: "a photo only captures a distorted visual snapshot of a moment, not the full sensory experience—the scents, the sounds, the feels . . . the animations."

Despite these objections, COVID-19 contact-tracing requirements in Europe forced Ann to carry a smartphone on her first walk for St. Martin. She wasn't thrilled, but decided to use the obstacle as an opportunity to log her daily pursuit of food and shelter. Over the late summer and fall, I received photographs and updates from her "two-thumbs journal." My own days remained monotonous and confined, and I devoured her descriptions of meals made sweeter by travail: windfall fruit gleaned from the orchards she passed through, day-old baguettes and gifted hunks of cheese, all of it washed down with a bottle of donated table wine. I wandered vicariously through ancient cathedrals and verdant countryside, reveling in her snapshots of *the animations* and *the feels*, and my torture was bittersweet.

Ann told the story of St. Martin to everyone she met: a soldier who once sheared his cloak in half with a sword to share with a beggar. Meanwhile, in Seattle, where I live, it was a summer of wildfire smoke and a lethal heat dome, and charity for the ever-increasing number of people who camped in tents and vans lining the streets was scarce. I was raw from lack of sleep. From caring for a vulnerable child in a terrifying world. I felt alternately bereft and enraged whenever Ann was rejected by an unfeeling priest or a condescending town official. And I joined in her celebration when her day was ultimately saved by a kind Samaritan.

I was still hatching plans for my own pilgrimage, but a destination continued to elude me. It would be too tedious to elaborate my brainstorming, but I will confess that one idea involved the childhood home of Jimi Hendrix, and another entailed several days of walking down a busy highway shoulder. Destinations on the short list were selected for ease of execution and had little personal relevance, because anywhere truly meaningful demanded either too much time away from home or too many potential hazards. In my life before, I had taken it for granted that mortal danger was the price of my freedom. But my world had changed. I had changed. How could I complete a pilgrimage if the moment I part from my child it's as though I draw a length of retractable leash? From that moment, no matter where I go—whether on a morning run, or deep into the Appalachian foothills—its tension pulls me inexorably home. For the sake of expedience, we can call this tether "love." But I would not characterize the experience as pleasant. More like tearing a vital organ from your body, then anxiously trailing it into a hail of shrapnel. And I had engineered this vulnerability.

Though I could probably get away with one of the shorter and nearer routes, I did not want to walk down a highway shoulder for several days. I wanted the fantasy, to have it both ways. To stay close and care for my boy, and simultaneously to live free of all expectations and attachments. An unoriginal predicament, to be so divided. Perhaps this accounts for the saints' trick of bilocation.

I could, I did not want, I wanted—sometimes we hear ourselves

talking. What a sad parody of the spiritual-not-religious set, spoon-
ing a little of this and that tradition onto my tray at the discount
buffet of metaphysical eclecticism! Emphasis inevitably on the *I*.
Here was yet another way I differed from Ann. Those of us who
journeyed in the hope of some personally relevant intervention or
message were mainly in it for ourselves, in order to encounter or
to beseech the divine, not to serve it. Ann walked in service of her
God, with saints for coworkers, on behalf of the whole world. Like
the parable of the drowning man who refuses human rescue in
anticipation of divine intervention, I kept waiting for an inspired
destination—some supernatural epiphany that would reconcile
me to my life. All the while, the example of Ann's steady, boots-on-
the-ground devotion was staring me in the face.

Like most human endeavors, pilgrimage depends on fantasy and
projection. Projection of the mercy and power of God upon the
object; the fantasy of deliverance upon arrival. Like the shoestring
travel guide, with its images of mountain trekkers and seaside
cliffs at sunset, pilgrimage suggests rewards that will outlive the
adventure or pleasure of the moment. We hope the journey will
manifest inwardly, deepen and change us. Sometimes it does. And
sometimes it distracts us from the depths of where we already are.
    My fantasy of becoming someone else through travel was born
long before my son. As was the revelation that no matter where I
put my body, there would be no escaping myself. Hadn't I come
to the same conclusion dozens of times? That even paradise can
become burdensome if you're inclined to experience consciousness that way—even if you're free to blunt that consciousness with
drugs, adrenaline, or the seduction cycle's cascade of dopamine
and norepinephrine. Isn't that why, for two decades, I couldn't
stop moving? Psychoanalysts call this tendency the "manic defense," an attempt to distract oneself from uncomfortable feelings
with frenzied activity. As I see it, the main difference between my
manically defended former life and my situation today is that I no
longer live in the shadow of my own insignificance. I've become
significant to others, and this significance demands that I retire my
expired distraction strategies.
    I don't mean that my former itinerancy was exclusively an attempt
to outrun discomfort—I also widened my horizons, encountered
many lovely Others, touched the mountains and the sea, and in so

doing experienced flashes of ecstatic communion. I only mean that at some imperceptible juncture, my choices became compulsions, and what had once felt enlivening came to feel like going through the motions. Parenthood, I am learning, likewise depends on fantasy and projection. And from the inevitable erosion of those projections, the dashing of those fantasies, comes both pain and the possibility of growth. Put another way, my son has not deprived me of my freedom so much as he has dispelled the illusion that I was ever free to begin with.

There's a story Ann likes to tell about a shepherd boy she encountered one day in the Extremadura region of Spain. She crested a lonely hill and came upon the boy and his flock. He was about twelve years old, all alone, cradling a sickly lamb in his lap with "obvious sadness." Ann offered to share some bread and oranges. He pulled a hunk of sheep's cheese from his rucksack and together they ate.

She presents this as an example of how her fleeting presence can provide companionship and comfort. "So many times, somebody needs an objective sounding board and *bam*, I show up out of nowhere, and *bam*, I leave." She is the deus ex machina who, passing through, facilitates peace, or love, or else poses a dilemma for the one who answers the door: *Will I open my heart to this stranger or turn them away?*

Of the shepherd boy, she continued, "Oddly, he never asked about me, where I was going . . . He didn't inquire about my nationality. He only told me about his sheep, the lambs born in the previous weeks, pointing to the ones he personally helped deliver. He told me the names of some of the ewes and how long he's known them. Somehow he could distinguish one sheep from another. They all looked alike to me. This boy knew his flock, and it seemed the flock knew the shepherd by the sound of his voice."

On the one hand, Ann makes herself vulnerable in order to help others discover their own generosity. But it doesn't seem to occur to her that these numinous strangers might have appeared out of nowhere in order to facilitate *her* growth, to remind her of *her* goodness, to supply *her* with companionship and comfort. Or that there might be more to the story of a shepherd, who knows each of his flock by name; who delivers, and loves, and grieves each one.

Or maybe she does sense this, and doesn't want to say. As Ann sometimes reminds me, she's not "a touchy-feely kind of person."

Pilgrimage is a runaway metaphor, and I know I've headed down a shady path. But I can't help feeling that where I already am, for once, is the only meaningful destination left to me—or at least, the only one I can pursue in good faith. Or that there might be more to the story of the boy, whose vulnerability and need transforms his host. That my charism, for now, is *to caretake*. Much is made of the parents' selflessness in this dynamic, but my experience has been otherwise. Becoming a parent has meant tolerating an uncomfortable surplus of myself. Every time I try to flee, my child bars the way, forcing me inward. A strange and uncertain country, indeed.

JASON WILSON

How Things Disappear

FROM *Everyday Drinking*

IN THIS TERRIBLE age of media—when we are told that travel writing is dead or dying—I made a travel writer's pilgrimage, winding through miles of olive-tree forests in Andalusia's interior, to the small hilltop town of Estepa. I'm still not exactly sure why.

Estepa is a relatively random town situated between the bigger cities of Córdoba and Málaga in southern Spain. I was in Córdoba on assignment, and I'd had a Saturday morning appointment with a winemaker in Montilla, a guy who made strange, dry wines in this hot climate from the Pedro Ximenez grape.

After the meeting, in the bar of an old restaurant in Montilla, I ate a big, carnivorous lunch alone. As a group of men argued over glasses of the local wine, I ate a plate of paper-thin jamón Ibérico de bellota, followed by grilled pluma Ibérico, washed down with a half-bottle of an oaky Tempranillo. After lunch, I had a free afternoon and no one awaiting me in Córdoba, so I decided to drive another hour farther south, through a series of bright, white-washed villages, to Estepa.

I had wanted to visit these so-called pueblos blancos of Andalusia for a long time—for at least three decades, ever since I read about them in Rick Steves's classic guidebook, *Europe Through the Back Door*. As a dumb and impressionable nineteen-year-old college student, about to head off on a European backpacking tour, Rick Steves was my sherpa. The copy of *Europe Through the Back Door* that I took with me in 1990 was one of Steves's early self-published editions that dated to the late 1980s, with hand-drawn maps, grainy black-and-white snapshots, and goofy, hippie-ish illustrations. I still own that dog-eared and marked-up copy. I will always love Steves's nerdy, idiosyncratic voice and his deeply sincere belief that the world could be a better place if everyone traveled more outside their comfort zone. I revere it as much as any work of travel writing on my bookshelf.

In that early edition, Steves writes breathlessly about the south of Spain. He implores readers to leave the tourist trail, to rent a car and to explore the interior of Andalusia, which he called "wonderfully untouched Spanish culture." He writes, "All you need is time, a car, and a willingness to follow your nose."

Steves loved the small towns of southern Spain's interior, but one stood out above the others. "My most prized discovery in Andalusia is Estepa," he writes. Estepa is known mostly for its hilltop convent of Santa Clara ("worth five stars in any guidebook, but found in none," according to Steves). In fact, if the town is known at all in Spain, it's because the nuns at this convent make a famous cookie that's eaten at Christmastime. "Enjoy the territorial view from the summit, then step into the quiet, spiritual perfection of this little-known convent. Just sit in the chapel all alone and feel the beauty soak through your body," Steves writes.

It's surprising how many words Steves commits to Estepa in this old edition of *Europe Through the Back Door.* He regales readers with anecdotes about "sleeping under the stars" on the convent porch and Estepa's "evening promenade" where residents "congregate and enjoy each other's company, old and young." He loves Estepa so much that he literally transcribes a page from his own youthful travel journal, in italics: "*Estepa, spilling over a hill crowned with a castle and convent, is a freshly washed, happy town that fits my dreams of southern Spain.*"

My own backpacking trail in those days took me elsewhere—to Italy, Switzerland, France, Germany. I never made it to Andalusia until years later. But because I was such a fan of Rick Steves, I tucked those joyous descriptions of the region's pueblos blancos away in my memories, vowing someday to visit. Whenever I would see a new edition of *Europe Through the Back Door,* I would flip to the chapter on southern Spain. Estepa was always there.

More than thirty years after my first backpacking trip to Europe, I realized I would be visiting Andalusia close to the pueblos blancos. Yet when I consulted the most recent editions of *Europe Through the Back Door,* as well as Steves's country guide to Spain, I was dismayed to see that all mentions of Estepa had been removed. I looked through several recent editions and found no Estepa. I

knew I wasn't misremembering, that this wasn't some false Man-
dela effect–like memory. After all, as evidence, I had my three-
decade-old, dog-eared, hippie edition of Steves' book.

I needed to know what happened to Estepa. It seemed like
precisely the sort of off-the-beaten-path destination that Steves,
at least when I was younger, always preached that readers should
visit. So, I reached out to Rick Steves, to see what happened to Estepa. Well, not Rick Steves, the man, directly. Rick Steves Europe
is now a large travel and media company, and the books they
publish are no longer hippie-ish at all. Still, the same day, I got a
friendly Facebook message back from one of Steves's top editors,
Cameron Hewitt, with an explanation:

> "In about 2015, we overhauled that book and reworked all
> those old 'Back Doors' sections that had been in the book
> for decades . . . I imagine Estepa simply didn't make the new
> editorial cut; we wound up replacing lots of 'heritage'-type
> content in that edition with fresher bits of writing from Rick.
> It was not necessarily because we feel that Estepa is no longer
> worth visiting; just one of those tough editorial calls you make
> along the way."

So Estepa had not been canceled for any noteworthy reason.
Rather, Estepa had been a casualty of the same cold, ruthless
"tough editorial calls" that many of us in publishing have faced
over the past few years—particularly those of us who work the
so-called "lifestyle beat," and particularly those of us who do long-
form travel writing. The lifestyle beat is a space that's become
increasingly homogenized, full of derivative clickbait tips and
listicles driven by social media. Estepa disappeared like so many
of the outlets that were once committed to publishing quality
travel writing.

In my own life, in one eighteen-month span, I'd watched two of
my anchor publications disappear. In mid-2021, I was told that *The
Best American Travel Writing*, the annual anthology I'd edited for
more than twenty years, would be discontinued. The reason given:
the publisher was about to be acquired by a larger company, and
they were "cleaning up the balance sheet." Then, in late 2022, I
learned that the *Washington Post Magazine*, the publication where a
few times each year I published the best of my travel writing would
shut down and cease to exist.

I can't say either shuttering was a surprise. Travel writing seems clearly to be in decline—both the supply and the demand. For years, during my annual process of reading and selecting for *The Best American Travel Writing*, I'd noticed a sharp drop in the amount of quality travel writing published in American magazines and newspapers. A decade or two ago, it was no problem to find a hundred notable travel essays and articles. By the late 2010s, I usually struggled to find fifty.

More than a genre of writing is being lost by our current era of corporate consolidation. I know in my small corner of the world, I've tried my best to amplify voices that were outside of entrenched media structures. But legacy media continues to cut corners as it tries to wring more from underpaid work.

Across publishing, the basic rate for freelance writing has stagnated at around $1 per word for decades (very often less at many outlets). Consider how long this "dollar per word" has been a standard. Ernest Hemingway, filing dispatches for magazines from the Spanish Civil War in 1936, was also paid $1 per word. That 1936 dollar is the equivalent of about $22 in 2023. Even if they're no Hemingway, today's writers earn a fraction of the per-word rate that writers did almost ninety years ago. What other creators have seen such a precipitous drop for their paid work? Young writers are having to rely more and more on canned press trips, subsidized by brands or regional organizations. It seems that the end result of all this will be that the only people who will have the time and resources to do travel writing will be the same sorts of affluent people that did it in the age of the British gentry on grand tour.

Given all this, is travel writing dead? Dying? When I think about this, I'm reminded that the distinguished UK literary magazine *Granta* posed this very question to a dozen or so writers in its Winter 2017 issue. Like so many of these faux-provocative questions ("Is the novel dead?" "Is pop music dead?" "Is baseball dying?") no definitive answer was reached. As Geoff Dyer, who was among the respondents, wrote: "Yes and no. Sort of."

Much of the discussion dwelled on nomenclature, the idea that the genre's name—"travel writing"—did not adequately capture what it is to write about place in 2017. "So, what matters to me is not whether a piece of writing is called travel writing," wrote Mohsin Hamid.

Dyer offers up Miles Davis's work from the 1970s as a possibility.

At that time, Davis no longer referred to his music as "jazz" but rather "Directions in Music." Said Dyer, "That's what I'm after: Directions in Writing."

So yes, this was a pretty weird discussion in the pages of *Granta*. The simple fact that it was asking the dreaded "Is travel writing dead" question was astonishing enough, but it was especially alarming to those of us who have been ardent readers of both travel writing and *Granta* since the 1980s. *Granta*, after all, led a revival of travel writing in the 1980s, advocating for what had become a badly atrophied, nearly moribund genre in the late twentieth century. With Bill Buford as its editor, *Granta* dedicated two special issues to new travel writing, in 1984 and 1989. Legendary travel writers regularly turned up in the magazine's pages: Bruce Chatwin, Colin Thubron, Martha Gelhorn, Jan Morris, Ryszard Kapuściński.

I can't overstate how exciting and freeing it was when I first discovered writers like Chatwin or Kapuściński or Gelhorn or Rebecca West or Ted Conover or Pico Iyer. While I was supposed to be focused on fiction in my graduate creative writing program in the 1990s, I found my mind drifting toward travel writing. This was still before the rise of so-called "Creative Nonfiction," several years before the mainstreaming of the memoir, and a decade before the emergence of personal blogs. Travel writing, in those days, was not a topic of polite discussion in graduate fiction seminars.

In any case, the travel writing published by *Granta* would inspire me, in the mid-1990s, to create my own journal devoted to travel, *Grand Tour*, which lurched along for a few years, then died and went to small-underfunded-literary-magazine heaven. Out of *Grand Tour*'s ashes, however, the *Best American* anthology emerged. In early 2000, I scoured through the travel stories of 1999 along with our first guest editor, Bill Bryson—one of those travel writers who I'd first read in *Granta*—to gather our first anthology.

I did the same for twenty-two editions, spanning 9/11, the endless wars in Iraq and Afghanistan, the lifting of the Cuban travel ban, the Syrian refugee crisis, the presidencies of Bill Clinton, George W. Bush, Barack Obama, and Donald Trump—chronicling the world as it has been transformed in so many previously unfathomable ways. Travel itself irrevocably changed over that time. I think about what did not exist when I began the *Best American Travel Writing* anthology: the euro, Brexit, Google Maps, translation apps, Uber, Yelp, so-called "Premium Economy," boarding passes scanned from iPhones, and TSA PreCheck.

This evolution is, of course, the sort of thing that's supposed to happen with travel writing. In my first foreword, to the inaugural edition in 2000, I wrote:

> Travel writing is always about a specific moment in time. The writer imbues that moment with everything he or she has read, heard, experienced, and lived, bringing all his or her talent to bear on it. When focused on that moment, great travel writing can teach us something about the world that no other genre can. Perhaps travel writing's foremost lesson is this: We may never walk this way again, and even if we do, we will never be the same people we are right now. Most important, the world we move through will never be the same place again. This is why travel writing matters.

Maybe the blunt assessment of *Granta*'s former editor, Ian Jack, during *Granta*'s 2017 travel writing discussion summed up the way a lot of people think: "Travel writing isn't dead. It just isn't what it was."

Looking backward at what travel writing "was" has always been fraught. Given the genre's history of cultural voyeurism, colonialist impulses, and straight-up racism, it's often not pretty. When literary people ask, "Is travel writing dead?" they're suggesting that the genre is outdated or old-fashioned or in need of an avant-garde "subversion." I don't know that this is possible; travel writing is a reflection of its time. Travel writing has existed longer than most other forms of literature, dating at least to Herodotus in ancient Greece. And travel writing has faced criticism for nearly as long. In the first century AD, the Roman essayist Plutarch was already calling bullshit on Herodotus, accusing him of bias and "calumnious fictions."

Maybe the most subversive, experimental, and most honest "direction in writing" one might pursue is to try one's hand at classic, traditional first-person travel narrative? That's what happened during the last real renaissance of travel writing, in the 1980s, the one driven by *Granta*, and by writers like Paul Theroux, Bruce Chatwin, and Bill Bryson. And don't forget Rick Steves in that pantheon of travel writers who came on the scene in the 1980s—

whose service-minded guidebook writing had always been driven by quirky personal narrative.

When I finally arrived in Estepa, I found exactly what Rick Steves had promised all those years ago. The hilltop convent of Santa Clara is gorgeous, as is the view overlooking the white towns of Andalusia. It was a windy day in February. There were no other tourists at the convent and so I stood and listened to the wind rustle through the tall evergreen trees. Near the convent is a park, where families were having Saturday afternoon picnics. Farther down the hill, a cheering crowd watched local kids playing a soccer game.

I wandered down to the town center, through small squares surrounded by orange trees. I passed a group of young people carrying huge ornate decorations into a pretty church. In the town center, I suddenly found myself caught in a crowd of children, all dressed in costumes for Carnival (knights, cowboys, superheroes, Mario Brothers, anything seemed to go) marching along with a band dressed as jesters and clowns walking on stilts. Afterward, I followed the parents who crowded into the local bars and I shared a few beers with the good people of Estepa.

Yes, Estepa still seemed to be as lively and just as "freshly washed, happy" as a young Rick Steves found it in the 1980s. It may have been excised from the guidebooks by Rick Steves Europe's "tough editorial calls," but the town still exists.

Let the TikTokers and Instagrammers—following the posts of other TikTokers and Instagrammers—pour into the bigger, better-known cities. Maybe Estepa is better off now. Maybe it's been freed from the samsara of tourists who follow Rick Steves?

In telling you the story of my uneventful visit to this Andalusian hill town, I guess I wanted to make the simple point that travel writing is a bit like Estepa. It hasn't stopped existing simply because of corporate editorial decisions. It's still there, waiting for someone to enjoy it again.

The impulse to travel and explore—and to write about those experiences—will remain. Pico Iyer (guest editor of *The Best American Travel Writing 2004*) was one of the writers who took up *Granta*'s question in 2017. Iyer's response can stand as mine: "Travel writing isn't dead; it can no more die than curiosity or humanity or the strangeness of the world can die."

Eating Badly

FROM *Esquire*

THE DAY MY grandmother in Beijing died, I went out to dinner in New York. The meal was meant to be in her memory, but really, it spoke to the paucity of mine. My partner asked for stories as we drove from Brooklyn into Flushing, a neighborhood that hummed with the slow pedestrian choreography of its predominant Chinese diaspora. Staring out at a mass of gray-haired grannies, each indistinguishable from a distance, I found I had no stories of the woman who'd raised me. I knew neither her age nor city of birth; nor could I recount a single shared conversation. She had me until I was four, a stretch of time unimprinted on conscious memory. Empty of anecdotes and tears, I believed myself empty, too, of grief for a woman I'd seen three times in the previous thirty years.

What I had: an impression of her salty brown cooking.

At the restaurant, I buried our table under the food of northern China. Pork ribs and potatoes, bitter long peppers, braised intestines. Meat pies breathed a hoary steam when split. Periodically, I'd add a dish I saw sailing out to the one other group dining at 4:00 p.m. on a Thursday. Three older Chinese men grew progressively louder as they drank Tsingtaos, their Beijing *r*'s ringing, harsh and distinctive, across the room. They knew the language and cuisine, as I didn't; they seemed content, as I was not. The food was just okay.

"Okay," I would say for months, when asked how I felt about my grandmother.

Weeks later, when a second craving hit, I ordered pork and potatoes delivered from a different spot. The food was, again, disappointing. By the time a third or fourth carton of ribs arrived on my doorstep some months later, I opened the warm paper bag and realized: I'd mixed up my order. What I thought was hunger had been a poorly translated form of grief.

Quiz: say "grief" in Mandarin. Say "dissociation." Say "inarticulation." Say, in a flawless Beijing accent, "the sense that you have put away, in the wrong place, some small, worn object you can no longer recall; and which you would, anyhow, fail to recognize if found." Good luck passing this quiz at the age I was when I moved out of my grandmother's house, still fumbling the crude blocks of a toddler vocabulary. I lost more and more of those pieces in moves to Kentucky, California, Rhode Island, the United Kingdom, Thailand, Iowa, New York. By thirty-two, I found myself without a grandmother tongue. I could express myself only through this primal cry: that of a child begging to be fed.

Displeased with restaurants, I decided to recreate my grandmother's cooking on my own. In this effort, I had a slapdash bravado inherited from her son, my father, a man scornful of recipes. The core of my culinary education has been gleaned from watching my father move in swift, digressive arcs around the stove. In life, his answer to "how much salt?" was popping raw meatball mix into his mouth, spitting it out, and adding another splash of soy to the bowl. (Say, in Mandarin, "food poisoning.") He died ten years ago.

For months, I read food blogs and cookbooks that gave my intuition the legitimacy of language. *Hydration* is the method whereby ground pork gets a splash of A) my grandmother's soy sauce, B) my father's cooking wine, or C) my shiitake water. Meat and liquid, I learned, must not overmix because you are A) arthritic, B) in a hurry, or C) avoiding the release of myosin, which toughens proteins. Let this rest for the time it takes to A) shift furniture in a cluttered Beijing apartment, B) call children to dinner, or C) hear the stopwatch go off, precisely thirty minutes later, on my phone.

Researching, cross-referencing, and obeying the laws of food science, I hydrated, to perfection, the memory of the meatball soup my dad had learned to make from my grandmother. I stood by my pot like a lifeguard. Snatched up each fat, bumpy sphere as it bobbed up. The meatballs, split, were so pinkly moist as to appear undercooked. Gelatinous, lush, they proved better than my dad's.

In penance for this thought, I ate the next day's meatball straight from the fridge. Cold and dense, it tasted closer to the family recipe. Still wasn't right.

Thus passed an odd, quiet summer of subterranean franticness that burrowed into the cool, gray weeks of fall. I'd hole up for days with elaborate, multistep cumin ribs; or blur asleep at four in the morning, clutching a phone that glowed with selections of aged bean pastes. Methodically, obsessively, I scanned for new northern Chinese restaurants on new Chinese food delivery apps—the more illegible the menus, the better—until one day, my partner asked what I wanted to order for dinner.

"Anything you want," he said.

He meant to soothe me. For months, A had been tasting my experiments and praising their successes as I listed failures; he knew I'd assembled detailed maps of specialty foods in a fifty-mile radius and knew how I used that knowledge to cut down his opposing culinary opinions. He was ceding the field. I should have been thrilled. Instead, I burst into tears.

"I don't want to choose," I said. "I want you to cook for me."

He reminded me that he was not a good cook, words out of my own mouth. I was nearly as ungenerous about others' cooking as I was about my own. That night, I was past caring. I have no memory of what A made for me. Just how it made me feel.

It wasn't until writing this that I remembered: my grandmother was not a good cook. Sandwiched between my father (lauded) and my great-grandmother (legendary), she was considered a clumsy interloper in the kitchen, lucky to serve a husband too concerned with scholarship to notice what he ate—plus me, a baby. Thinking back, it seems possible that the chicken soup my grandmother boiled up for me with salt and white pepper, nothing else, was bland; that her dumplings were *too* brown and salty; that I might be a better cook than she was.

Certainly, I've shaped myself into a more discerning eater. I spent my twenties in pursuit of the perfect meal. While contemporaries chose continuing educations in cocktails, rock climbing, Settlers of Catan, and Spanish, I learned *amuse-bouche, Maillard reaction, gastrique,* and *agrodolce* with the intensity of an immigrant kid determined to test out of ESL. Newly flush with disposable income, I found myself seduced as much by fine dining as by the culture it represented: a certain socioeconomic stratum of European-inflected worldliness expressed in white tablecloths, small portions, and *good taste*—the same words used to describe the intellectual dimensions of that life in which the books on the table are as old and revered as the wine. I'd spent years peering in the window. Eating was, I suppose, the most direct way to internalize what I desired.

I became an insufferable eater. Long before I criticized my partner's cooking in New York, I fought with a friend in a too-hot kitchen in Nashville. N and I were in our twenties, students of medicine and writing, arguing at absurd, incendiary levels over when to add garlic to vegetables. We were obsessed with the idea of one *best* option. I can see now how unhappy we were in our perfectionism. It all felt scarce, back then: expensive farmers market produce; student stipends; faith in graduate programs meant to deliver us into the lives we wanted; hope that those lives remained possible; time itself in that claustrophobic year. In 2016, hunger had become another word for fear. Frantic in me was the idea that I hadn't lived enough, done enough, consumed by rightful portions. Each meal, each day, carried the immense pressure of defining who I meant to be.

These days, I live in a place more expansive in its epicurean landscape, and its emotional one, too. I am trying to cultivate a belief in abundance. In the bleak years of 2020 and 2021, it was biographies I craved: stories of women artists for whom long droughts of grief and penury, war and heartbreak, could not blight the fruitfulness of their lives. The novel I wrote coming out of those years, *The Land of Milk and Honey*, is framed by a chef who, at the end of her life, looks back on how she lived through famine. I am not religious—I'm a hedonist, in fact—but this is the faith I try to keep. May I believe that these things will pass: a week of wildfire smog, four years of cruel politics, a bad dinner, a bitter night; may I believe in a future that grants the time to taste more. My meals, freed of the fear that can masquerade as perfection, are more often simple things.

Often, what I want is to eat badly. I crave my mother's limp broccoli, undersalted out of concern for my blood pressure. Lumpy plantain porridge A orders in from the Jamaican spot, so that I come home to warm plastic tubs and a puppy's yelps. Six pounds of mediocre bread sent by friends in another city who misunderstood the size of a loaf, and the French toast another friend makes from its stale slices. My friend K and I are close enough to laugh at our toast's utter mediocrity and hunt up an ancient bottle of balsamic vinegar. We stir the dregs into overripe cherries, making a jam whose recipe I won't share, and don't advise that anyone eat again—which makes it one of a kind.

It seems cruel to have learned this lesson so late, after losing the taste of my grandmother's mian and the ability to ask what, exactly, my father sprinkled into his bing; but I remind myself that I am done optimizing meals in an exhausting, impossible quest for perfection; that what I was fed matters less than that I was, by people who loved me. I think of the chai a friend made for me when I was grieving my grandmother. S brought her own tea. Used whatever milk sat in my fridge. Chai was not a word in my grandmother's vocabulary, yet I was struck by the familiarity of the weak tea S brewed in my inadequate kitchen. Bland, tender, lukewarm, it rang out a soft, coppery warmth that can't be purchased. Deeper than spice, more pungent than tea, as long-forgotten and long-remembered as the dry sheaves of my grandmother's hair between my fingers, this was the taste of her care. Give me, please, bad food made by a person who loves me.

Contributors' Notes

Other Distinguished Food and Travel
Writing of 2023

Contributors' Notes

NAVNEET ALANG is a Toronto-based writer and educator who writes on a variety of topics including tech, food and drink, immigrant identity, and literary criticism. His work has appeared in *The Atlantic, New York Magazine, Eater, Bon Appétit, The New Republic, The Globe and Mail,* and many other publications.

BETSY ANDREWS is a James Beard-, IACP-, and SATW-awarded food, drink, and travel writer. She is a contributing editor at *Food & Wine* and *SevenFifty Daily,* and she writes for many other publications, among them *The Wall Street Journal, Travel + Leisure, Condé Nast Traveler, Imbibe, Plate,* and *Serious Eats.* She is the former executive editor of *Saveur* and a former *New York Times* dining critic. With chef Scott Clark and photographer Cheyenne Ellis, she is cocreator of the forthcoming *Coastal: A Road-Trippy California Cookbook.* She is also an award-winning poet. Her latest book is *Crowded.*

JOHN BIRDSALL (he/him) is the author of *The Man Who Ate Too Much: The Life of James Beard* and the forthcoming *What Is Queer Food?* He lives in Tucson.

MARIAN BULL is a writer, editor, and potter living in Brooklyn. She writes *Mess Hall,* a weekly cooking newsletter, and is at work on her first book.

SHARANYA DEEPAK is a writer and editor from and currently in New Delhi, India. She is also editor at *Vittles Magazine* and a fellow at South Asia Speaks. Sharanya is currently working on a book of essays.

MELISSA JOHNSON is a screenwriter and documentary filmmaker who tells stories about rites of passage, the wilderness, and sports through an irreverent lens. Her first-person essays have appeared in the *New York Times, Outside Magazine, Longreads, The Rumpus, The Guardian,* and elsewhere, including the inspiration for her autobiographical animated film, *Love in the Time of March Madness,* about her dating life as a 6'4" tall woman, which won the Tribeca Online Film Festival Best Short Film award and went on to be shortlisted for an Academy Award. Her award-winning and

Emmy-nominated films have appeared on Showtime, ESPN, and MTV. Melissa lives in Los Angeles, where she obsesses about which national park to bring her baby daughter to first. Learn more at melissajohnson.net.

TALIA LAVIN is a Jewish New Yorker who believes in the need for a better world, fresh buttered green peas, and cold coffee on summer mornings. She is the author of the book *Culture Warlords* and the forthcoming book *Wild Faith*, and the writer of the food-and-politics newsletter *The Sword and the Sandwich*.

KIESE LAYMON is a Black Southern writer from Jackson, Mississippi, and the Libbie Shearn Moody Professor of English and Creative Writing at Rice University in Houston. Laymon, a 2022 Macarthur Fellow, is the author of *Long Division* and *How to Slowly Kill Yourself and Others in America*. His bestselling *Heavy: An American Memoir* won the Andrew Carnegie Medal for Excellence and was named one of the 50 Best Memoirs of the Past 50 Years by the *New York Times*.

JORI LEWIS writes narrative nonfiction that explores how people interact with their environments. Her reports and essays have been published in *The Atlantic, Orion Magazine*, and *Emergence Magazine*, among other publications, and she is a senior editor of *Adi Magazine*, a literary magazine of global politics. In 2022, she published her first book, *Slaves for Peanuts: A Story of Conquest, Liberation, and a Crop That Changed History*, which was supported by the prestigious Whiting Creative Nonfiction Grant and a Silvers Grant for Work in Progress. It also won the Harriet Tubman Prize and a James Beard media award.

LIGAYA MISHAN writes for the *New York Times*. She has won a James Beard Award and was a finalist for the National Magazine Awards. Her essays have been selected for the Best American anthologies in magazine, food, and travel writing, and her criticism has appeared in the *New York Review of Books* and *The New Yorker*. The daughter of a Filipino mother and a British father, she grew up in Honolulu.

KAREN RESTA is a writer with an interest in the vast panoply of food, cooking, and eating. A former executive chef, she lives in Brooklyn.

ALEXANDER SAMMON is a writer based in New York.

ADAM SELLA is a journalist covering Israel and the occupied Palestinian territories. He's written about topics ranging from food to war for the *New York Times, Haaretz, Al Jazeera, Eater*, and *Wine Enthusiast*, among other publications.

MAYUKH SEN is the author of *Taste Makers* (2021) and the forthcoming *Love, Queenie: Merle Oberon, Hollywood's First South Asian Star* (2025). He has won a James Beard Award for his food writing, and his writing was previously anthologized in the 2019, 2021, and 2022 editions of *The Best American Food Writing*. He teaches food journalism at New York University and lives in Brooklyn.

JAKE SKEETS is the author of *Eyes Bottle Dark with a Mouthful of Flowers*, winner of the National Poetry Series, Kate Tufts Discovery Award, American Book Award, and Whiting Award. He is from the Navajo Nation and teaches at the University of Oklahoma.

FELICITY SPECTOR has worked as a producer and chief writer for ITN Channel 4 News since 1989. She is also an ambassador for the nonprofit organization Bake for Ukraine.

BEN TAUB is a staff writer at *The New Yorker*. His works have won a Pulitzer Prize, a National Magazine Award, two consecutive George Polk Awards, a Livingston Award, a Robert F. Kennedy Award, an Overseas Press Club Award, and other honors, and they have appeared in recent editions of *The Best American Magazine Writing* and *The Best American Travel Writing*.

MOSAB ABU TOHA is a Palestinian poet from Gaza. His debut poetry book, *Things You May Find Hidden in My Ear*, was a finalist for the National Book Critics Circle Award and won an American Book Award, a Walcott Poetry Prize, and a Palestine Book Award. His poems and essays appeared in *The New Yorker*, the *New York Times*, the *Washington Post*, *The Nation*, *NYRB*, and *The Atlantic*, among other publications.

LISA WELLS is a poet and essayist living in the Pacific Northwest.

JASON WILSON is the author of *Godforsaken Grapes, Boozehound,* and *The Cider Revival.* He is the creator of *Everyday Drinking* and a senior writer at the *New Wine Review*. He's written for the *Washington Post, The New Yorker,* the *New York Times, Travel + Leisure, Wine Enthusiast,* and many other publications.

C PAM ZHANG is the author of *How Much of These Hills Is Gold* and *Land of Milk and Honey.*

Other Distinguished Food and Travel Writing of 2023

EXPLORE THE REST OF THE SERIES!

THE·BEST·AMERICAN
FOOD AND TRAVEL
WRITING™ 2024

EDITED BY
PADMA LAKSHMI

THE·BEST·AMERICAN
ESSAYS™
2024

EDITED BY
WESLEY MORRIS

THE·BEST·AMERICAN
Mystery and
Suspense™ 2024

EDITED BY
S. A. COSBY

ON SALE 10/22/24

THE·BEST·AMERICAN
Science and Nature
Writing™ 2024

BILL MCKIBBEN

THE·BEST·AMERICAN
Science Fiction
and Fantasy™ 2024

EDITED BY
HUGH HOWEY

THE·BEST·AMERICAN
Short Stories™
2024

EDITED BY
LAUREN GROFF

MARINER BOOKS traces its beginnings to 1832 when William Ticknor cofounded the Old Corner Bookstore in Boston, from which he would run the legendary firm Ticknor and Fields, publisher of Ralph Waldo Emerson, Harriet Beecher Stowe, Nathaniel Hawthorne, and Henry David Thoreau. Following Ticknor's death, Henry Oscar Houghton acquired Ticknor and Fields and, in 1880, formed Houghton Mifflin, which later merged with venerable Harcourt Publishing to form Houghton Mifflin Harcourt. HarperCollins purchased HMH's trade publishing business in 2021 and reestablished their storied lists and editorial team under the name Mariner Books.

Uniting the legacies of Houghton Mifflin, Harcourt Brace, and Ticknor and Fields, Mariner Books continues one of the great traditions in American bookselling. Our imprints have introduced an incomparable roster of enduring classics, including Hawthorne's *The Scarlet Letter*, Thoreau's *Walden*, Willa Cather's *O Pioneers!*, Virginia Woolf's *To the Lighthouse*, W.E.B. Du Bois's *Black Reconstruction*, J.R.R. Tolkien's *The Lord of the Rings*, Carson McCullers's *The Heart Is a Lonely Hunter*, Ann Petry's *The Narrows*, George Orwell's *Animal Farm* and *Nineteen Eighty-Four*, Rachel Carson's *Silent Spring*, Margaret Walker's *Jubilee*, Italo Calvino's *Invisible Cities*, Alice Walker's *The Color Purple*, Margaret Atwood's *The Handmaid's Tale*, Tim O'Brien's *The Things They Carried*, Philip Roth's *The Plot Against America*, Jhumpa Lahiri's *Interpreter of Maladies*, and many others. Today Mariner Books remains proudly committed to the craft of fine publishing established nearly two centuries ago at the Old Corner Bookstore.